Threading My Way

Nuremberg: The Facts, the Law and the Consequences
Survey of International Affairs 1947-48
Survey of International Affairs 1949-50
Survey of International Affairs 1951
Survey of International Affairs 1952
Survey of International Affairs 1953
Middle East Crisis (with Guy Wint)
South Africa and World Opinion
World Order and New States
Suez: Ten Years After (with Anthony Moncrieff)
World Politics since 1945
Total War (with Guy Wint and John Pritchard)
The British Experience 1945-75
Freedom to Publish (with Ann Bristow)
Top Secret Ultra
Independent Africa and the World
From Byzantium to Eton: A Memoir of a Millennium
A Time for Peace
Who's Who in the Bible
Resilient Europe: A Study of the Years 1870-2000

Threading My Way

Peter Calvocoressi

Duckworth

First published in 1994 by
Gerald Duckworth & Co. Ltd.
The Old Piano Factory
48 Hoxton Square, London N1 6PB
Tel: 071 729 5986
Fax: 071 729 0015

A catalogue record for this book is available
from the British Library

ISBN 0 7156 2627 2

Typeset by Ray Davies
Printed in Great Britain by
Redwood Books Ltd., Trowbridge

Contents

(Plates between pages 120 and 121)

Prelude

Autobiography is not biography written by the subject. Biography is a kind of portraiture. It aims to portray a man or woman as completely, vividly and truthfully as possible. Autobiography cannot do this, if only because it cannot fulfil that third purpose. Somebody once said that there is no point in writing autobiography unless one is prepared to tell all. But telling all about oneself is likely to be tedious and, besides, nobody does tell all.

Echoing Gibbon's famous meditation on the steps of Santa Maria in Araceli by the Roman Forum when he resolved to write the history of the Decline and Fall of the Roman Empire, Stendhal, surveying Rome from San Pietro in Montorio on the Janiculan hill on the eve of his fiftieth birthday, resolved to write about himself as a way of discovering what sort of man he was. In which quest he failed, abandoning it at the point where he had reached the age of 17 and remaining as much an enigma to himself as he was to his friends and has been to posterity. His narrow probe got almost nowhere and, however divertingly, illuminated little.

This memoir starts from a small point but sweeps wide. It probes into centuries. I like the study of the past but that would not be reason enough to go into my antecedents at such length. There is another reason. My ancestors lived for centuries in a small self-governing island which became singularly prosperous – and they with it – until a huge misfortune threw them abroad where they were at first refugees and migrants. But they fell on their feet. Forced into new worlds, they resolved to be not only in them but of them. They assimilated. Their story has wide lessons, never more so than today.

A new world is a kind of limbo. For a generation or two my forebears were facing two ways, an uncomfortable stance. I myself lived as a child in a Greek home in England and saw little beyond other Greek homes. Then, in English schools, I moved abruptly into an entirely English world. The education which I got there was Classical – that is to say, it was based on Greek and Latin literature and ideas – but the ethos and people were English. I have long reflected on this education, which was good, and I have written about it here at some length because it may well be that my generation has been the last to have it.

When I emerged from my education I was more English than Greek. Yet, as I uneasily discovered, some occupations were barred to me. I found others where my origins did not matter. I also found, strangely, that the barriers were less stringent in wartime than peace.

In retrospect I can see that my origins – Greek, cosmopolitan, mercantile – have played more than a small part in my choice of activities, in my enjoyment of them and perhaps in my usefulness in them. This has been particularly so with my interest in world affairs and contemporary history, one of the main strands of my professional life. In another – publishing – I found myself more interested than most publishers in European writers and making them available in English. I also found in publishing a happy fusion of my mercantile genes with my intellectual education and inclinations. The pattern of my life has been a coherent diversity.

The first chapters of this book make use of material which I used earlier in a booklet which was published by the Centre for Greek Studies at King's College, London. Chapter 8 contains material derived from the archives of Chatto & Windus and The Hogarth Press deposited in the Library of Reading University. I am grateful to the present directors of these firms for their permission to see these archives and specially grateful to Mr Michael Bott, the librarian in charge of them, for his help when I came to consult them. My overwhelming debt is to my wife without whom the tremendously happy, and I hope fruitful, life told in the later chapters of this book would not have been lived.

1

A Long Look Back

The first Calvocoressi appeared in 1461. Before that year there was no such thing. The Calvocoressis do not go back to Adam. They go back to the union in 1461 of a Kalvos with a Koresis, a union which before the year was out produced Nicholas, the Ur-Kalvokoresis. The spelling Calvocoressi is a nineteenth-century western adaptation. Calvocoressi is, therefore, a double-barrelled name without a hyphen – fortunately, since double-barrelled names with hyphens are apt to attract a certain kind of derision. My name has given me some trouble but it has not become a sitcom joke.

Since 1461 and until 1822 hundreds of ensuing Calvocoressis lived in the island of Chios in the Aegean within swimming distance of what is now Turkey. There, too, lived the Rallis, my mother's family, and a network of interrelated clans. In 1822 the Chiots were massacred after a rising against Turkish rule. The population of the island was decimated, not in the usual sense of being reduced by one in ten but in the sense that only one in ten remained. The other nine-tenths were killed or fled, some of my forbears being in both categories. Of the former you may still see many skulls preserved in a spirit of not entirely admirable piety.

Survivors who migrated westward had their ups and downs over the next few generations. My mother's family had the most ups and the least downs, my father's a more uneven history. My father was born in France at a time when his father had a business in Manchester, but this business failed, my grandfather went mad and his wife and children retreated to Constantinople around the year 1881. My father was then seven. He lived and learned in the Ottoman empire until he was seventeen when he went with his elder brother to the Sorbonne in Paris. They studied civil and commercial law and in their third year were bracketed joint prize winners in third place. The citation records that the papers of the two brothers were equally worthy notwithstanding '*la diversité de leurs qualités et de leurs défauts*' – the variety of their virtues and their shortcomings. This was in 1894. Soon afterwards my father got a job in the flourishing firm of Ralli Bros. which sent him to New York and then to India. My parents married in 1911 and in 1912 I was born in Karachi.

My father was at that time a French citizen because, although he never lived in France, he chanced to be born there. He later became a naturalised British subject. I, however, was a British subject by birth because I was born in India. Many years later the law which made a Greek born in India British was changed, and when I made a routine application to renew my British passport I was told I had become by Act of Parliament a 'potential Pakistani'. The Foreign Office would not renew my passport until I registered with the Home Office my renunciation of this potentiality. I have never resolved the question of what to put in documents which ask for my country of birth. Should it be India or Pakistan? It does not seem to matter. I get the impression that if I put Utopia nobody would notice.

My mother, like myself and for the same reason, was British from the hour of her birth in Calcutta. So was her mother. My mother died before Indian independence but my grandmother, who lived to be 97 and so survived the Raj, became a 'potential Indian'. Rallis had been domiciled in England since just after the Napoleonic wars and, as I shall later relate, they made London the headquarters of a commercial empire which flourished until after the Second World War.

I came to England, aged three months, on the eve of the First World War and I have been here ever since. I was part of a community which was both prosperous and foreign. The foreignness was a decree of history: these Greek families were thrown off their Greek island by forces beyond their control and contrary to their will. The prosperity on the other hand was more than accidental. Chiots knew how to prosper. They had been doing signally well for themselves for hundreds of years before the catastrophe of 1822 and in a variety of settings.

Chios contrived a special position for itself in the late Byzantine empire. It was a key point in Genoa's commercial empire in the east. It enjoyed unparalleled autonomy in the Ottoman empire up to 1822. In all these phases it was a nucleus of prosperity in a wider region. In the eighteenth century its horizons expanded and Chiots were foremost among the traders of the eastern Mediterranean who ventured into the booming economy of western Europe and established offices in Livorno, Marseilles and London, where big new opportunities were being created by the industrial revolution, the worldwide spread of French and British empires and the beginnings of free trade.

For the visitor to Chios today there is one cultural 'must'. This is the church and monastery of the Nea Moni, so called because it was new when it was built nine hundred years ago. The Nea Moni is one of Greece's outstanding Byzantine relics. Like the churches at Osios Loukas near Delphi, Dafni near Athens and some in Kastoria in Macedonia, the Nea Moni was built in the eleventh century in a period of artistic renaissance. It was severely damaged by an earthquake in 1881 and is now somewhat forlorn, gloriously situated ten miles inland from the main town but tended by only two or three very old nuns, hospitable but pathetic, who look as though they expect to have no successors. The church itself, although dilapidated, has vestiges of grandeur in its unusual octagonal design and in the glory of its mosaics which recall its opulent origins. No other Greek island had anything like it. It was commissioned by an emperor who, perhaps because he was lucky to become emperor, wanted to make a splash. He was Constantine IX, last emperor of the Macedonian dynasty begun by Basil I – assassin, usurper, lawgiver, conqueror, patron of the arts. Basil re-established Byzantine rule in southern Italy and gave a spur to an artistic revival which spread from churches and palaces in his capital to Sicily, Venice and Russia. The prototype of this renaissance was his new basilica, commonly called the Nea, in Constantinople (destroyed in the Turkish conquest of 1453). The chief characteristics of this middle Byzantine period were the simple Greek cross of four equal arms encased in a square and surmounted by one large dome and four smaller ones and their clusters of semi-domes. Inside, ceilings and walls were clothed with mosaics, gold and marbles to make a sumptuous display of Christ's mission on earth. The broken glitter of the mosaics, reflecting thousands of candles from surfaces not yet grimy, made up for the lack of depth which was achieved by the masters of western fresco when they discovered the alternative magic of perspective.

By the middle of the eleventh century the dynasty called Macedonian was coming to an end in a splutter of princesses. The elder of two sisters, Zoe, had had two husbands without issue and the church did not allow a third. But the Patriarch was prepared to bend the rules in an emergency and when Zoe chose Constantine for a third attempt to keep the dynasty going the Patriarch blessed the union – but stayed away from the coronation. Constantine's face was his fortune. Although not royal, he was noble and handsome: he is one of the few Byzantine emperors whose features we may know since they are depicted in Aghia Sophia in Constantinople. (But the body is not his – his face was overlaid on a portrait of his imperial predecessor. He appears also on a gold and enamel inset on a crown in Budapest.) Before his marriage to Zoe he had spent some years in exile on Lesbos, the island north of Chios. He was sent there by Zoe's current – second – consort who had murdered the first and suspected Constantine of wanting to be the third. While on Lesbos Constantine learned of a miracle on Chios which led a few monks to erect a shrine on the spot where the Nea Moni now stands. Constantine promised to help this new foundation and after he became emperor he did so in style. He was a lavish patron of the arts whose benefactions reached east and west to Palestine and Italy and included the restoration of the great church of St George Manganas in the capital where he was eventually buried with his favourite mistress.

The point of this potted excursion into Byzantine history is its bearing on the fortunes of Chios. In antiquity Chios had been nothing much: it was the birthplace of Homer (so they say), got good marks from Thucydides for being good at governing itself and making money, stuck to Athens for most of the Pelopennesian Wars but changed sides just in time, manoeuvred skilfully in the feuds between Alexander the Great's successors and the wars between Rome and Mithridates, and caught a glimpse of St Paul on one of his missionary journeys. This was a record of survival at the margins rather than anything more resounding. But its fortunes were about to rise. When Constantine IX died (1055) the Macedonian dynasty did not long survive and its demise gave the empire a shove into an instability which was now inherent in it. By this phase in its long history the empire's rulers were essentially baronial lords who lacked the charismatic authority of a Constantine the Great or Justinian. They had lost much of that dignity and divinity which hedged about Roman emperors for centuries after Augustus, so that at the first signs of failure by one family or dynasty there was always another looking to pick up the crown. A local power base outside the capital became more important than enthronement in the capital itself, while the tendency of dynasty after dynasty to run to females gave ambitious generals added opportunities to cement by marriage claims to the throne which rested ultimately on the claimant's private army and wealth: in other words, on his disruptive competitiveness. Most damaging to the empire were the financial consequences of this baronial feuding, as the lords of great estates kept their wealth for themselves instead of remitting parts of it to the central treasury.

The next phase in imperial history, an Italian phase, introduces incidentally the Calvos. The Calvos came from Genoa. Other Chiot surnames are as recognisably Italian: Argenti, Casanova, Grimaldi, Salvago. This is the time of the rise of the Italian maritime city states which challenged and repelled the seapower of Arab caliphs and sundry pirates in the Mediterranean and Adriatic Seas. Genoa's first essay in expansion was to southern Italy and thence to the coral fisheries of north Africa, but like its rivals Venice and Pisa it ventured further afield by cashing in on the crusaders' need for sea transport to the Holy Land and for supplies of men and materials to sustain the precarious footholds won by the First Crusade in the eleventh century. Italians acquired privileges and special quarters in the seaports of the Holy Land and the Genoese pushed on from Syria into Asia Minor, Constantinople itself and the Black Sea. By the year 1200 there were about 60,000 Italians in Constantinople, jockeying one another for privileges by proving themselves alternately helpful or hostile to the imperial government. The takeover of the empire by the crusaders and Venice in 1204 (called the Fourth Crusade) was a short-lived victory, for in 1261 on the Feast of the Dormition of the Virgin the Greeks recaptured the city and re-established the old empire for close on 200 years more. Throughout this final Byzantine period Genoa was the empire's least unpopular outside power and also a necessary ally. As the empire, assailed on all sides by Mongols, Turks and the French rulers of southern Italy, trundled towards its final collapse, it was forced to look to Genoa to provide the naval cover which it could no longer afford out of a defence budget already overburdened with the cost of large land armies. The Genoese presence in the east became firmly established round three main bases: Pera (a suburb of Constantinople), Kaffa in the Black Sea and Chios.

In 1346 Genoa seized Chios from Byzantium and from under the nose of Venice and stayed there, first under Byzantine and then under Ottoman suzerainty, for 220 years. In partnership with Greek families Genoese merchants and financiers created one of Europe's most flourishing economies. This was the year when Edward III of England defeated the French King at Crecy and went on to besiege Calais which surrendered to him in the next year and remained English until 1558, eight years short of Genoese rule in Chios.

The first Genoese to arrive in Chios had been private adventurers and they were followed more or less accidentally by the Republic itself. Early in the fourteenth century a Genoese family called Zaccaria took the island and prospered so far as to harbour political as well as commercial ambitions. The imperial crown had been tossed around so much that even an Italian bourgeois might aspire to it and the incumbent emperor, taking no chances, threw the Zaccarias out of Chios and repossessed it. But not for long. In 1346 a Genoese fleet captured the island. Rival Genoese and Venetian fleets were hovering in Aegean waters. The Venetian admiral suggested to his Genoese counterpart, Simone Vignoso, a joint assault on Chios and its partition. But Genoa considered that the Zaccaria interlude had given it a special claim to Chios which it was not prepared to share. So Vignoso, who commanded 29 vessels and about 6,000 men, sailed to Chios, betrayed the Venetian scheme to the Chiots and offered them his protection. They refused, whereupon Vignoso landed and seized the island for the Genoese Republic. There was little fighting and although the fort held out for three months the rest of the island was subdued in a matter of days. The instrument of surrender was signed by five Chiot notables, two of whom were Koresis. A few years later the Byzantine emperor John V, who needed all the help he could get from the west to stave off the Turks, ceded Chios to Genoa for a peppercorn. Genoa remained sovereign over Chios until it was taken by the Turks in 1566.

This sovereignty was exercised in a peculiar way. It was delegated by the Republic to a company or Maona, a joint stock venture formed in Genoa by private citizens on much the same lines as the English and Dutch East India Companies – but more than two centuries earlier. The members of the Maona acquired Chios accidentally. A consortium of wealthy citizens had paid to equip Vignoso's fleet which the Republic had raised on mortgage to meet an emergency in the west which never materialised (an alleged assembly of Genoese malcontents in Monaco). So the Republic had a fleet for which it had no ostensible purpose and had not paid. It despatched Vignoso to the east with instructions to seize property out of which to repay its creditors. Chios was part of the loot, and the Republic did a deal with the creditors by which – until their debt was paid off, which never happened – they were to receive all Chiot revenues and exercise civil and criminal jurisdiction in the island. The Maona, formed to exercise these rights, became the effective government of Chios in much the same way as Clive's East India Company became the government of Bengal. A little later other Genoese Maonas were created for Corsica and Cyprus.

This strange arrangement developed into an informal partnership between the Maona and the local bigwigs. Where these bigwigs came from is unclear but at least some of them seem to have descended from Byzantine aristocrats who fled the capital as the imperial power declined. Chios, an offshore island – a sort of Taiwan in times of trouble – was an attractive refuge and there they became a successful landowning and commercial bourgeoisie. Chios had long been famous for its produce: oranges and lemons; the mastic shrub whose gum goes into alcoholic drinks, perfumes and varnishes; silks and linen; and for its trade in slaves, grain, rice and alum. The Greek and Italian streams mingled and intermarried, although how frequently it is impossible to say. Koresis met Calvo, so leading to the union of 1461 and to wider contacts.

Other Calvos from Genoa included one who was involved in the first recorded shipment of goods from the Aegean to Flanders, a foretaste of an avocation to come; and, less indicative perhaps, another who was a troubadour and became involved in amorous intrigues in Spain and worked off his frustrations by starting a war between Aragon and Castile. A George Koresis (otherwise Gennadios Scholarios) was the first Patriarch in Constantinople under Ottoman rule and another can be traced preaching Protestantism in Wallachia (modern Romania) in the 1570s and translating the scriptures into Romanian. Yet another George Coresio became a professor at Pavia in 1609, wrote books on the Turkish invasions of Europe and the playing of ball games, and dropped stones from the Leaning Tower of Pisa – not, as Galileo is said to have done, in order to prove Aristotle wrong about the behaviour of falling bodies but in order to prove him right: a futile exercise, by whomever conducted, since Aristotle never said what he was supposed to have said. George Coresio lost his university chair six years after getting it, ostensibly because he went mad, but one cannot avoid the suspicion that he was deprived less on account of losing his wits (always a venial professorial offence) than for refusing to abjure his Greek Orthodox faith for Roman Catholicism. The airport at Pisa is named after Galileo but whenever I land there I reflect that it ought in fairness to be named after George Coresio, mad or not.

In Chios time gradually reduced the Italian element, so that the Chiots came to think of themselves as entirely Greek instead of what they really were – healthy hybrids. But one peculiarity of Genoese family life seems to have embedded itself firmly in this society. In Genoa, alone among Italian cities so far as I know, the main social unit was the extended family called the *albergo*. The *albergo* embraced a number of houses or palaces, sometimes up to fifty or more, all roughly in the same quarter of the city. The inhabitants of these households, including even the servants, had the same clan name and the *albergo* as a whole was a self-governing unit with a family council. It entertained semi-diplomatic, semi-economic relations with other *alberghi*. The Chiot families into which I was born in the twentieth century had a clannishness and a deference to family authority which may have owed something to these Genoese antecedents.

The Genoese occupation inaugurated a new era of prosperity. By the treaty of 1346 Genoa secured possession of the kastro or fort which remains to this day a prominent, although ruined, feature of the town and harbour of Chios. They also secured 200 houses in the kastro, for which they agreed to pay. Evidently they intended from the first to settle in some strength and not merely install a token garrison (which is what the Turks did later). They built a two-storey palace for the *podesta* or governor, offices for the Maona and a Roman Catholic cathedral. The Genoese government appointed the constable of the fort and a few other officials and had the controlling voice in the selection of the *podesta*: the Genoese authorities drew up a list of twenty names, from which the Maona picked four, from which the Republic made the appointment. But the Republic played a minor and declining part in government and the *podesta* was no more than a symbol and figurehead.

The real business of government was finance, which was in the hands of the Maona. The Maona itself was governed by a general meeting of shareholders and, when these became too numerous, by an elected body of thirteen, meeting either in Genoa or Chios. In Chios the Maona appointed a small council to control public spending and two treasurers to receive all taxes. The Greeks accused the Maona of rapacity and corruption, but it was in a tight corner and vulnerable to bullying by both Greeks and, later, Turks.

Apart from financial squabbling, the two communities on the island co-existed harmoniously and profitably enough. The Genoese multiplied and were joined by other northern Italians, by Neapolitans and even some Spaniards – mostly traders like the Genoese. The indigenous notables by contrast were making their fortunes from landowning and horticulture. The Chiot mercantile tradition which was to become so pronounced in a later age seems to have come from Genoa rather than Byzantium. Vignoso guaranteed these landowners in the possession of their properties and so won their support. A later age might have called them collaborators; but what developed was a partnership between distinct groups of landowners and merchants with banking largely, but not exclusively, in Genoese hands. Genoese law was introduced but the Greeks and Genoese were equal before the law and Greeks suffered, it appears, no adverse discrimination.

Religious discord between Greek and Latin Christians had been virulent for centuries but on Chios the two communities settled down to a surprisingly amicable relationship which lasted through the Genoese period and for a hundred years thereafter – so much so that other Greek Orthodox communities frowned on it. The Genoese built numerous churches and chapels. Dominicans, Franciscans, Capuchins and Jesuits all established themselves. Some Greek children went to Jesuit schools. At one time Roman Catholics were allowed to celebrate mass in the Nea Moni with Orthodox monks taking part. In some churches altars were shared and there are others, still to be seen, where the presence of two naves suggests that Orthodox rites were celebrated on one side and Roman Catholic on the other.

Both communities founded hospitals as well as schools. Leprosy and plague were endemic in the island. Plague did not die out until the nineteenth century, and leprosy was still prevalent in the twentieth. When I first became involved with certain London-based Chiot charities one of these supported a leper hospital a few miles west of Chios town. Some time after the Second World War the authorities in Athens decided to close it because the declining number of lepers no longer justified its maintenance. Its few inmates were to be moved to another part of Greece. I remember their poignant – but unavailing – pleas to be allowed to remain in their native island and not be transported miles away from scenes and people whom they knew and loved.

There are no reliable data about conversions from one brand of Christianity to another during the era of good relations which lasted from the mid-fourteenth to the mid-seventeeth century. The most notable Greek convert was Leo Allatius, born Alatzes (1587-1669) who became vicar-general to the Roman Catholic bishop of Chios, friend of popes and savants in Rome, a relentless traveller and a scholar renowned as far afield as Paris. But he was something of an embarrassment to his relations who thought he had gone too far, and shortly before his death the brotherly love between the two churches gave way to a more normal animosity, provoked in this case by the Greek bishop who started a violent quarrel with the Catholic bishop. The latter appealed to the Turks in Constantinople, who enjoyed the luxury of taking a detached view of rumpuses among Christians. The sultans were in any case not much excited by clerical controversy, for although Islam has had its full share of theological acrimony, the protagonists have more often been Arab or Iranian than Turkish. Sultan Muhammad IV – or more probably the viziers and sultanas around his rickety throne – came down on the Roman Catholic side but the Roman Catholics in Chios then allowed their exhilaration to run away with them. Having triumphed over the Greek Orthodox they thought they could insult the Turks. They over-played their hand badly, even beating up a Turkish judge, and engaged in intrigues with the Venetians who briefly occupied the kastro and harbour in 1694-95.

They never recovered from this mistake. Many left the island. At the time of the Turkish conquest (1566) there had been about 6,000 of them. Their number increased during the seventeenth century but then fell away. The religious orders departed one by one and the Roman Catholic cathedral was burnt down during the disasters of 1822. Nevertheless,

Chios was long noted for its comparative tolerance of Roman Catholics and their see was not abolished until 1939.

When the Turks ousted the Genoese in 1566 their admiral, who was repeating the role played by Simone Vignoso in 1346, was a Hungarian convert to Islam who had risen to the rank of Kapudan Pasha or First Sea Lord under the name of Piali Pasha. He commanded eighty ships but took Chios by a ruse and almost without striking a blow.

For the Turks this action was a minor incident in a struggle for power in the Mediterranean between the Ottoman and Spanish empires. Ostensibly it was a punishment for Chiot delay in paying its annual tribute to the sultan but, more concretely, it was a tit-for-tat after the defeat, a year earlier, of a Turkish attempt to take Malta. By this time Chios was a sort of Hong Kong, a flourishing offshore island and entrepot whose activities benefited the ruling powers in Constantinople much as an independent Hong Kong benefited Mao Zedong's China after the communists' conquest of the mainland in 1949. Genoa recognised the realities to the extent of paying a tribute to the Turks (even before they took Constantinople in 1453), but the relationship became increasingly uneasy and the sultans suspected the Maona of acting as spies for the Knights of Malta and other Christian foes. The immediate impact of the Turkish take-over was rough. Leading Chiots were mulcted of larger sums which they were often unable to pay without selling their estates at knock-down prices. Some were deported into exile round the Black Sea. But Turkish rule, which lasted until 1913 (just after I was born), was only sporadically harsh. A Florentine attempt to dispossess the Turks in 1559 led to the beheading of 500 Chiots, and the more serious Venetian invasion and occupation in 1694-95 invited similar reprisals, but until the general Greek insurrection against Turkish rule in the 1820s the Turks left the Chiots to get on with their own affairs, economically and administratively. Chios continued to enjoy an extraordinary degree of self-government. In the year of Piali's conquest a joint Greek and Latin delegation went to Constantinople to ask for independence – an audacious request which, however absurd on the face of it, says something about the island's status and self-importance. Nor did the delegates come back empty-handed. They secured exemption from the conscription of boys for the corps of janissaries, thus preserving not only family life but also valuable labour for their family businesses. They won also special concessions on taxation and freedom of navigation.

We approach 1822. Ironically, that fearful catastrophe was preceded by a Great Leap Forward. From being smallish traders in a limited region Chiots became capitalist entrepreneurs operating all over Europe. Any growing economy needs a zone into which to expand – to sell more and buy more. Western economies boomed in the eighteenth century. The main sources of this boom were the industrial revolution and the teachings of Adam Smith who explained that the best way to build on success was to discard protection and monopolies and so swell the volume of trade and drew profits from the increase: to enlarge the cake rather than cut it up differently. Gradually the main trading nations – the Netherlands, France and ultimately the most successful of all, Britain – stopped insisting that their trade must be monopolised by their companies and their ships. Greeks, as too Armenians and Jews, were no strangers to European trade but so long as protectionist theories prevailed they had perforce to be content with the role of second-class traders, making the best they could of chinks in the protectionist system. They operated at severe disadvantages; but they did operate, and so when the system changed they were ready to take advantage of the change. They were knowledgeable and above all they were there.

The main points of leverage for the Chiots were Odessa in Russia and Livorno (Leghorn) in Italy. The two Ralli brothers who opened their first office in London in 1818 came from these two ports and one of them had a wife from Pisa. The Russian advance into what became southern Russia had got under way with Peter the Great who founded the city of Taganrog in the first years of the eighteenth century but lost it almost as soon as he founded it. Permanent Russian occupation had to wait for the end of the century and Catherine the Great, the German wife of Peter's grandson. Catherine's annexations were given the name of New Russia (Novorossiya). They were divided into three provinces, one named after her and the others – Kherson and Tauride – given ancient Greek names. The jewel of New Russia was Odessa, founded in 1794 and developed with astonishing speed and success under Catherine, her grandson Alexander I and the governors whom they appointed for New Russia – notably the Duke de Richelieu, later Prime Minister of France. From about 5,000 in 1800 the city grew to 10,000 at mid-century. It became one of the most liberal cities of Russia and one of the most cosmopolitan in Europe. Pushkin and Gogol lived, and Liszt performed, there. It became the chief port for the export of wheat from the rich black soil of the lands to the north (which needed no manure) to the whole of Europe via the Mediterranean ports of Livorno, Trieste and Marseilles. But at first the Russian authorities found it difficult to get Russians to settle in New Russia without special enticements: freedom or semi-freedom for serfs, a blind eye to the antecedents of dubious characters, religious toleration for Jews from other parts of Russia. The authorities also enticed foreigners with grants of land, exemption from taxes and military service, and commercial opportunities. Most numerous among these foreigners were Greeks, which was not surprising since Greeks had been coming and going there for centuries, ever since Chios itself and Kaffa in the Crimea had been twin centres of Genoa's eastern empire (not to mention Jason and the Argonauts). They were moreover Christians of the same brand as the Russians and shared the Russian appetite for fighting Turks. Besides their flourishing commerce the Greek families in Odessa and other Black Sea ports raised units to fight in Russian wars and were recompensed with lands and status. They had their own schools, churches and libraries, intermarried among themselves and lived in enclaves in the best sections of the cities. Their main activity was the grain trade where profits were quick and large and which they dominated until mid-century. Then they began to drift away. During the Crimean War the export of wheat from Russia was prohibited and a decade later the opening of the American west after the Civil War provided western Europe with cheaper wheat delivered by the new steamships. Greek merchants sought new commodities and new fields, notably – in the case of Ralli Bros. – cotton which took them to Egypt and India. They abandoned their Russian activities in 1866 and others in Persia and Turkey a little later. Greek businesses in New Russia were largely taken over by Jews, some of whom had learned the trade in Greek firms and, unlike the Greeks and other Europeans, multiplied in Odessa during the century: from being a tenth of a small population at its beginning they grew to a third of a much larger population at its end. Some racial rivalry was evident before the Crimean War when the first of Odessa's anti-Jewish pogroms occurred, the assailants in that instance being Greeks. A number of Greeks stayed on in New Russia as substantial landowners, gentry and government servants and marrying into the Russian landed classes, even the aristocracy. Their descendants were still there at the time of the Bolshevik revolution, when some of them made their way back to Greece.

Livorno in the eighteenth century was a small but busy port with a population around 30,000. It was the main port of the comparatively liberal Duchy of Tuscany which came under the rule of minor Habsburgs after the death in 1737 of its last Medici duke. This prince bequeathed his patrimony to the Habsburgs. It was bestowed on Francis Stephen, husband of Maria Theresa and heir to the Holy Roman Empire (she having no brother). On his marriage Francis Stephen was obliged to give up his own duchy of Lorraine because the French were not prepared to have an adopted Habsburg ensconced on their borders in Nancy, and he was given Tuscany instead. He did not much like his new domain and visited it only once. His son and successor as Grand Duke, however, took the opposite view. It had been decreed that the Grand Duchy must be kept separate from the main Habsburg line and so Francis Stephen was succeeded there by his second (surviving) son who was called Peter Leopold – after Peter the Great, whose daughter, the empress Elizabeth of Russia, was his godmother. Peter Leopold eventually succeeded his childless brother as emperor, but before this promotion he and his Spanish wife lived in Florence and Pisa (which they preferred) for 25 years, during which Peter Leopold set himself to regulate his duchy, and his family of sixteen, in accordance with the enlightened precepts of the French *philosophes*. He reformed agriculture, the finances and the judiciary (abolishing torture and the death penalty); built roads, introduced public health services, regulated prostitution and refurbished the Uffizi Galleries. This atypical Habsburg hated priests and superstition and introduced the mass in the vernacular 200 years before it was sanctioned by any Pope. He was also rather a bore, superficial in his enthusiasms and puritanical in the behaviour which he observed for himself and tried to impose on his Tuscan subjects.

Already famous among connoisseurs, Tuscany flourished materially, particularly in and around Livorno, and the combination of the grand duchy's ancient culture and its new wealth attracted visitors from all parts of Europe and gave a somewhat provincial principality a metropolitan flavour. Florence had a resident English coterie and a flow of more ephemeral visitors who included the Pretender to the English and Scottish thrones under the name of Earl of Albany, and his estranged wife and illegitimate daughter; Sir William Hamilton, with his Emma, in search of Etruscan vases; Horace Mann, diplomatic agent, dilettante and indefatigable letter writer; Edward Gibbon, who visited the Uffizi fourteen times during a two-month stay in the summer of 1764; Johan Zoffany, who painted English notables in well-chosen surroundings and whose own self-portrait can still be seen in nearby Cortona; and a string of royal dukes and lesser grandees. In Pisa Smollett was writing *Humphrey Clinker*, while in Livorno a substantial (in both senses of the word) English merchant colony – which staged a football match with fifty players on either side to mark Peter Leopold's first visit to the town – flourished alongside 4,000 Jews and other traders who basked in the commercial and intellectual liberalism which characterised the port. The variety of its attractions was attested by a palace designed by Inigo Jones and the use of the harbour as a naval base by Admiral Orlov's Russian fleet in the Russo-Turkish War of 1770-74. In this vivacious little place a handful of Chiots characteristically elbowed their way around. A subsidiary point of penetration was Trieste which, under direct Habsburg rule at the head of the Adriatic, was the entrepot for trade between the east and thence overland into Germany, Switzerland and the Netherlands. In this last country several dozen Greek merchant houses established themselves during the second half of the eighteenth century, chiefly in Amsterdam and Rotterdam.

Greeks made themselves useful to their more powerful French and English competitors. English companies, for example, were irked by the monopoly granted to the Levant Company and used Greek traders to circumvent it. Anglo-French competition presented further opportunities. As the English gained the upper hand French merchants, particularly those of Marseilles, dropped their restrictive practices in order to encourage foreign merchants and so keep Marseilles alive in the face of its declining share in Mediterranean commerce. Greeks had an edge over Armenians and Jews because of their dominance in Syria, the centre of the important trade in cloth from west to east, and in Odessa. The Greeks were also more adventurous, or at any rate success made them so. In a period of almost continuous wars from 1750 to 1815 they did not shrink from the hazardous but lucrative business of privateering; they diversified their businesses from trade in goods to lending and even speculating in foreign currencies; and, turning profits into capital, they bought their own vessels and by the early years of the nineteenth century the more successful partnerships had multiple branches extending from southern Russia and Persia to London and points in between. Greeks in this context meant above all Chiots.

All this thriving in foreign parts created at home something like a paradise. The more affluent Chiots had country houses in the Kampos – a district measuring about five miles by one just south of the main town and port. This area was divided into plots of a few acres round a medium-sized stone dwelling of two or three storeys. Round these small estates were high walls, built not for privacy but to keep wind, sand and salt from the oranges and lemons which gave the whole area its beauty, savour and wealth. The outlines of these properties are still to be seen but most of the houses and walls are dilapidated or gone and the great water wheels in their gardens no longer go round. In their heyday, however, life in and around them was sweet and apparently stable. Here, the year before the outbreak of the Greek War of Independence, is an account of what life was like in Chios. The writer is a 25-year-old French diplomat of good family who was posted to the French embassy in Istanbul but found his duties there compatible with extensive trips in the Levant as far south as the Holy Land. He became a keen philhellene and a prolific, if not very scholarly, author whose chief claim to fame is that he carried off the Venus of Milos to Paris. Two extracts from his travel journals give some of the flavour of life at the top in Chios and life at less secluded levels.

In the first he recounts a visit to the country house of Tchelebi Rodacanaki, Tchelebi being roughly the equivalent in Turkish of the French word Sieur for which English has no rendering – a form of politeness which falls short of a title:

The house was outside the town, in a valley full of oranges and lemons which runs from the southern edge of the town from the sea where the hills begin. The house belonged to Tchelebi Rodacanaki, the richest of the Greek merchants in Chios, one of the island's elders (*primats*), and one of the most generous of the founders of the high school ... I went through large groves of lemon and orange, along paths flanked by walls like those in the surroundings of Marseilles, and then through fields with terebinth and scattered palm trees. After two hours' walking, without a guide, I reached the villa ... Its appearance is simple: a stone flight of steps against the wall led me to the first floor and the masters of the house hastened to receive me. They led me to a small rotonda painted in fresco with a view into the far distance; the wind, blowing from the sea through orange groves in bloom, brought us fresh and balmy breezes. First I was made to rest on a white and pink sofa covered in material made at Brusa at the foot of Mt. Olympus in Bithynia. This material gave a soft and pleasant glow to our surroundings. I noticed the care which had been taken to keep from me the crowd of importunate servants which always clutters up the town houses of the opulent Greeks: I saw no single servant during my entire visit. Sweetmeats and coffee were handed to me by Coccona-Tharsitze (Lady Theresa) herself, the wife of Tchelebi Roda-canaki, while the husband, reclining beside me on the sofa, prepared and lit a long pipe for me with his own hands. After this first ceremony Tharsitze bade us repair to a gallery where I was shown a number of pictures, mostly of the Venetian school. From there we went up to the terrace at the top of the house, where a telescope had been erected. I turned it upon the port of Tchesme, the ruins of Ephesus ... .

The writer goes on to describe the gardens with their flowers and artificial waters and other parts of the house, including a library with 2,000 books. At parting his hostess insisted on stuffing his pockets with lemons and bergamots. No wonder that other Greeks, with a touch of envy, accused the Chiots of becoming soft.

Comparatively few lived so well but lower down the social scale the style was still happy and relaxed:

Every evening I went (to the promenade along the seashore) to breathe the fresh air, and immediately I would find myself surrounded by girls from the town. They walk about in noisy groups amidst young men who often accompany them singly. They are only rarely followed by their parents. They sing, dance and laugh and chatter. Sometimes they sit on the grass and tell love stories. Nothing inhibits the freedom and gaiety of their spirit – not even the janissaries who gravely parade past them and smile in Chios at pranks which in Istanbul they would punish. This stretch is the rendezvous for lovers. In Chios love is not expressed in sighs, languishing glances or stammered phrases; passions are declared amid laughter and during the public promenade. Yet these imprudent and apparently permissive customs never lead to scandal. As the sun sets and the Turkish patrol begins its rounds, normal order is restored, female quarters are closed and not even a brother can enter his sister's apartment. The girls coming home from the seashore and those who have been sitting on the stone benches outside their houses and smiling at the young men of the neighbourhood, all disappear at once and are not seen again until the following evening ...

Besides its havens of private civility Chios had a lively academy or high school with 500-600 pupils, a number of them attracted from other parts of Greece; it taught theology, philosophy, mathematics, physics and the Latin, French and Turkish languages. There was a public library with some 6,000 volumes, some of them in Latin or French. There was a printing press with a German director and a stock of founts from Paris. There was a hospital, a madhouse and a leper colony.

Then came the crash. The massacre of 1822 was an episode in the War of Independence. It destroyed for ever an exceptionally prosperous economy and benign society, killed or enslaved or drove to flight nine out of ten Chiots and laid the island waste. The war started in 1821 on the mainland – precisely where is a matter of parochial dispute – but the islands assumed at once a special role because they could put together an Aegean squadron capable of causing the Turks a lot of bother. Chief among these pugnacious islands were Hydra and Spetsai off the coast of the Peloponnese, and early in the war their squadron was joined by vessels from Psara which lies a short distance to the north west of Chios. They summoned the Chiots to join the war.

Patriotism has its price. Chios was the most prosperous corner of Greece and Chiots had the most to lose by rebelling against their Turkish suzerain. This was true for the humbler Chiots as well as for the leading merchants who were among the richest in Greece, and it was no less true for those Chiots, often members of these same families, who were residing permanently or temporarily in Istanbul and other Turkish centres. The heads of families and businesses in the island knew that a successful rising in Chios would immediately imperil the lives of compatriots overseas. An unsuccessful rising would bring ruin upon them and the island too. These prospects counselled caution upon a community already disposed that way as a consequence of its privileged status and prosperous condition. It was too comfortable to want to rebel.

The population of Chios at this date was about 120,000, of whom a quarter lived in the town and the rest in 66 villages, including the twenty mastic villages with their special privileges in this specially privileged island. To all intents and purposes the Chiots ran their own affairs. The Turks were few and kept themselves to themselves and to their quarters in the fortress overhanging the harbour. Istanbul provided a governor and a *cadi* (a superior magistrate), but day-to-day administration and taxation were in the hands of the Council of Five, a little group of leading merchants meeting daily or almost daily to take decisions trivial or momentous, an oligarchic guided democracy in which elections for an executive Council, an assembly and the judiciary were tempered by discreet interventions to ensure that the right persons got elected. Revenue was raised by a poll tax on adult males, levied by the Council and paid to the Turkish governor. The public services and interest on the public debt were paid for by excise duties, also fixed by the Council. The Council had also to find the salary of the Greek Orthodox bishop who was appointed by the Patriarch of Constantinople. His more important acts, such as ordinations and excommunications, required endorsement by the Council: in Chios, unlike most of Greece, the decisive voice was that of the business community, not the bishop. The mastic villages in the south enjoyed a special regime. They were placed under the aegis of the sultan's mother who appointed a special Aga to represent her. These villages paid their taxes in mastic instead of cash and at harvest time the Aga paraded round the area collecting his mistress's share from the elected headmen of the villages. He was not a popular figure and his progress often led to clashes. (This regime was abolished in 1841 and normal taxes replaced the mastic levy.)

So long as the tribute due to them was punctually paid the Turks did not interfere in local affairs. The small garrison in the fortress was a symbol rather than a force, and travellers' accounts of island life suggest that its members had nothing to do except sit outside cafes at the appropriate end of the harbour. According to one orientalist and traveller the government in Istanbul would remove a governor who did not get on with the locals rather than risk a rumpus. For the Turks the main thing was to let well alone. But in 1821 things were not well and could not be left alone. Nor was this a time for half measures. The first Greek risings on the mainland had been met with reprisals in Istanbul where the Greek patriarch and others were hanged. When the Hydriot squadron appeared off Chios in 1821 the Turkish governor parleyed with the Chiot notables and demanded that a number of them deliver themselves up as hostages. They complied and were confined in the fort. Turks were brought across the water from the Asian mainland. Their misbehaviour, sometimes savage, provoked disorders. The notables, caught between the devil and the deep sea, continued to place their faith in the governor and tried to discountenance hostile action from outside. The governor, still playing for time, asked for more and more hostages. At first these had been four of the leading merchants and the archbishop. Then ten more were added, and twenty more, and forty more, until 75 persons in all had surrendered to Turkish custody in the fortress (although allowed for a time to go about their business by day). In some contemporary accounts the number of hostages is considerably higher, but whatever the true figure the governor's purpose is clear: to prevent the Chiots from making common cause with insurgents from elsewhere, by removing and scaring their natural leaders.

With the Turkish garrison too weak to act on its own and the Chiot leaders distraught, the island's fate passed into the hands of those outside it. In Istanbul the government laid hold of all the leading Chiots in the capital – these, like their fellow hostages in Chios, ended up dead – and ordered the Kapudan Pasha or Grand Admiral to set sail for Chios. This he did with 6 ships of the line, 21 lesser vessels and 27 transports. He hove in sight of the island on 8 March 1822 (new style).

Three weeks earlier Chios had been invaded from the neighbouring island of Samos. 500 Samian patriots landed about a mile south of the town. They were accompanied from Samos by 150 Chiots under the leadership of a megalomaniac in French uniform who, after seeing service with Napoleon, had taken refuge in Samos. The invaders, equipped initially with only two cannon, drove the Turks into the fortress mainly, according to a contemporary, by yelling at them. They then established a provisional government, collected more cannon from nearby islands and sent emissaries to the provisional Greek government assembled in Corinth to ask for help. In Corinth they were neither well received nor taken very seriously but, after some delay (which turned out to be serious), they were given two mortars, five other siege engines and a handful of foreign officers who wanted to make themselves useful. Meanwhile back in Chios Samians and Chiots were quarrelling among themselves and the provisional government was making itself unpopular with the locals by trying to tax them. But some villagers joined them.

The arrival of the Kapudan Pasha off Chios was followed by a pause of three days. The Chiots waited uncertainly to see what the Turks intended to do. The Turks, certain about their intentions, waited only to ensure maximum effect. Then they let loose one of the most appalling massacres of the century. Men, women and children were killed wholesale and in the most brutal manner. The town and villages were devastated. Atrocity stories continued to be told for a generation and more; they still make ghastly reading today, and even allowing for inevitable exaggeration a terrible truth comes through: the aim was the virtual annihilation of the population and their homes.

Nine tenths of the population were killed, enslaved or forced into flight. The death tally was around 25,000 in addition to the 75 hostages in the fort and all the Chiot notables who had been arrested in Istanbul and were decapitated there. The harbour was crammed with corpses and in the villages the mounds of dead were left to rot and stink and threaten pestilence. Thousands of their skulls can still be seen today stacked in grisly rows in two chapels in the interior. An even larger number of victims, mostly women and children but including also some males, were sold into slavery in the markets of Istanbul and Adrianople, Smyrna and Cairo. The sultan took a cut of the proceeds of sale. So large was this traffic that the price of a slave fell precipitately and vendors found that they had too many unprofitable slaves on their hands. They solved the problem by killing them. In Istanbul a rare note of protest was raised by an Ottoman princess, the beneficiary of the annual mastic tribute. She was furious at the spoliation of her appanage and refused to be mollified by a gift of sixty beautiful virgins. Among the slaves were two of my great-grandfathers; it took their relatives years to find them and buy them back. About a century and a half later I startled a UN Sub-commission of which I was a member by observing in the course of a debate on modern slavery that two of my great-grandfathers had been slaves. My colleagues were not sure whether this remark by Britain's white representative was a fact or some sort of allegory or just a joke.

Many Chiots fled out of the island. The population may have fallen as low as 10,000 by the time the killing stopped. Over thirty years later there were, according to the Earl of Carlisle who visited Chios in 1854, still only 18,000 Greeks there. A few years after the catastrophe an English traveller came upon a wandering party of sick and destitute Chiots in the southern Peloponnese. Another Englishman complained in 1829 that too much fuss was being made: the world was full of such enormities, he said, and the Greek version of events was being swallowed wholesale because the Greeks were Christians while the Turks were not. He found a lot of rebuilding in progress in the town and a number of well-housed notables.

In 1848 a Swiss cleric reported that survivors were still camped in corners of ruined houses, even though much of the town itself had been rebuilt and about 9,000 Greeks were living in it.

There was some retribution. On the night of 18 June 1822 the Psariot and Hydriot captains, Constantine Kanaris and George Pipinos, sailed fireships into Chios harbour and destroyed, among other vessels, the flagship of the Kapudan Pasha, who was himself struck by a falling mast as his ship exploded. He died as he was carried ashore. This stirring exploit led to more killings on the island.

The massacre of Chios sent a shock throughout Europe which was not equalled until the Bulgarian massacres at the latter end of the century. Delacroix was inspired to paint one of his greatest pictures, Victor Hugo to write a heartfelt ode. In Bath the self-taught painter Thomas Barker covered thirty feet of his private gallery with a splendid fresco. Nor should we omit parenthetically to mention the stanzas, rescued by Mr Osbert Lancaster, from the pen of Miss Amelia de Vere, the poetess of Drayneflete.

Chiots who were neither killed nor enslaved and who managed to get away sought refuge in nearby Aegean islands. Some moved on to Egypt or Malta, where descendants are still to be found. Others went yet further – to Trieste, Marseilles, London. This diaspora, so abrupt to begin with, spread gradually, each generation taking a fresh step. Thus one Calvocoressi, born in Chios in 1807, escaped to the neighbouring island of Syra, where he died. His son, born in Syra, died in Marseilles; and his son, born in Marseilles, died in London after a career divided between Paris and London. He – my sixth cousin once removed – was M.D. Calvocoressi, music critic, one-time secretary to Sergei Diaghileff and close friend of Maurice Ravel whose *Alborada del Gracioso* is dedicated to Calvocoressi. Ravel's *Cinq mélodies grecques* are Chiot songs which were supplied by Calvocoressi to Ravel for a lecture on folk song which Ravel had undertaken to deliver. Besides persuading Ravel to write accompaniments for these five songs, which he did in 36 hours, Calvocoressi taught the singer how to pronounce the Greek words and later provided an introduction when they were published.

But the main engine of the Chiot diaspora was not art but commerce, in which my mother's family was pre-eminently successful and my father's, albeit intermittently, not much less apt.

2

Migrations

My father, who lived into his nineties, used as a boy to listen to his grandfather Matthew, who lived to be around 90 too, recount what happened in those days of horror in 1822. Matthew was then in his teens. The family – his parents, a nonagenarian grandmother, an older half-brother and four younger brothers and sisters – divided their time between a house in the town and another in the Kampos. There was much uneasiness and fear. The Samian patriots who had arrived under the banner of liberation were suspected of baser motives – Chios was a richer island than Samos – and their incursion was thought likely to provoke the Turks into who knew what. The family decided to leave the town for the country but the country house was not far away and as the atmosphere got scarier the family decided to trek further into the countryside and make for Matthew's mother's home to the west. They were a group of about twenty persons including servants. After scrambling down precipices and hiding in caves they reached the west coast but were then spotted by one of the bands of Turks from Asia Minor who had been let loose in the island and were hunting down Chiots to seize money, trinkets and other valuables. Matthew's old grandmother was the first to be killed. She was walled up alive, refusing to abjure her religion. Matthew's father had some of his fingers cut off one by one, protesting that he had no money about him, and when this appeared to be true his head was cut off. Matthew's mother escaped because she was hidden behind the door through which the Turks had burst in upon them; she had her youngest child in her arms and had almost to smother it to prevent it from crying out. The survivors of this fearful scene automatically became slaves and were taken back to the town where they were sold in the slave market. Some of his brothers Matthew never saw again. Matthew himself passed from one owner to another and was taken from Chios to Smyrna and then gradually towards the interior of Asia Minor. Luckily for him successive masters proved milder than his first alarmingly ferocious owner. In this turmoil he came upon one of his small sisters, escaped with her back to the coast, was appropriated by yet another master, but after a number of other adventures got back to Chios where his mother managed to raise the money to buy him back.

Slaves were often well treated by their masters and mistresses, especially if they became Muslims. One of Matthew's brothers became a

Muslim, took a Turkish name and married a Turkish girl. Years later Matthew and his mother rediscovered him and persuaded him to revert to Christianity and return to Chios, but at the last moment he could not bring himself to abandon his wife and children and a promising career as an official of the Ottoman state. But his dithering cost him dear, for he became suspect to the Turkish authorities and may have been murdered. Another brother became a Turkish general and distinguished himself at the battle of Eupatoria in the Crimea. Other renegades did better still. About a century later an uncle of mine met in Istanbul a distinguished scholar in the Ottoman archaeological service who turned out, under his Turkish guise and name, to be a Greek and a cousin. He was, it seems, the son of a former Ottoman foreign minister and Grand Vizier who, born in Chios before the massacre, had been educated in Paris before embarking on a career in the Turkish army and civil service. There must have been far more accommodation to fate of this kind than family records tell or folk memory allows.

To western Europeans horror stories like Matthew's read like something out of the murkier recesses of the Middle Ages, but every Chiot family had one or two and nobody doubted their truth in every terrible detail. Some had happy endings. George Calvocoressi, for example, about six years old at the time of the massacre, was sold as a slave but was tracked down by his family, ransomed and put on a ship bound for Baltimore in the United States with seven or eight other boys. Such was the horror roused by the massacre that charitable foreigners established funds for the rescue and adoption of lost children, and George was adopted by Captain Alden Partridge of the US Navy who provided him with a home and an education at the Military Academy at West Point. His family lost touch with him after his arrival in the United States but recovered contact by advertising, and some years later George met them again when his first tour of foreign duty took him to the Mediterranean. George became a lifelong seaman, served with a famous four-year voyage of discovery to the Pacific and Antarctic, wrote a book about it, saw his name inscribed on the map in two hitherto uncharted reaches, served later in African waters and in Chinese and throughout the American Civil War. He was promoted Captain in 1867 but was disappointingly retired, probably because there was a surplus of officers when the Civil War ended but also not without suspicions of discrimination in favour of officers with better connections and ancestry. Five years later he was mysteriously murdered, leaving a son who became an admiral and transmitted the seafaring bug to descendants to the twentieth century. This branch of the family spells its name Colvocoresses because George's benefactors failed to get their little protégé's name quite right. I happily record that although urged, generation after generation, to change their name to something more manageable all these cousins have (like me) consistently refused to do so.

By contrast, the story of one who stayed behind. Before and during the

Second World War the mayor of Chios was Leonidas Calvocoressi, whose grandfather was for a time a child slave in Smyrna. The child's mistress became attached to him and wanted him to become a Turk and make a new life in Turkish Asia Minor, but he was discovered by his family, rescued by ruse and so brought back to Chios where he died at the age of 90. One of his descendants now lives in a Calvocoressi house in the Kampos.

My father's branch of the family had its ups and downs and my father's boyhood corresponded with one of the downs. Matthew, his grandfather whom I have already mentioned, found his way to England; he was married in London and his first two children were born in Manchester. Presumably he was in business there, but the business did not do well; his two younger children were born in Istanbul, and that looks like a retreat. One of the younger children, John (my grandfather), repeated the cycle. He was born, married and died in Istanbul, but between these events he was in business in Manchester; all but the youngest of his children were born in western places. About 1881, when he was no more than 35, his business failed and he went mad. I do not know the causes of either of these calamities. Perhaps he failed because he went mad, or *vice versa*, or perhaps there was no connection. It is more than possible that his failure was caused by the Depression of the 1870s and after, which used to be labelled the Great Depression until the (much shorter) Depression of the 1930s appropriated the name. The peak of English Victorian prosperity was reached around 1872 and was followed by a depression which lasted to about 1896. It was not the uniform catastrophe once supposed but it was bad enough to force the smaller fry to the wall. Economic growth, although reduced, did not disappear and England's share in the world's manufacture and trade, although challenged by the United States and Germany, remained pre-eminent. But the extraordinary and solitary peak of England's nineteenth-century economic miracle was reduced and with it the peculiar confidence of the English middle classes and their spirit of adventure and innovation. Profits were squeezed and investment likewise, including foreign investment in English enterprises. Exports of textiles, the core of Manchester's wealth, fell off. A weak banking system failed to come to the rescue of hard-pressed businessmen; many local banks collapsed and the nationwide banks of a later age were not yet in place. It is a plausible guess that my grandfather's business was a victim of this slump. His sons, including my father, were all cautious men in business.

However that may be, the whole family left England for San Stefano (now Yesilkoy) where on the seafront of the Bosphorus John's wife had a house. It was, judging by later photographs, quite a grand house or at least elegantly commodious, and it had just made a brief appearance in history, for in it was signed the Treaty of San Stefano which marked the end of the war between the Russian and Ottoman empires in 1878.

When Maurice Baring was in San Stefano during the Balkan Wars (and,

as it happens, in the month of my birth) the place was devastated by
cholera, the streets filled only with the sound of old-fashioned tunes from
pianos behind shuttered windows, and the one Greek school turned into a
hospital. The men in the hospital, which had no beds or medicine or
sanitation, were dying soldiers, mostly Turkish, some Greek, cared for by
a Swiss lady and an Austrian lady (who both caught the pest), a Scottish
minister of religion and an American army surgeon. Baring noticed the
better houses along the front, elegant, whitewashed, two-storey summer
residences of better-off Greeks. A few years and one war later my family's
home had been ransacked and destroyed. It was lost to the family after the
First World War when Greeks fought an ill-conceived and unsuccessful
war against Kemal Ataturk's new Turkey and Greeks in Turkey suffered
for this imprudence. Various members of my family tried for decades to lay
claim to the site, which became quite valuable when Turkey's international
airport was built at Yesilkoy after the Second World War. When my wife
and I went to have a look at the site it consisted of a public playground in
one corner and an ice-cream stand in another and nothing much in
between. Attempts to recover it have been predictably futile.

My father was about seven when his father was engulfed by his double
disaster. From then on he had only dubious prospects but a Chiot network
to fall back upon. He went to the Greek school of the Patriarchate in
Istanbul, then to the Sorbonne and at the age of twenty he had to find a
job. Like all his brothers and other young Chiots he turned to the Chiot
business community, was taken on by Ralli Bros., and spent the whole of
his working life in that firm. He was sent first to New York and then to
India and although he must have visited England on various occasions he
did not live in England from the time when he was seven until he was
posted to Liverpool just after I was born more than thirty years later.

I knew nothing at all about my grandfather's madness or even his
existence. That was not a matter that anybody talked about. More than
that, his own children did not know that he lived on for about forty years.
At the end of the First World War my youngest uncle, who was serving in
the Grenadier Guards, was posted to Istanbul and there discovered by
chance that his father was in an asylum there – he died very soon
afterwards. His wife and brother had cared for him all these years but
entirely in secret. There is in the family no obvious explanation for his
madness since the Calvocoressis were not specially in-bred or hereditarily
feeble. My mother's family on the other hand were extravagantly in-bred
and yet remarkably robust. On my mother's side cousin marriages were so
numerous that I lack the regular number of ancestors, the same individuals appearing in different places in the family tree. Rallis tended to marry
Rallis, partly because they were exceptionally numerous and perhaps also
because they deemed that they could not do better. My maternal grandmother, both my great-grandmothers on that side, and two out of four at
the next remove were all Rallis before they married Rallis. This seemed to

do them no harm. They were a vigorous and intelligent lot, a challenge to conventional eugenics. My grandmother, for example, lived to be 97 although she gave up her favourite pastime, golf, in her eighties. My parents, however, were no closer than fifth cousins which is remote kinship in a close island community. Some experts say that endogamy, although normally detrimental, may be the reverse when repeated cousin marriages breed out the weaker strains: in other words, if the community is tight enough endogamy does more good than harm. My own family has ceased to be a testing ground for such theories since my wife is as entirely English as I am Greek and our daughter-in-law is Ghanaian.

The firm of Ralli Bros., which I have mentioned more than once, took its name from five brothers. Two of them – the eldest, John, who had his main office in Odessa – and the youngest, Stratis, who had his in Livorno – came to London together and opened an office there in 1818, a few years before the Chios massacre. John went back to Odessa and, as the Icelandic Sagas say, is no more in this story. The Black Sea branch of the family's enterprises drifted apart. John, who was for many years American consul in Odessa, died in Paris in 1859; his widow returned to her native Tuscany. He had a son who flourished in Odessa and had twin sons, of whom the one abandoned commerce for a life in the army and the court of St Petersburg while the other remained in Odessa, wealthy and philanthropic but without a son to keep the family name going in that city.

London, meanwhile, flourished and superseded Marseilles as the hub of the Ralli businesses. John's youngest brother Stratis opened a branch in Manchester and was joined in London by another brother from Marseilles. Yet another brother, the second in order of birth, lived his whole life in Marseilles but sent his son Stephen to London where he became the firm's senior partner in the next generation. He carried the story into the twentieth century, dying in London in 1901. He was my great-grandfather. The Rallis became the doyens of the Greek community in London, which was preponderantly Chiot. It was a secular and domestic community whose strongest links were provided by the family and the business. Family ties were unusually strong and wide. They embraced remote cousins and looked after them, even those who were not altogether deserving. The male workers were provided with jobs but with the expectation that they would work hard and – no less imperative – honourably. Religion and the church were another bond, but less strong. Piety was optional, but church-going on a respectable number of Sundays and in Holy Week was a social obligation. It was in decline in my childhood but still in evidence. The leading merchants were automatically the most prominent worshippers: they were nature's churchwardens. They were also more than that, for Chiots – unlike most other Greeks – regarded the church as an extension of the lay community, not the other way round. Not only did they build and pay for and own the church itself, they also insisted on running its affairs without interference from the Greek state or even the Greek

Orthodox synod, and they even claimed the right to participate with the synod in the choice of priests. They acquired a cemetery, or a special section of a cemetery, at Norwood in south London, where a number of sepulchres bloomed in the course of the nineteenth and twentieth centuries, including a mini-Parthenon built by my great-grandparents as a memorial to their eldest son who died at Eton. It is now a listed building. I inherited various rights in this building and assigned them to the Greek community.

When these Chiots first put down roots in London early in the nineteenth century they found there no Greek church, although there had been one in earlier times. Greeks probably used the Russian church in Welbeck Street which was attached to the Russian Embassy and, where for a time at least, the priests were not Russian but Greek. A first Greek church had been built in 1677 in Soho in Hog Lane, later Crown Street and now Charing Cross Road: the site was until recently occupied by the St Martin School of Art. The community of those days was small, transient, poor and churchless, but it managed to press into its service a singularly energetic cleric called Joseph. This Joseph had been archbishop of Samos, but finding the post too much of a strain he had retreated to St John's island of Patmos where he wrote a book and recovered his energies. He then travelled to London, perhaps in search of a publisher, and was prevailed upon to stay and raise funds for a Greek church. Joseph must have been an intrepid character, for although he knew no English he collected £1,500 by the direct method, beginning with the king's brother (the Duke of York, later James II) and the bishop of London. But he soon got into trouble. He became embroiled between rival entrepreneurs – first with Nicholas Barbon, economist, physician, property developer and son of the Cromwellian Praise-God Barebones, and then with one of Barbon's competitors. Also, and not surprisingly, he did not understand the difference between freehold and leasehold and when, with the help of the bishop of London, he acquired the site in Hog Lane he misunderstood what he had bought. More alarmingly, when he accused an associate of embezzling some of the church funds, this associate got his own back by accusing Joseph of being involved in the bogus anti-Catholic ramp known as the Popish Plot.

Joseph soon realised too that he had bought land in the wrong part of London. None of the Greeks lived or worked near Soho. So he decided to sell and build another church, probably further east. The parish of St Martin-in-the-Fields wanted to buy. A jointly appointed valuer assessed the property at £626 but the parish then secured a second and separate valuation of £168, offered the Greeks £200 and, when this offer was refused, made itself master of the building by breaking down the door. This was a financial catastrophe for the Greeks and aborted their plan to build another church somewhere else. This first church was handed over to French Huguenots in 1682 but was still for a long time known as the Greeks' church. Greek Street nearby has more lastingly preserved their name. In the nineteenth century the church was used by Dissenters, was annexed to the Anglican parish of St Anne Soho and finally became the separate parish of St Mary Soho. The original building was all but submerged by reconstructions and was demolished between the two World Wars.

Meanwhile the new Greek bourgeoisie had resolved in the 1830s that it must have a church of its own and so a Brotherhood, an unincorporated association, was formed by 24 persons, nearly all of them Chiots and among them seven Rallis. This Brotherhood still exists, with its rules practically unaltered over 150 years. It built a church at No. 9 Finsbury Circus in the City of London and imported a priest from Chios who stayed until 1848 when he resigned because of advancing years and the dampness of the climate. Similar Brotherhoods catered for Manchester's needs and Liverpool's.

Within a few years it became clear that the church in Finsbury Circus had been too modestly conceived. It was too small for the expanding community, and another was built not far away in Winchester Street. This one functioned for thirty years (1849-79), but the Brothers began to feel that a church near their homes would be more convenient than one near their businesses. They therefore bought a half-acre plot in Moscow Road, Paddington, turned one third of this site over to the local authority for road-widening and erected a church more than twice the size of the one in Winchester Street. The total outlay of £35,000 was subscribed by the community with only one solitary non-Greek benefactor, Edwin Freshfield, solicitor to many Greek firms and families (his father-in-law had been the agent in Smyrna of the Levant Company). The architect, a son of Giles Gilbert Scott, was paid £1,000.

The London Chiots became members of the Victorian bourgeoisie, some of them decidedly rich, others at least what the Victorian bourgeoisie called comfortably off. External and material progress were for most of them steady. In the next century the senior partner of Ralli Bros. died a millionaire and a baronet. I heard it said in awe that his executors signed a cheque for over £1 million of death duties, an act to make the mind boggle and the hand tremble. But in other ways they were not comfortable. However close and self-sufficient their community, they could not but be aware of what we now call the host society which enveloped them and of which they wanted to be part. Unlike many migrants they roused little hostility. Since they looked after themselves financially they made no calls upon the resources or the consciences of the English natives. Unlike, say, the Jews who fled to England after the Russian and Romanian pogroms of 1881-84, the Greeks did not penetrate into England at the bottom of the social and economic pile. They were more like the Huguenots who moved into Spitalfields in the seventeenth century with useful skills and some capital. In religion the Greeks might practise a strange brand of Christianity but they were at least Christians – and not Papists. Nor were even the richest among them ostentatious. They behaved like honorary Victorians who knew how to enjoy good fortune without getting uppity. As the century wore on they increasingly rubbed shoulders with their English counterparts in the business world and in the comfortable leisured classes and, in some cases, the racing fraternity. They found friends too in artistic circles, as witness the friendship of the Ionides family with G.F. Watts (the Ionides collection of pictures, including a number by Watts, is now in the Victoria and Albert Museum), or of Marie Zambaco with Burne-Jones. One of my Ralli relatives became a close friend of a VIP, although an eccentric one. This Ralli was known as Ashstead Ralli from the place where he lived in Surrey: Leigh Hunt, on a walk one Sunday from Dulwich to Brockham beyond Dorking, had noted Ashstead Park's fine walnut trees and 'one of the noblest limes I ever saw'. Ashstead Ralli followed the Chiot domestic pattern of taking a Chiot wife but not, as did his father and brother, another Ralli. He also struck up a special friendship with Herbert Kitchener who made a habit of always staying with him on his rare visits to England. Kitchener, an Irishman, was an untypical British officer. As much archaeologist as soldier, he spent most of his life abroad in Cyprus, Egypt, South Africa or India, but he counted as a famous Englishman and contacts with so notable a person were a source of quiet pride among Greeks who were not sure where they belonged in England. Such contacts seemed significant and important, the more so as long as they were exceptional.

This was a community in transition. You could hear the transition taking place. My mother, for example, and her mother knew no Greek or very little but in my grandmother's home I heard many of her friends speaking English, however fluently, with the strongest foreign accents. My father, who spent all his adult life in English-speaking countries, never lost all trace of an accent but did not like to be told so. Physically the London Greeks moved from the genteeler suburbs to the next-to-smartest parts of London. My great-grandfather used to take his carriage every working day from Streatham to Finsbury Circus in the City where, although he was the senior partner, he signed his name in a register before a line was drawn across the page at 9 o'clock. One of the original Ralli Bros. lived on Putney Heath in a house called, when he bought it, the Gothic Villa but renamed Scio House – Chios is Scio in Italian and was the form used in England and France at that time. Designed by the neo-classical architect H.L. Elmes, designer of St George's Hall in Liverpool, this house was within a stone's throw of the Bowling Green where William Pitt and William Tierney duelled in 1798 and Castlereagh and Canning in 1807. Pitt lived and died in nearby Bowling Green House. (Duelling in England became more parliamentary than knightly before it was stopped. The last public duel, fought in 1852, also involved a Member of Parliament.)

With time and prosperity these Greeks moved either outward to the home counties or inward to London's core. For me as a child London was epitomised by my grandmother's home at 33 Porchester Terrace, Bayswater. I do not know when my grandparents bought this house but they did not enjoy it together for long since my grandfather died suddenly in his forties; he died before his father-in-law, whom he was expected to succeed as head of the family firm. My grandmother, still only 35, remained in Porchester Terrace until the Second World War when the house was bombed. She took up photography and became proficient in a special treatment called bromoil transfer for which she used a couple of dark rooms at the back of the house into which my sister and I were occasionally allowed to penetrate if we opened and shut the door quickly. Her work was exhibited all over the world and we were much impressed when we saw examples labelled for despatch to Tokyo.

From my grandfather's death 33 Porchester Place was a home without a man, inhabited by my grandmother, my mother aged fifteen, her younger sister and half a dozen female servants. My mother lived there for the next twelve years. These years no longer shed much light. There are glimpses of a high-spirited, affectionate and also studious girl in a benevolent but small circle of family and friends. She learned from governesses what girls were taught at the beginning of this century. She was attracted to music, played the piano and the guitar and played in a guitar orchestra. Besides French, which was an automatic acquirement, she learned German and read German literature, past rather than contemporary. Among her books there is no Italian, not even Dante, but she had a smattering of Italian and was familiar with Renaissance painting from London galleries, from books and perhaps from talk with her father. English literature meant mainly Victorian novels and poetry with some extensions at the earlier end. A pocket Herrick and Longfellow which I still have are inscribed: 'Prize for the croquet tournament, Westgate, 1903.' At Christmas that year, when she was 21, her mother's present to her was the works of Thackeray in thirteen volumes, bound in red leather, half calf, with gilt tops. When she died 34 years later in her fifty-fifth year some of the pages of some of these volumes were still uncut but most were cut. There is, it seems to me, a hint of puzzlement in her mother's mind in choosing a present of this kind, verging even in 1903 on the stodgy. George Eliot followed next Christmas and there are sets of Dickens, Fanny Burney, Charles Kingsley (the last with gilt sides and bottoms as well as tops), two dozen volumes of standard poets, plus a Tennyson in nine volumes and a Swinburne in seven. My mother would have taken these presents to Bumpus' bookshop, then on the north side of Oxford Street, to choose a leather binding and the ornaments to be impressed in gold on the spines. She would have been met by an assistant who knew her and whom she knew by name (years later when I went with her on similar errands he was Mr Garland); and she would have gone back to collect her books only a week or so later. She treasured her books but which of them she loved I do not know. Most of them have descended to me. I am very glad to have them. They are finely printed and bound; they put me in mind of my mother; and being always

at hand I have read them more often than I would have done if I had had
to go to a library for them instead of reaching out upon a whim to take
them from their shelves.

Porchester Terrace, ample and quiet, led its inhabitants gently into
Hyde Park at its southern end. Trollope and Galsworthy found it appropriate for some of their less exciting characters. After the Second World
War it was amputated at its north end where a school and an apartment
block were built, cutting it off from Bishop's Bridge Road. The houses in
Porchester Terrace were a mixture. Some, like my grandmother's, stood in
their own large gardens with a garage (ex-stables) round at the back.
Others were in pairs, semi-detached. Others were humbler still but none
was really humble. Unlike W1 or SW1, Mayfair or Belgravia, W2 was
comfortable rather than grand; but the comfort was pronounced. My
grandmother's home was as comforting as my grandmother herself – all
calm and affection, almost entirely uncensorious although far from uncriti-
cal. The furniture and furnishings were more solid than elegant and so
were the servants. These were of my grandmother's own generation. At
least two of them had been her mother's servants; the elderly parlour maid,
who had not, was referred to as young Rose. This house, destroyed by
bombs in the war, stood between two equivalent houses belonging to
Franklins and Samuels, well-to-do Jews. The Samuel in question was
Herbert Samuel, statesman, proconsul and philosopher who, when in office
as a Minister, enjoyed the protection of a policeman whose presence added
as much dignity to the Terrace as the great man himself. Such houses were
very private domains; you knew whom you might meet there. They were
glimpsed rather than seen, reticently shrouded by high walls and big trees
– in my grandmother's case, a high mulberry tree which children were
warned to keep away from when the fruit was ripe and most tempting. The
garden had another and more dubious attraction. My grandmother had a
relative, a sort of niece, who was fond of cats. The cats, of course, died from
time to time. I remember an occasion, a Sunday afternoon, when a few
friends were solemnly having tea in the drawing-room and the niece
arrived with a dead cat loosely wrapped in a newspaper. She wanted to
bury it in the garden. My grandmother motioned her through the French
windows with a kindly smile but probably with the thought that the timing
of this unheralded visit was unfortunate. I myself was disconcerted less
by the poor cat in its dingy wrapper than by the fact that my elderly relative
was wearing shabby white gym shoes which were not in those days seemly
drawing-room attire, least of all on a Sunday. This departure from conventional proprieties disturbed me more than the fate of the cat.

This existence – comfortable, cloistered, protected – was repeated in the
Greek colony in Liverpool where my parents and I arrived at the beginning
of 1913 and remained for the next fifteen years. I had been named Peter.
There was a touch of eccentricity about this choice. There is, so far as I can
discover, only one Peter among my Calvocoressi forbears and he was eight

generations back from my father. During a long life which occupied most
of the eighteenth century (1706-94) and began and ended in Chios he
acquired the title of Hadji, indicating that he had been on a ranking
pilgrimage – not presumably in his case to Mecca, as the word strictly
implies, but rather to Jerusalem or some equivalent Christian shrine. On
my mother's side there was a sprinkling of Peters but since I was my
parents' first-born they did not count since convention decreed that I
should be named after my father's father. My mother chose Peter simply
because she liked the name. When relations wrote in puzzled protest to
ask why I was not to be called John my parents took the precaution of
adding both my grandfathers' names in order to forestall similar arguments in the future. These names have never meant much to me. Only a
first name is truly personal: others tend to be either part of one's inheri-
tance or, with an eye on godparents, of expectations, or just passing fancies
to give body to an infant who might seem a bit base with a single name.

My parents were comfortably off with the added bonus of never expecting to be anything else. My father was clearly in Ralli Bros. for life. He had
no thought of moving from one firm to another in pursuit of a bigger salary
or a fortune. He must have had a good salary and as a senior manager he
had also a share in profits before these were divided among the partners,
who were just three. My mother had what were called expectations
although she did not live to inherit them. My parents lived without fear of
failing resources or the itch of ambition to go higher. My father, careful
with money but not mean, generous but not flashy, was a good example of
the virtues and values of pre-Thatcherite capitalism.

Our house in Liverpool, Holme Hey, was on the edge of Sefton Park
which was on the edge of the city: the trams stopped just short of it. The
Park was one of the first public parks to be laid out, in the 1860s, after a
public competition for its design. Holme Hey is no longer there although
its neighbour has survived. When I went to visit it more than sixty years
later it had gone without trace and the whole plot in which we had roamed
and played as children was strangely and disappointingly small. The park
where we had fed, or overfed, the municipal ducks was shabbier than I had
expected and the Palm House, Liverpool's reply to the Crystal Palace, was
dilapidated. Holme Hey had been a largish stone house in a largish garden.
Spaciousness, I have come to see, is one of the greatest prizes of wealth,
not necessarily in the size of one's house but in the size of its rooms, be
they few or many. All my life I have lived in houses with big rooms, two
before I married and two since with only a single year in a small flat in
London the year before the war. That is not the least of the ways in which
I have been lucky. My home in Liverpool, decently shrouded by vegetation,
had a lawn in front, a tennis court behind, a rocky dell with big trees on
one side and a garage with rooms above it in one corner. It was an
undistinguished architectural jumble with some slight, almost apologetic
castellation. Its key note was substantiality. It had three floors above

ground and one below. The top floor was shared between my sisters, myself and our keepers (nurse and nursery maid, the latter usually French) and the servants. The servants had their bedrooms here and also a large workroom at the end of a corridor where at certain hours of the day two or three of them would be engaged in mending sheets or such chores. It was not clear whether the workroom was out of bounds to us children. There was an invisible line between children and servants and a thin one. It was there partly to ensure that we did not 'bother' the servants or unduly invade their territory and partly so that they might get on with their work; there was also the indefinable distance to be preserved between servants and nursery staff who were a cut above the servants, or at any rate above the indoor servants if not perhaps the chauffeur. The servants' workroom was a cheerful place with large windows opening to the west and an easy welcome for us, whatever the theoretical demarcation lines might say. That servants were servants went without saying – it was a fact of life – but more to the point was that we saw them all the time and regarded them as friends. In one sense they were our closest friends. We had other friends who were friends because they were the children of our parents' friends, but they were not part of our daily life and being, like us, mere children, were not confidants. We accepted the master-servant relationship without embarrassment and I have little doubt that the servants did so too so long as their treatment, more important than their status, was just and civilised, which in our household it was. This does not mean that no servants ever gave any thought to their inferior status. The younger ones must occasionally have wondered why they should be facing lives so very different from ours, while the older ones must have felt a twinge of apprehension as they approached a retirement without pensions or a home of their own. And we too sensed something amiss which I can best illustrate from an episode so painful to me that I have never forgotten it or even recounted it to anybody.

It happened on my birthday when I was still a very small boy. I collected in those days small bronze animals. One of my birthday presents was a bronze horse and cart which delighted me. I had had them only a few hours when, carelessly swinging them by the reins, I knocked them against a piece of furniture and broke off one of the horse's legs. I felt overwhelmed by grief and remorse, the more so because this was the present given me by our nursery maid and I was horrified that she might think that I had not cared for her present as much as I would for things given me by my family. I learned early that, as Jonathan Swift said, the giving or receiving of presents is an affair of as delicate a nature as most in the course of living.

From the windows of our nursery I made my first intellectual observation. Seeing the tall trees of Sefton Park swaying in the wind I deduced that the trees caused the wind. Although I subsequently found out that this was not so, I have never been able to detect any logical defect in my reasoning. But I was no nursery intellectual and was then – as since – as much intrigued with practical efficiency as abstract reasoning. I remember, for example, waging a secretive war with my nannie over an elementary time-and-motion problem. I saw that getting up in the morning could be made easier and quicker if the night before I took off my shirt and vest together and left the one inside the other so that both could be put back on again in a single operation. This procedure was, however, vetoed on the grounds that vests must be aired and not left inside shirts. Unconvinced, I continued to do things my way as often as I thought I could get away with it. Inefficiency and incompetence are minor human failings but all the same they have irritated me immeasurably all my life. One curious feature of our nursery quarters, which I have never seen anywhere else, was a round shaft or tunnel about a foot in diameter running at eye level between the day nursery and night nursery and closed at either end by a small glass door. By looking along this ingenious passage grown-ups could assure themselves that all was well without disturbing sleeping children. As we grew up this night nursery was handed over to me as my sole territory, equipped among other things with a bookcase in which I began to store and treasure my own books. All our rooms upstairs had sepia reproductions of famous pictures, chosen at first by my mother but later by her in conjunction with us, searching through catalogues which came from a shop in Oxford Street in London. We had Hobbema's *Avenue*, one of Raphael's more famous Madonnas (the one in Dresden), Millet's *Angelus*, a picture by Mauve called (I think) *The Sandcart*, a picture of a sailing ship called *Off Valparaiso* whose artist I cannot recall, Rosa Bonheur's *Horse Fair*. There must have been quite a few more if I am right in recalling that we added one new one every year.

Holme Hey had two special features: an aviary and a music room. The aviary was part of a conservatory which opened off the hall on the ground floor through a pair of big glass doors and housed, besides the usual potted plants and cane chairs, a netted enclosure which was my father's delight. He was a man who loved to exercise homely ingenuity and in his aviary he constructed a system of perches in which every perch was directly or indirectly connected with every other perch so that each slightest movement of each tiny bird set the whole system in motion and gave them, so he thought, the sensations which they would get from the branches of softly agitated trees. He also provided the birds with a choice of climate by extending the aviary through one of the conservatory's walls into an external annex, which, however, was closed in very cold weather. They were very little birds, about an inch and a half long, mostly from India or Australia, brightly coloured seed-eaters, several dozen of them, plus a few Harz canaries noted for their roller song; the canaries were twice as big as the rest and added song to the twittering. From time to time we would go to a shop in Liverpool or to Gamages in High Holborn in London to buy new birds or gadgets for them. When one of them got ill it had to be caught and put in a special box or cage in front of the fire in the drawing room where it might lay an egg and get better. The hope was that they would not only lay eggs but raise young. This would have been a triumph but, as far as I can remember, it was perennially disappointed.

The second special feature of our home was the music room. Much the biggest room of the house it was stuck onto the back of it and ran along its whole length and up in Gothic style through two storeys. It was used for dancing classes (select friends included), for listening to the gramophone, for romping on its polished floors and for parties. The gramophone was a massive instrument of the kind now used to give a period flavour to stage sets. The records betokened my mother's love of German Lieder – sung by Elena Gerhardt, Elizabeth Schumann, Lotte Lehmann; Neapolitan songs from *O Sole Mio* to Tosti's *Ideale* sung by Caruso; Strauss waltzes and Souza marches; opera arias on single-sided records to be played at speeds varying between 78 and 82 – I remember Adelina Patti singing *Voi che sapete* rather slowly; and current foxtrots, waltzes and tangos. The parties were splendid Christmas functions which went on for the best part of twelve hours. This was because they were stratified. The earliest stage was a children's party for my younger sister (seven years my junior) and her friends, with a conjuror or some such entertainer, a generous distribution of presents, and a considerable meal. Next came the section for my older sister and myself, whose main components were dancing and eating. We both loved dancing and were good at it, and I recall that – excessive though it may seem – there was both a buffet and a sit-down meal. When we and our friends had been driven off, the third and final section took the form of a dance and supper for the grown-ups. Much of the food came from Messrs. Barbellion in London in dozens of small cardboard boxes full of delicious titbits just not too squishy to be eaten with the fingers and preferably small enough to be popped into the mouth in one go. Unpacking all these goodies and preparing the party was almost as much fun as the party itself, an enlivening bustle involving my mother, ourselves and a small gang of servants. My mother loved getting things ready and right, while my father was happily engaged in seeing that doors were taken off their hinges and stowed safely away. As preparations moved towards the event itself, there was a tiresome interval devoted to 'getting ready' which meant washing, donning best clothes and being reminded that hosts have responsibilities. We were enjoined to keep an eye on all our guests and make sure that the shy and awkward ones were having a good time. Fifty or more years later, after I had given a short radio talk of reminiscences, I got a letter from a distant cousin who used to come to our parties and remembered my mother 'dark haired and very pale' and my father 'rather short and making jokes to draw the shy ones into the fun' – and me, 'the possessor of much envied fairish, curly hair'. My father loved dancing and went at it with vigour, but since he was as unmusical as could be he responded to the music by marking time with his and his partner's

outstretched arms in a way which seemed to my sister and me embarrassingly exuberant.

In the more prosaic 364 days of the year we lived a life which seemed to
us normal but was in fact anything but normal for most Liverpudlians. We
were waited on not only by our own servants but also by the shopkeepers.
Food was ordered by telephone and delivered by van as soon as ordered.
Our clocks were wound by a clock man who came every week to wind them.
Obviously we were not incapable of winding up clocks, but we just did not:
it was somebody else's job. Even the shoemaker came to the house and
traced our feet on pieces of paper when we children needed new shoes. So
too did a hairdresser, although when I grew older my father took me to a
barber 'down town' who had a contraption which I have seen nowhere else.
From a rod near the ceiling descended elastic loops, one over each chair,
and into these loops the barber fitted a big brush with a long handle. He
then pulled the brush down, causing the loop to rotate the brush and so
pound one's scalp. When we chose to go shopping we might take the tram
but if we did so we waited at the tram stop for a first-class tram, which
was painted white instead of plum and had blue cushions on the seats
instead of none. Shopping expeditions by car – a Daimler, a Rolls Royce
being considered rather out of our class – might be extended to the docks
so that we might look at the big Cunard or White Star liners which were
still using Liverpool, not yet Southampton, for the crossing to America. We
knew that Union Castle or Holt ships went to other parts and we knew
how to recognise all these lines by their funnels. Other expeditions took us
to the Greek church which was more than ordinarily boring since we knew
no Greek, but mercifully these duty calls were kept to a socially necessary
minimum – as were the infrequent but uncomfortably formal visits by the
priests to our house. For holidays we went to North Wales, later to Sussex,
later still to a marvellous place called Abroad (which I reserve for another
chapter). At Criccieth in North Wales we children and our train occupied
year after year the same small cottage for a month or two, while our
parents took the twin cottage for the shorter period allowed for my father's
leave from the office – a few weeks only. Holidays meant a different routine
in a different place: on the shore in the morning, going for a walk in the
afternoon. The one excitement came when a siren blew for the lifeboat to
be launched, a strenuous business of hauling the boat from its shelter and
over the rocks by manpower but, in summer, not frequent. At Criccieth, so
legend has it, I was kissed in my pram by Miss Megan Lloyd George.

From 1922 onwards we began to take our summer holidays in Sussex,
most of them on or around Ashdown Forest. At the appropriate time the
search would begin for a suitable house to let. My mother would go to
London to make the round of agents who specialised in summer lettings
of this kind. The owners presumably used the rent we paid either to prop
up declining fortunes or to make a splash in the south of France. The
essentials were a tennis court and spare rooms for favourite uncles and

cousins. If not essential, yet automatic, was a good greenhouse with luscious fruit and the services of a gardener who 'went with' the house. Of our own servants some came with us in relays while the others had their own holidays or stayed in Liverpool on what were called board wages, a skeletal rearguard. (I hope they had a good time but since the servants were themselves a strict hierarchy I suspect that there was little letting down of hair.) The main point of going to Sussex was that my grandmother summered every year at Colemans Hatch in easy reach of the Ashdown Forest golf courses where she pursued her favourite activity and had it taught to me.

A small world, however happy, can be an ill preparation for a bigger one. Those who inhabit small worlds seldom realise that they do so, and venturing out may bring unpleasant surprises. I took my world for granted, found it good and sufficient and did not think about what lay beyond. It had not occurred to me that being Greek was odd or that my foreign origins and name would evoke jibes and ridicule. My fair and curly hair did not help, nor the fact that I was both too timid by half and too clever by half: out of twelve terms at the prep school to which I now went I spent eight in the top class and discovered the hard way that being bright at lessons is no passport to popularity at school. To be called a greasy Greek was as astonishing as it was wounding and scaring. (I have distrusted alliteration ever since.) Not until many years later did I discover, with equal surprise, that to some people being Greek was romantic and a good thing. Some of the masters were as bad as the boys, in the masters' case unforgivably. On one occasion the headmaster's end-of-term report, commenting on my failings in some subject, ascribed them to my race (he used that word) and even at that age I sensed the meanness of prejudice as well as the unfairness of the comment. Silently I criticised my father for not being angrier at this slur and I still recall its perpetrator with unforgiving distaste. When I left that school my parents, conforming with custom, gave presents to all the masters. My father gave a lot of thought to choosing something appropriate to each of them but I, nervously and perhaps ungenerously, felt that he somewhat overdid it.

The school had a scheme of rewards and punishments called Stars and Stripes. A Star was red and good, a Stripe was blue and bad. There was a board with every boy's name on it and opposite each name two strips which were gradually filled up with red or blue chalk as the term progressed. But a blue square took up twice as much space as a red one, so that it was twice as hard to be good as to be bad. I thought this bias hugely unfair and typical of the way the school was run. Many accounts have been written about schools of this kind and many people who have never seen them from the inside have dismissed these descriptions as the exaggerated caricatures of literary licence. When I say that I hated every minute of my life at my prep school I realise that I must be exaggerating, but none the less that is how I remember it and I am sure it was a dreadful place. I found compensation in private addictions. I became a collector. At one time or another I had been mildly interested in collecting stamps or birds' eggs or cigarette cards, but my heart was not in these pursuits. Then I discovered the joys of collecting facts. Although many facts are dull, the pursuit of facts and putting them together is an intriguing exercise and so I learned and arranged in their proper order the names of Roman emperors because Roman emperors happened to come my way. The beauty of knowing things and the excitements of discovering them absorbed me. I read long and often boring books in order to extract bits and pieces from them in much the same spirit as I might spend a rainy afternoon doing a jigsaw puzzle and I began a lifelong dabbling in compilations of odd facts such as Isaac D'Israeli's *Curiosities of Literature*, Haydn's *Dictionary of Dates*, Fowler's *English Usage*, the Penguin *Dictionary of Saints*. Among the things I collected was a vocabulary. I was fond of words and their derivations. I discovered the new craze for crossword puzzles and bought square blanks (newsagents sold them in pads), fitted words to the spaces, contrived clues for these words and hunted new words and meanings in dictionaries. Such were the private, almost furtive, occupations which were a refuge from the incivilities of prep school life. That they did not turn me into a bore and a pedant I owe to my next school which was very different.

Of eight Calvocoressi cousins in my generation only one married a Greek and much the same was happening in other families. This was the big shift and its biggest single cause was education. Going to an English prep school was the first step in a new migration which took me away from being more Greek than English and made me more English than Greek. The Greek community provided its members with many things including jobs and brides, but it did not provide education beyond the most elementary stages in reading, writing, doing scales on the piano and learning to dance the hornpipe (a dance which I never had occasion to perform outside our dancing class at home). The boys had to go to schools and I went to boarding schools because that was what the system provided. Mothers might sigh at losing a son for more than half the year but the system was famous and highly prized and there. For my parents, as for Edward Gibbon's, it was 'the convenient and customary mode of English education'. Paradoxically what I got in this English system was a classical education whose roots were Greek. And perhaps the beginnings of something else. I remember taking my leave of the headmaster who asked me if I was sorry to be going and I remember the utter astonishment with which I heard myself saying that, no, I was not sorry. That may have cut the interview short, for I did not get the expected explanation of the mysterious mechanisms of sex, about which, therefore, I remained ignorant for some time to come.

3

A Classical Education, with History

The outstanding features of the English public schools' education are often confused. They are boarding schools and they provide what is called a classical education. These characteristics, although they overlap considerably, are not the same, since the one concerns what is taught and the other where it is taught.

The case against boarding schools is simple and persuasive but not wholly decisive. The boarding school takes a child away from home, beginning at a distressingly early age. It offends against the deeply ingrained view that home is better. But, to give the devil his due, a boarding school may provide something which even the best home does not: a community of contemporaries. At home children make friends, visit their houses and may go on holiday with them, but these few friends do not constitute a community or an independent forum. They are an annex to the home rather than a separate world, the children of one's parents' friends rather than one's own friends. At school there is, for good or ill, a distinct community where one learns to live with people other than guardians and to talk and think on equal terms on matters trivial and serious. At Eton I benefited from this companionship as much as I benefited from the teaching. I got to know boys from different homes, boys maturer than myself, conversant with ideas and books which I became eager to explore – if only to keep up, which may be a base reason but opens vistas all the same.

Boarding schools used to be quite small. The eighteenth-century house in which we lived for 39 years during and after the Second World War in Aspley Guise in Bedfordshire was a boarding school or Classical Academy for most of that century and half the next. Its normal complement seems to have been around 100 boys but rose on occasions to 230 or 250, taught at its peak by eight masters. In its earlier days pupils were sought by private correspondence, notably in 1723 after 'some vacancies (were created) by the smallpox'. The school taught English, Latin, Greek, French, Arithmetic, Merchants Accompts, Geometry, Trigonometry and Navigation for (in 1810) 25 guineas a year with Dancing, Drawing and Music available for another one guinea each per quarter. The owner/headmaster lived in the small early Georgian house, perhaps accommodating one or two of his assistant masters in it. Classrooms and dormitories, no longer in existence, were across a yard. The boys must have had access to the house as well as the out-buildings since some of their names were still to be made out crudely cut in the woodwork round our bedroom windows. They included a Paxton, presumably a member of the local family of Paxtons which produced Joseph Paxton, gardener to the Duke of Devonshire and designer of the Crystal Palace. In 1799 the village church had to be enlarged to take the school on Sundays. The school changed hands in 1815 for £4,300 but it began to run into difficulties and closed about 1840. One of the difficulties was the building of railways which enabled parents anxious to dispose of their children to send them further away to the larger and more famous schools which were proliferating in this period. Many famous schools were either founded or revived in the nineteenth century.

But some were old and venerable, founded in the late Middle Ages (Winchester, Eton) or soon afterwards (Harrow, Westminster) in order to educate poor boys to the level needed to make them useful to their betters and incidentally provide them with careers a notch above farm labourers or shop assistants. Henry VI founded Eton in 1440 to educate 24 poor scholars – soon increased to seventy. The school began to expand from this nucleus soon after it came into existence. Enterprising landladies took in non-scholars called oppidans (townsfolk) and so became the precursors of the later House Masters. They were called Dames and to this day a House at Eton is referred to by its inmates as M'Dame's. In the eighteenth century assistant masters entered the house-keeping business to supplement their pay but it was not until the next century that the Provost and Fellows began to build Houses themselves and to buy up existing ones. There was still in my time one House which was owned by its House Master.

The competition for the seventy places in the College where the scholars lived ran thin in the early modern period, so that a boy of no more than average ability could sail in before entering his teens, proceed automatically to a similar scholarship at the affiliated King's College at Cambridge and then, after taking Holy Orders, relax for the rest of his life in one of the vicarages in the gift of Eton or King's. The first stage was the hard one since life in College at Eton was by most accounts disgusting and vicious. But the nineteenth century saw expansion and reform as the propertied classes – the aristocrats and the wealthy, two overlapping but never co-terminous categories – expanded and the social elite was enlarged to take in merchants and manufacturers as well as land-owning nobles and squires. In the same period the new opportunities and techniques and leisure of the industrial age fostered those twin pillars of education: the search for useful knowledge and a more purely intellectual curiosity. The public schools multiplied and grew to meet these needs and to net the material revenues. Eton, when I went there in 1926, had over a thousand boys. There were eighty assistant masters, including 25 House Masters.

But professional conservatism ensured that what we were taught changed more slowly than the school's size and composition. The public schools remained Classical Academies, like the school kept in the fourth century in Rome by Aelius Donatus and attended by St Jerome (like myself a migrant from the Balkans) and renowned no less than Eton for its teaching standards, social exclusiveness and high fees. And in both, the basis of the curriculum was the Latin of Cicero and Virgil which, if not dead in Jerome's day, was already antiquated.

The classical education has been derided for being pedantically remote and irrelevant. It is easy to see the force of this indictment but it misses the mark – or an important mark – by a sizeable margin. The classical education was an education in what are called the Classics (they got this name at the Renaissance), which is to say the languages and literature and history of ancient Greece and Rome which were regarded as unique repositories of wisdom and beauty. That was what the learned believed. They much exaggerated the continuity between the Classics and modern Europe: most medieval priests and monks knew little Latin outside their breviaries and had no scholarship worth the name, most medieval lawyers knew far less Roman law than their modern successors. But a few in the Middle Ages knew enough to preserve a shaky bridge between a golden classical past and a post-Renaissance revitalised classicism which recovered ancient writings and thinking and went on to assert the superiority of the European Classics over all other civilisations. The twentieth century has played down such arrogant claims, but it is at least sound to argue that the Classics have made a crucial contribution to modern Europe and a much greater one than any other civilisation. Other civilisations are not to be neglected or decried but for schoolboys Greece and Rome were enough to be going on with.

The Classics were taught for a wider reason than their supposed uniqueness. Unique or not they were a way to train the adolescent mind, show the pupil how to think straight and cultivate his powers of expression in speaking and writing. The classical education was good at these things and that is why it lasted so long. There are also subsidiary reasons for honouring it. The remoteness of the Classical Ages, far from being a mark against it, stretches the imagination further than comparable events in more recent times. Hannibal's wars provide a better education than the Wars of the Roses because Hannibal's wars move you a thousand miles and two thousand years further off. Nor can you read the Classics without catching a glimpse of Socrates and at least a hint that he had things to say which are still immensely cogent. And, finally, the classical education fulfilled the major purpose of showing that learning things is less important than learning that there are always more things to learn.

Although the Classics were commonly referred to as Greek and Latin there was more Latin than Greek at the school level. No public school except Winchester made Greek a condition for admission, although most (perhaps all) of them required Greek for a scholarship. Latin had an unbroken history in western Europe and even when Greek writers were rediscovered at the Renaissance Latin remained the *lingua franca* of Christianity and the leading element in education. The study of Greece and Greeks made a surge in intellectual circles and it also found some favour among Protestants who associated Latin with Roman Catholicism, but it did not begin to catch up with Latin until the eighteenth century when Germans in particular and the Romantic movement in general adopted Greece as a counterweight to the austere virtues of the Roman Republic and the militarism of the Roman empire. England followed the German example and made a distinctive contribution when aristocrats and others pushed the Grand Tour beyond Italy into Greece. By my time Greek occupied a peculiar position *vis-à-vis* Latin. It had attained a cultural priority, partly because of the chronological priority which made the Romans into pupils of the Greeks (notably in the arts and philosophy), but all the same we did more Latin than Greek. There were some boys who did no Greek. Ironically they were designated in the School List by a letter of the Greek alphabet: they were *kappa* boys.

The education which I shared with St Jerome and thousands in between us was classical in the sense that its institutions, its methods and the core of its curriculum were all derived directly from the educational ideas and institutions of ancient Greece and Rome. There is incidentally no better introduction to the mind of the ancients and their persistent influence over two thousand years than the *History of Education in Antiquity* by H.I. Marrou, a book whose dour title belies its entrancing contents. The educational traditions of the ancients shaped medieval education and maintained their sway in Europe into modern times. Perhaps my generation has been the last in this country to enjoy – or endure – a schooling which its father, Plato's contemporary and adversary Isocrates, would recognise.

The basic tool of this education was language. Learning a language is a discipline for sharpening a pupil's mental and intellectual capacities, his unique heritage. The classical *trivium* – comprising what the ancients called Rhetoric, Grammar and Dialectic – meant the use of words and phrases in order to make things clear and get them right. It was at the root of medieval scholasticism, which eventually got a bad name because it declined into a dreary formalism and narrow theological apologetic; but it was revived and reanimated by the Renaissance of classical learning towards the end of the Middle Ages. Classical literature was inseparable from this schooling in language because the surviving classical texts, poetry and drama, philosophy and history, were the natural extensions of learning words in order to master knowledge and ideas. The main purpose was not to breed classical scholars (who were a by-product) but to train the mind, lead it to the fountains and perhaps make it drink. There is everything to be said for learning modern languages but the common antithesis between teaching modern languages or dead ones is false. The object of learning a modern language is to be able to speak it, but practically

nobody has for centuries learned Greek or Latin in order to speak these
tongues. Even for Roman Catholic clerics Latin is not a conversational
facility and the last lay body to have Latin as a regular spoken language
was the Hungarian Parliament which dropped it after the first World War.
The purpose of learning Latin and Greek is intellectual and in the widest
sense educational – to extend the mind, not the vocabulary. Thus learning
a modern or an ancient language are not educational alternatives. They
are alternatives only because, since there is no time for everything, a choice
has to be made between one thing and another. Neither choice can be made
without some loss. The claim of the Classics is that they are the authors
of our civilisation and so have a special relevance (which the Chinese
Classics, for example, do not have) by virtue of this relationship. Our
western civilisation has remained essentially Greco-Roman in spite of
additions and modifications, of which Christianity has been the most
influential. In eastern Europe, in Slav lands in particular, Christianity
may perhaps have become as potent as the Greco-Roman classic matrix,
but further west the way we think and what we prize derive principally
from the ancients whom I read at school. And, finally, the classical writings
have a precision, linguistic and logical, which is an excellent mental
training. They are not the only great writings or the only beautiful ones
but they possess qualities of clarity and discipline, together with a richness
of vocabulary, which makes them supremely good guides and masters.
They have intrinsic as well as historical virtues. As inflected languages
they are peculiarly malleable: if the function of a word does not depend on
its position in the sentence, the writer or speaker has a wider choice in the
arrangement of his words with consequent opportunities to shift the
emphasis or mould the lilt. Latin in particular possesses a fertile variety
of words meaning nearly the same thing but not quite the same, so that
once more the writer or speaker has choices which, if knowingly used,
convey nuances or hints which broaden his art. Since words are man's main
vehicle for his thoughts, his speculations and his emotions, these advantages are incalculably valuable. In sum, the classical education improved
the critical faculty, roused the aesthetic, gave a grounding in the origins
of our own civilisation and taught how to use to the full our own language.
I would even go so far as to say that it is virtually impossible to write pithily
in English without knowing the Latin which gives English words their
prime and inner meanings. Playing with words or with verbal associations
– *paronomasia* as it is technically called – may become insufferably
pedantic but this pitfall does not alter the fact that a language cannot be
understood or wielded to its full capacity without knowledge of its roots.
You can choose your words carefully only when you know their core
meaning.

Yet when all these points have been made in favour of the classical
education it remains true that during my *Lehrjahre* and before them this
education was in the terminal stages of a slow decline. Latin was current

only among the clergy of the Roman Catholic church and for the polite
expression of indelicacies: the *pudenda* might figure in the decent obscu-
rity of a learned language but not otherwise. So the writing was on the
wall since clerics and pornographers provide a manifestly inadequate
constituency for a great language. In his lectures on Homer at Oxford
(1861) Matthew Arnold noted this decline and he himself was the first of
the university's Professors of Poetry to lecture in English and not in Latin.
The classical thinkers and writers were still masters but no longer supreme masters which they had once been. It was no longer enough to go to
them to learn about the way the world was constructed or the way it
worked, or how human beings were likely to behave or ought to behave. In
the heyday of the classical education it was believed that the ancients had
the answers to all the important questions of knowledge and behaviour
and possessed a uniquely marvellous store of wisdom. This eminence was
enhanced by the rediscovery of the classics in the later Middle Ages and
their apotheosis in the High Renaissance. But it did not go unchallenged.
It was, first, sharply challenged by Christians who inveighed against the
veneration of pagan authors and disputed the value of learning Latin and
Greek (except, in the latter case, in order to read the New Testament in
its original language). This hostility was powerful throughout the seventeenth century and beyond. It lost ground when the study of ancient art,
chiefly architecture, caught on beyond the confined circles of *dilettanti* and
it was enormously boosted by the assiduity of travellers with sketchbooks
and, later, by photographers. In the nineteenth century the middle classes
could become familiar with classical temples without stirring from their
homes (Goethe in the eighteenth had to go all the way to Paestum to see
a Greek temple) and by the time I went to school boys like me knew
classical myths and legends as a matter of course. We knew where Achilles
went to school and we knew more of Homer and Virgil than of Milton.

Yet there was throughout this period a second challenge to the classics
which undermined their status, the more so because it was not sectarian
but went to the root of knowledge itself. From the seventeenth century –
the beginning of an age which was modern in the sense that it looked
forward as much as it looked backward – it began to dawn on the bolder
spirits that the ancients could think excellently without, however, always
coming to the correct conclusions. The Renaissance, although it exalted
the classics, also stood on the threshold of a new age in which future
discoveries appeared even more exciting than the recovery of the past.
Take, for example, the greatest of the classical polymaths, Aristotle.
Aristotle described the world in categories which were accepted for 2,000
years as its basic physical constituents and the basic stuff of intellectual
discourse about it. But these sense data – tables, trees, horses or whatever
– turned out not to be the units of ultimate reality, since they have in
common ingredients which modern science has discovered. Therefore,
Aristotle did not have the last word and it is not enough to learn what he

said. Similarly with the most influential of all the ancient Roman masters, Cicero. Cicero's example in matters as diverse as proper behaviour in adversity and exemplary prose style dominated medieval classrooms and it is a timeless source of instruction; but there is a vast difference, as the modern age slowly dared to believe, between turning to Cicero to be told what's what and turning to him as one only among many guides. In the seventeenth century, in France and England specially, seeking knowledge meant digging deeper than reading classical texts and it included above all the recognition that the ancients had been deficient in method: that they had failed adequately to annex to their intellectual brilliance the necessary business of experimental testing of hypotheses. At this point modern science (Latin for knowledge) was born and was divorced from what the ancient and medieval worlds called philosophy (meaning thereby the totality of the search for knowledge and right behaviour). The distinction was made between ancient and modern and the Classics became, however valuable, ancient in the dual sense of incomplete as well as antique: antiquity lost some of its shine. A new wave, of which Descartes and Boyle may claim paternity, sired a new philosophy and a new physics (Greek for nature) and so diminished the ancients and cut them down to size – great figures still but no longer the be-all and end-all of knowledge and wisdom. Parallel material and technical advances and inventions evidently put the moderns in a different world from the ancients and all these profound changes in attitudes and resources slowly subverted the prevailing notions and system of education. One of the crucial differences between medieval and modern Europe is that modern Europe knows a great deal more than did the ancients whereas the Middle Ages did not – and did not believe that they could.

The scholars of Eton were selected by competitive examination and at this point I must qualify my strictures on my prep school. Odious though it was, it did its job and more. Its job was to get its boys into public schools and in my case it got me to Eton with a scholarship. Nearly 500 years after its foundation the notion of Eton as a charitable institution for the education of the poor had worn desperately thin; no poor boy could get anywhere near Eton and the main prize for a scholar was not money but honour. The parents of scholars were spared most of the fees but parents who could afford the full fees were asked by the Provost to do so: or so I have been told. How the Provost used the money I do not know (perhaps in aid of some impoverished but boneheaded aristocrat). The standard fee for a scholar was £150 a year but it might be reduced. The non-scholars, or oppidans, paid £254 a year. In other words the scholarship was worth, in money, £104 a year in 1926.

The scholarship candidates, attended by parents or schoolmasters, stayed at hotels in Windsor for the inside of a week and trekked to Eton each day to do the set papers. The largest contingent came from one of the prep schools which specialised in getting its pupils into Eton. They processed from Windsor to Eton in a crocodile under the guidance of a master and were said to be fed during the week on fish in order to improve their intellectual agility, a recipe for success which was considered by everybody else as only dubiously fair. They were regarded as the main opposition and with justice since five of them won scholarships in my year.

The crux of the competition for places was the Latin verse paper. No literary, let alone poetic, talent was required. This was an exercise in ingenuity. It consisted in taking a piece of English verse or prose and choosing equivalent Latin words which could be arranged to fit the strict rules for fabricating Latin hexameters or heroic couplets. I was good at this game and I had in addition an outrageous stroke of luck. Before each paper the candidates gathered outside the School Hall, a capacious, grandiose and over-decorated twentieth-century building erected as a memorial to Etonians killed in the Boer War but verging on the vulgar. Here we eyed one another warily as we waited for the doors to be thrown open with the gestures which that sort of occasion engenders. We then advanced rapidly but decorously to our appointed desks and took a first quick glance at the paper to assess its difficulties. With amazement I saw that the first piece to be versified was the hymn *Abide With Me* – which I had rendered into Latin only a few weeks earlier as an exercise. So I wrote out my version with a fluency which must have astonished and impressed any invigilator who happened to be looking my way. Not long afterwards my name was posted at Eton, and in *The Times*, as second scholar of the year, and since I held that position almost unchanged for the next five years I may conclude that my luck with *Abide With Me* was not the sole cause of my high, if not supreme, ranking. Yet in some degree I owed my initial success to the absurd feat of rewriting a nineteenth-century English hymn in couplets supposedly redolent of Ovid.

The seventy scholars of Eton were a community within a community. We lived in our own quarters. The rest of the school lived, slept and ate in Houses, some more ramshackle than others, with between thirty and forty boys to a House. We had a section to ourselves in the School Chapel. We wore gowns in class and on other formal occasions and surplices in Chapel on Sundays and Saints' days. We were exposed to a certain amount of the hostility inevitably directed at those who are different, specially when they are cleverer or supposed to be, but this kind of prejudice was much reduced from earlier generations and no longer carried the stigmata of poverty, dirtiness and social inferiority. We began life halfway up the school instead of in the bottom half. Within the College each of us had a room of his own after the first year but in that year we inhabited a common chamber divided into cubicles and barred to older boys. We were ruled by the top ten boys and by a Master in College. The top ten – the Sixth Form – were more civilised than their predecessors of earlier times and somewhat less prone to assert their status by beating smaller boys, although they were still entitled to do so. The Neanderthal strain was not wholly extinct.

For most of my time the Master in College was a strange and ungainly bachelor with a thick black moustache known to us from his initials as H.K. but to the rest of the school as Bloody Bill. Some feared him, some perhaps hated him or came to believe later in life that they had done so; all must have found him a bit sinister; one or two may have been sophisticated enough to feel vaguely sorry for him. He was a mathematician who had got a First in Maths at Merton College, Oxford, and he was a good teacher. But he was utterly hopeless as a communicator, furtive as a housemaster and so cruelly miscast as a schoolmaster. Part of his routine was to patrol the College after the hour when we were confined to our rooms. He would open a door at random, ask a stilted question to which he got barely a reply from a tongue-tied boy, linger mutely for a minute and then back out again with a toneless goodnight. He had been an Eton scholar himself and was fiercely loyal to the College and took special pride in seeing it triumph over Oppidan Houses in games or the quasi-military exercises at which Oppidans were expected to excel Collegers.

The scholars of Eton with whom I consorted did not in after-life attain the heights of distinction which our rigorous selection and special training foretold. Since there were always seventy scholars at any one time and since I was one of this shifting population for five years I must have known, closely or cursorily, about 120-130 boys who were pointed towards fame. Yet only a single one of us achieved it. In my own year – we were sixteen – my most talented contemporary had a notable career in architecture and the arts and we produced two generals and a well-known naturalist but no cabinet minister or ambassador, no judge or professor or even a bishop. The single international celebrity to emerge from these years was A.J. Ayer, precocious philosopher and *bel esprit*, who shot to fame while still an Oxford undergraduate with his book *Language, Truth and Logic*. He was amazingly young when he wrote it and it was written in what was considered amazingly clear and elegant English for a philosopher. Yet he created no new school of philosophy, certainly not at Oxford which was still recovering from a late nineteenth-century addiction to Hegel while uneasily sniffing new breezes wafted from Cambridge by Moore and Russell. Ayer popularised the phrase 'logical positivism' but neither tutors nor students paid much attention to it.

Although segregated in living quarters and for competitive games, scholars were jumbled with non-scholars for lessons. These consisted of regular sessions in classes, tutorials, optional extras (a way of getting extra marks in exams if that was what you wanted or were expected to want) and holiday tasks. In spite of this array of imposts the Eton way of life included a surprisingly large number of uncharted hours. We had lots of work to do but how or where we did it was only partially regulated. Nor was it swamped by the Classics, although the Classics dominated until the last couple of years.

This is how the week went. There were 24 class-room periods. Every other weekday was a half-holiday, which meant no class-room period after midday. In my first year ten of the 24 periods were devoted to Latin and Greek. Next came Science with four periods, Maths with three, French with three, History and Geography with two, Divinity with one, and one 'saying lesson'. This last consisted of learning by heart a piece of English prose or poetry of one's own choice and reciting it and then pushing off – a not very arduous exercise, particularly when the master involved paid little attention and failed to notice how often you recited the same piece.

Although the classical curriculum was the norm for most of the school most of the time, the classical grip was relaxed well before my days by the incursion of other subjects and, more decisively, by the introduction of specialisation for the last couple of years after the School Certificate exams had been put behind. (The School Certificate was taken by nearly every boy and lay somewhere between the GCSE and A Levels of a later age.) The pattern of the last stage contained two main subjects, one major and one minor, plus subsidiary subjects which you picked out for yourself and varied from term to term as the fancy struck you. I chose History as my main subject with German, and thenceforward these two subjects together took up more of my class-room time (History thirteen periods, German six) than Latin and Greek had taken before. Those who carried on with the Classics were a select few. Dropping Latin and Greek was common, partly because of a feeling that the Classics had had their day and partly because we had had a surfeit of them: most of us relished the chance to make a change. In my last year (1930-31) we were 108 History specialists; next came Modern Languages (57), Science and Maths (39), Classics (35). I am sorry now that I allowed my Latin and Greek to fade away, but there had to be a choice and who can say whether I lost or gained by making the choice I made?

In my last years my two special subjects took up 79 per cent of classroom periods. That is a great deal less than the proportion of time given to A level subjects in the modern system but it is nevertheless a severe inroad on a general education and I have become increasingly converted to the view that specialisation on this scale at so early an age is a mistake. In France a general education remains dominant throughout the school years and entry to a university requires general, not special, knowledge.

There were three principal History masters at Eton in my time. They were so different from one another that they hardly seemed to belong to the same species. The senior was C.H.K. Marten, of whom it was related that he was so enthusiastic about the teaching of history that he had volunteered to teach it at Eton for nothing. This story, although a fable, was *ben trovato*, for while Marten did not invent History at Eton he was the leading figure in transposing it in the early years of this century from the fringes to the centre of the curriculum. He spent almost his entire life at Eton. He was a boy there, went to Balliol to read History and got a First, and was then immediately appointed to the Eton staff and remained there as Assistant Master, House Master, Lower Master (second in command to the Headmaster), Vice-Provost and ultimately Provost, in which office he died after a *gradus ad Parnassum* spanning 53 years. Besides teaching generations of Eton boys he taught the future Queen Elizabeth II and so earned a knighthood and other distinctions of that kind. He belonged to the homely type of schoolmaster, neither frightening nor pompous. He wrote one or more of those textbooks which were more familiar in those days than they are now – relentlessly condensed narratives of conflicts and legislation and, in the more recent centuries, general elections, the whole signposted by shoulder-notes in small italics in the outer margins of the page. Marten's great contribution to teaching, as far as I was concerned, was not his class-room manner (of which I remember nothing) but a single weekly period when he received us in his copious private library and left us to take from his shelves any book which aroused our curiosity and then just sit and read it. This was not the way most teachers taught but it was a stimulating supplement. It taught me the value of roaming round the edges of a subject and years later when I was teaching International Relations at Sussex University I would occasionally try to leaven the lump of 'reading lists' by mentioning a book which had little or nothing to do with what we were studying. G.H. Hardy's *A Mathematician's Apology* was one of my favourite suggestions in the hope that knocking up against something totally unexpected might exhilarate. Another was *The Greeks and the Irrational* by E.R. Dodds for its sparkling scholarship and compelling parallels with our own times. I remembered the mixed surprise and enchantment which I myself got from stumbling on *The Road to Xanadu* by John Livingston Lowes, *The Tyranny of Greece over Germany* by E.M. Butler, *The Rise of the Greek Epic* by Gilbert Murray, *The Allegory of Love* by C.S. Lewis; books of originality and insight. In later years the practice of reading aloud which my wife and I pursued throughout our married life added to this list: for example, *The Gift Relationship* by R.M. Titmuss, *The Art of Memory* by Frances Yates, *Black Athena* by Martin Bernal, *The Face of Battle* by John Keegan. Much of this I owe to spending an hour a week in Marten's library where I learned what a library is and what it is for – a store of books where you may wander, freely but quietly, in the expectation of discovering something valuable.

The second of my History masters was G.W. 'Tuppy' Headlam, member of a distinguished family of scholars, bishops and so on and the one Eton master of whom the Headmaster, the redoubtable Cyril Argentine Alington (Headmaster from 1917 to 1933), was said to be wary. Headlam no doubt had a good brain and virtues, but he was a terrible teacher, cynical and lazy. His idiosyncrasy was well established. It was related that, as a young master sharing digs with other young masters, he was deputed in lean times to think of ways of cutting back their living expenses. When he appeared to have done nothing and was taxed with his dilatoriness, he allegedly pointed out that he had discontinued the group's subscription to one London evening paper, price one penny. He demonstrated his departure from the common run by refusing to allow any boy in his House to become a Boy Scout, nor (provided this latitude was not unduly abused) would he allow senior boys in the House to be penalised for failing to go to early school. Slips of paper from the School Office requiring the attendance of the truant before the Headmaster would mysteriously disappear and inquiries why they should prove so continuously evanescent at one House only were aborted by undeviating inattention. Headlam was also remarked and no doubt envied for having as his not infrequent guest the seductive actress Anna May Wong, his main claim to fame in the school. In a conformist world he contrived to be different. In teaching he was different with a vengeance. His class performed a languid communal incantation of no merit whatsoever. As he came into the room the whole class rose – an otherwise unheard of courtesy – and solemnly intoned: 'Here comes the Master [the *a* short] like a great ship in full sail.' He was not in the least like that and he made for his desk as though he noticed nothing. He would then open a bulky textbook and call out a page number. From this point onwards he did nothing while the class recited in unison, slowly and in a ludicrously expressionless tone, what was on the page, deviating only to take in any footnotes which cropped up. Thus: 'Maximilian became emperor in one four eight six full stop note one (pronounced 'wan') he was the son of ...' and so back to the main text until the hour was over. This farce represented a substantial part of the handsome fees which our parents were paying to have us taught history but presumably in ignorance of how it was being done. Grotesque and even scandalous though it was, I look back on it with a modicum of forgiveness. If you go to an English patrician establishment you may as well have a dash of superbity. Unlike two of his brothers 'Tuppy' Headlam has not been deemed worthy of a place in the *Dictionary of National Biography*.

Finally, Robert Birley, not much older than we were, an excellent scholar, brilliant teacher and fine man. He was to become Headmaster at Eton and later a professor at Witwatersrand University in South Africa and the City University in London. At the end of the Second World War he was hired by the British Military Government in Germany to re-educate the Germans, an excellent choice since he immediately saw through this ridiculous notion and devoted himself to the more practical and useful business of providing Germans with books, pencils and paper. Later, in South Africa, he supplemented his professorial duties at the University of Witwatersrand with some clandestine teaching in black schools. At one of these he found that he had to expound the European revolutions of 1848 to black children for whom they were absurdly remote in time and place. He tried to give the topic some sense by talking about the ideas of freedom and tolerance. In this context, he once told me, he discovered one of the valuable lessons of the English public school – practice in getting out of houses and over walls in forbidden hours. Since he was about six-foot-six tall and distinctly ungainly this training was a peculiarly necessary adjunct to a temperament which naturally warmed to the mischievous side of life. Birley was the first of my teachers – others followed at Balliol – who so entranced me with history that I never for the rest of my life ceased reading and relishing it. The public schools provided excellent teachers – and duds.

There is a tailpiece to these accounts of how I learned history at Eton. The headmaster, Cyril Alington, was a classicist but he took the top history division once a week. He liked teaching the grand sweeps of history with dates and he had invented a special way of remembering dates. Each digit in a date was represented by a letter (or choice of letters). So 0 was *s*, 1 was *t*, 2 was *n* and so on. You turned the digits into letters and then concocted a catchphrase in which the initial letters of the words stood for the required digits. To make this easier you were entitled to ignore all words beginning with a vowel. Example: Three Ottos Saxon sovereigns end now. Leaving out 'Ottos' and 'end' because they begin with vowels you are left with TSSN which converts into 1002 which reminds you that Otto III died in 1002. Or again: Take it Lannoy, noble Lannoy. This makes 1525, which is the date of the battle of Pavia where the French king Francis I was defeated and surrendered his sword to the emperor's general, Lannoy. Clearly the headmaster had great fun making up these catchphrases. He produced dozens of them which he declaimed and we wrote down in our notebooks. I have forgotten nearly all of them but he was a dab hand at coining the catching line, even though some of them were less happy than others. One of his comparative failures was his cumbersome mnemonic for the arrival of the monk Augustine and the conversion of England to Christianity. It went: Let Augustine preach a desire. But the fact that I still remember it shows that it was, if clumsy, nevertheless memorable.

The Headmaster also set Sunday Questions. These were a most unfair imposition which grievously interfered with what was supposed to be a Day of Rest by requiring an essay on a topic such as: 'The fathers have eaten sour grapes and the children's teeth are set on edge (Comment).' One did not dare to make the obvious comment. But the Headmaster's central duties were, I suppose, two: to recruit the best teachers for the school and to see that parents and old boys did not interfere. This second task was far from easy in a school whose old boys had an excellent opinion of themselves and were, some of them, dukes or not much less. I suspect that Alington was good at both his main jobs, particularly the second.

Any school child likes best what he is good at. I coupled History with German because I was good at languages and because History made me interested in 'abroad' and I wanted to go there and talk to people when I got there. I had too a (perhaps partly snobbish) conviction that the foreign books which I wanted to read ought to be read in the original and not in translation. Since I had spoken French from my earliest days – our nursery had a row of books of the *Bibliothèque Rose*, an amalgam of the sentimental and the adventurous with, to my surprise, dashes where English books have inverted commas to indicate conversation – it seemed silly to choose French and I chose German as the next most relevant language. I had made a start with German in the course of childhood visits to my grandmother in London where I had my first lesson in German from a little old lady called Georgina Berry (Georgie to my mother and grandmother), a gentle and intelligent being who had taught my mother years earlier. She appeared to live what would be called modestly and I got the sense that this was a euphemism. A certain dowdyism betrayed a lack of means rather than lack of taste or care. I suspected that my grandmother paid her more than generously for teaching me and was happy to have the excuse to do so. I still have some German classics which belonged to her or perhaps to her father whose name – Mr Dulcken – is written inside one of them. So I learned that the German for what I knew as 'ho, hee, to' was 'der, die, das'. Mrs Berry's method – and she was very methodical – was grammar first, then vocabulary, and in this way we set out from basics towards German literature but without getting far since my visits to London were few. But they were a help when I got to Eton and I have fond memories of Georgina Berry, *geborene* Dulcken. Way back in the nineteenth century the Prince Consort had popularised the idea of Germany as a standard-bearer in the arts and sciences and had founded at Eton special prizes in French and German. Although not as prestigious as the principal Classics prize – the Newcastle Scholarship – these prizes ranked with the Rosebery History Scholarship as crowns to be aimed at by specialists in their last school year. I won the German prize in my two last years and was enormously flattered when in the course of some bilingual chat in a train in Germany in one of these years I was asked where I had learned to speak English so well.

Italian was regarded as suitable for those heading for fancy subjects like Art History, Spanish for less fancy careers in lowly commerce; of Russian so far as I remember there was none. Russia was hardly on our map, a circumstance which made it happily acceptable to read *War and Peace* in translation, a concession not quite proper in the case of *Le Rouge et le Noir* or *Faust*. I recognise here an element of false pride, akin to what Ruskin lamented when he said that reading foreign writers in their own languages cost him more time and trouble than he could spare: but Ruskin's reading was to acquire knowledge rather than savour literary art. Of Italian I got my first smattering at Oxford not from literature but by listening to broadcasts of Italian operas. Reception from Italy was poor but improved sufficiently after dark. There were in the thirties half a dozen radio stations in the major Italian cities which combined their resources to broadcast operas from the best houses and with the most famous singers: Maria Caniglia, Gina Cigna, Ebe Stignani and even more famous tenors such as Tito Schipa or Beniamino Gigli – *anglice* Benjamin Lily, a euphonious name for a full-throated performer. The recital of the cast would be followed by the conductor's name and then an invariably lilting phrase ending with a thumping spondee, 'maestro del coro Guiseppe Conca'. For some reason I have never forgotten Signor Conca, chorus master. Listening to Italian operas is not, however, a very good way to learn Italian. 'Un bel di vedremo' is a possible conversational gambit, although not a stimulating one; 'in questa tomba oscura' positively deadening. Later I pursued Italian with the help of Messrs Linguaphone who supplied gramophone records, illustrated booklets to go with them and correspondence tests. After the war I tried to take up Russian in this way but as my main place for doing so was a commuter train I found the going too tough and gave up.

Eton was a tolerant place but this verdict needs to be qualified since although the school was tolerant towards the boys, the boys saw no reason to be tolerant towards the masters and in appropriate cases they mercilessly adopted nature's hunting and pecking laws. One example will do. Before a certain master arrived to take his class one boy would remain outside. When the master arrived a brick was heaved through the window and all the other boys jumped up and, with cries of 'I'll get him, sir', rushed out of the room and did not come back. After this behaviour – called in less exalted quarters hooliganism – had occurred more than once the master in question concluded that his path in life lay away from Eton. He was an unluckily extreme case but his fate shows that the boys learned a nice discernment and how to practise it.

Most boys spent five years at Eton while a master might spend nearly fifty. Yet each generation of boys received from its predecessors a more or less accurate assessment of the masters. Some – the French, of whom there were in my day two, and the clergymen, of whom there were perhaps ten – started with unfair handicaps, particularly the former, but on the whole there was more shrewdness than prejudice in these juvenile markings of their seniors. Boys encountered several form masters per term and, less fleetingly, one or two House Masters and one or two personal tutors.

Prospective House Masters opened lists of boys – that is to say, they solicited parents for the custody of their sons. Since the boys were at that point only just born it was all but impossible to tell how the House Master who had not yet got a House would himself turn out twelve or so years later. He might not even be there any longer. At Eton the general rule was that every master, unless apparently he were French, should get a House in his turn and that, once he was installed, he would be irremovable except in the direst circumstances until his stint expired. For the boys the hazards were considerable, ranging from simple incompetence to the more unmentionable kinds of unsuitability. A House Master might change once or not at all during the boy's time at the school. A personal tutor probably changed when the boy became a specialist for his last two years. I had two tutors who, like my History teachers, exemplified the variety of the species. The first was a quiet, genial clergyman, the kind of man who makes only a modest mark on the young because he neither inspires nor hurts them: his benign appearance earned him the nickname of 'the sheep'. There was something of denigration in this appellation but also something of commendation. Sheep are nicer than wolves. My second tutor was a more flamboyant figure, often to be seen with a flower in the buttonhole of his braided tailcoat or commanding the Officers Training Corps from atop a horse. He went on to be a Head Master somewhere else. Different though they were in almost every respect both were good tutors. The function of the tutor was to help his younger pupils with their class-room work and to prod the older ones into extra-curricular topics of less obvious, less immediate relevance. The tutorials took place either around midday or, for older boys, in the evening when they had the additional attraction of expeditions since they entailed leaving the House at an otherwise forbidden hour. Tutorials at the later stage had the further charm of small encounters with far fewer pupils than were gathered in set classes, and sitting in easy chairs instead of at hard desks. There were, too, Sunday tutorials at which the tutor might read aloud anything which he thought appropriate – appropriate either to Sunday in which case it would be holy or at least morally improving, or appropriate to the marginal progress of adolescence in which case it might be anything at all from Sir Philip Sidney to Hilaire Belloc.

No less important than this range of instructional sessions were our leisure hours. I have said that we had 24 class-room periods a week. But the number of hours in the week is seven times 24 and so we had a lot of leisure. By leisure I do not mean idleness. The Romans contrasted *otium* with *negotium*, being free with being busy, time of one's own with time mapped out by somebody else. Time could be wasted and often was, but the invitation to waste time or spend it usefully or enjoyably was an important part of education. There is a kind of loitering with or without intent which should be encouraged at an early age in order to demonstrate the difficulties and necessity of making use of time rather than letting time make a mess of you. This is one of the things which the boarding school can do better than the day school since the latter's restricted routine can hardly accommodate unmapped time; time away from school is essentially different from unmapped time in school. Eton was not afraid of granting this latitude and of increasing it as you went up the school, even to the extent of exempting the top boys from the compulsory organised games which had too powerful a grip in the lower orders. It was enhanced by the fact that Eton is a beautiful place. I was a town-bred boy and, however subconsciously, I was struck by Eton's splendid old buildings, the river, meadows and trees. Eton opened my eyes as well as my mind. I began to learn some of the art of looking at things – looking to enjoy, not merely to recognise – although it was not until after marriage that I made much of these pleasures to be got from pictures and buildings, ancient and modern.

Leisure was punctuated by two things besides work – games and chapel-going (it would be a distortion to call it religion). Compulsory games are a famous feature of the public schools. They have often been derided and decried but most of those who write about them come from the few who were no good at them. For the few at the other end of the scale they had great rewards and gratification, if not without the pitfalls of getting too big for your boots. For the majority between the stars and the duffers, they were simply enjoyable, sometimes touched by earnestness but most of the time just fun. For the authorities they were a convenient way of knowing, or hoping to know, what all the boys were doing all the time and of channelling adolescent energies into approved activities. There was too another side of the coin. School games were cooperative as well as competitive and so contrasted with school work which was purely competitive. Games and success in games were admittedly the more glamorous and there was nothing quite so warming as being awarded your 'colours', usually at the end of a match when your captain advanced towards you, handed you a coloured cap or scarf, your colleagues clapped mildly and you tried not to look too pleased: leaping around and punching the air would have been unbelievably bad form and spraying good champagne into the air and over other people even more vulgar. Whatever may be said against the ethos of the public schools their aristocratic disdain of ostentation is a big mark in their favour. It restrained emotion without dulling pleasure. There is even a serious educational point to be made about games. At their core is the co-existence of conflict and rules. The first question anybody asks about an unfamiliar game is: 'What are the rules?' Without knowing the rules you cannot play the game and if you know but transgress them you are not playing the game and may even be dismissed from the field of play. At the same time a game embodies a conflict which may be intense; the aim of the game is to win. Yet in a game fighting to the finish does not mean fighting on until victory but fighting until the whistle blows. The outcome is decided by the clock. In sum, the rules are more important than the result. There is a lesson there.

Eton encouraged individuality and initiative. The older boys were allowed to take off on their own provided the stated object of the expedition was respectably cultural. I remember taking a Green Line coach in my penultimate year to go to London to see the exhibition of Italian art at the Royal Academy in the summer of 1930. Thinking for oneself was regarded as a good thing even though it might lead to unconventional conclusions. To its credit Eton preferred to encourage thinking rather than control it. So I am grateful to my school for something which it neither intended nor would have wished. It happened in the chapel. The chapel of Eton is one of the loftiest and purest fifteenth-century churches in England (the vaulting, however, was added after the Second World War). In front of us and behind us as we faced the central aisle, sitting, standing or kneeling, we had rare and intriguing wall paintings which had been rediscovered in the nineteenth century and, where not obliterated, restored in the twentieth. The services were jolly and sometimes uplifting, with a ceremonial appealing to the young. The Sixth Form – the ten top Collegers and the ten top Oppidans – had a place in the preliminary pomp, assembling in the ante-chapel and proceeding through the nineteenth-century screen and under the massive organ loft into the chapel itself with the (professional) choir, the Provost and other robed notables, before whom the Holy Poker – a gravely gowned, venerably whitehaired servitor shouldering a bronze emblem – set a measured pace as the organ proclaimed the worthiness of our corporate being. Once in the chapel there was time for reflection as well as participation in the familiar singing and rituals, for we went to chapel every day and twice on Sundays. One result was that chapel became a kind of homeopathy: with recurrent small doses it cured me of religion. It dawned on me that I did not believe that a single one of the statements in the creed which we were for ever reciting could be true. This was a disrupting thought. It seemed to set me apart from general, if not universal, opinion and it invited punishment either in this world or, more awfully, the next. For many years, even decades, I pondered the arguments used down the ages to prove the existence of a god who is supernatural and a creator, but my disbelief has never been shaken and I have no use for those who try to get round this great question by redefining god to mean something hazy enough to be acceptable. They seem to me to be saying: If we can no longer believe in God let us believe in something else and call it God. Defenders of religious belief say that unbelievers evince a sad lack of faith and so demonstrate the limitations of the human condition which so rarely rises above the need for rational satisfaction. The alternate view, more simple, is that the believer demonstrates his inability to cope without a god whom he must therefore invent. I conceived special disdain for the arguments, when I came across them, of Christian apologists who argue that if the truth of Genesis cannot be proved, neither can its untruth and that therefore leaves divine revelation in sole possession of the field. Such lame arguments fail to dislodge the elementary fact that the term supernatural is a contradiction in terms. The most generous judgment on these matters is Mill's: The whole domain of the supernatural is thus removed from the region of Belief into that of simple Hope. My own conclusion is less generous: To set hope as an alternative to belief is a form of cowardice.

But the validity of beliefs is not the only issue. Beliefs, including religious beliefs, may be valuable without being true, and while remaining convinced that belief in god is preposterous I am equally sure that religion gives very many people much needed comfort and consolation. The disbeliever must, therefore, fight shy of undermining the beliefs of others. It is a sad fact that those in need of comfort and consolation are very numerous and so long as belief in a god helps them the falsity of their belief is outweighed by its blessings. Yet I admit to uneasiness in the case of educated people who profess such beliefs, since they are to me unintelligible without a degree of willed self-deception and such self-deception in an educated person is unbecoming, even disreputable, the *trahison des clercs*.

Some people seek to justify and dignify belief in the supernatural by calling it a leap into faith, but this is no more than a determination to believe without having any reason to do so. For myself I am grateful to Eton for dispossessing me of this bogus baggage, and I also think that if you abandon religion a school is a good place to do so. It provides substitutes: in regard to oneself – discipline in thought and conduct, the uses of discretion, control over emotions and their display; in regard to others – the value of friendship, the importance of loyalty, the balancing of the claims of the group against the rights of the self. Like all virtues these can be exaggerated, but they should not be disparaged.

But the death of god, as it has been called, poses a reverberating question. There are two kinds of death of god. When the sailors off the island of Paxos in the Ionian Sea heard the great cry 'Pan is dead. The Great God Pan is dead', they were learning that one god had been over-powered by another: in this instance the God of Nature by the Supernatural God of the Christians. But the death of god in modern Europe, and the death of god in classical Greece, means the death of all gods, not one god or set of gods, and so poses the question how, without god, may we know of the existence of a distinction between good and evil or know which is which. Plato's answer is still the most gripping. If you take Plato's Theory of Forms as a description of the real world it is obviously nonsense; and if you take it as propounding the Idealist view that what you perceive is made and projected by the mind, it is hardly less unacceptable. But Plato's method was not to describe or analyse. Plato was one of the great myth-makers who use images to pierce the veils of ignorance and confusion. They do not portray; they suggest. Their suggestions cannot in themselves be right or wrong; they are more or less compelling or revealing. Plato's myths are an attempt to find in metaphysics a substitute for god. Yet this metaphysics has been around for two and a half millennia commanding respect but less than firm conviction and now we are told that metaphysics, if perhaps temporarily, is dead too. Nor have psychologists done any better than philosophers in explaining why so many human beings see a distinction between good and bad and try to be good. The problem is this. If, as Nietzsche proclaimed and many before him less concisely accepted, god is dead whence comes this distinction between good and evil: not merely knowing which is which, but perceiving the existence of an antithesis? Nietzsche supposed that god's place could be filled only by man and so imagined and hoped for a superman to sustain the values of society and civilisation. This is not the beefy superman of fascism or a spiritual moron. Nietzsche's supermen, like Plato's guardians, were morally superior beings but distinguishing them from their fellows presented unsolvable problems. The alternative to finding moral values and direction through the special powers of special men is to predicate a moral propensity in all but to admit that its source remains mysterious.

My grumbles about my schooldays are chiefly two. First, the education which I got faltered badly when it came to telling me about the world about me. When Isaac Newton was a schoolboy he spent his spare hours making knick-knacks and wooden models. He made a windmill by watching men making a real one and he made it work by giving it cloth sails and, alternately, by putting a mouse inside it. What the mouse did is not clear. Either its tail was attached to the mechanism or it operated a treadmill by scrambling for some food placed above the wheel. I find it hard to believe that any of my contemporaries at Eton, even one with the precocious genius of a Newton, would have done anything like that. We were not excited by science, still less by machines. I remember only one of my various science teachers. He was a short, round and ruddy man called Dr Porter, more familiarly Daddy P. He was memorable on more counts than one. He was the only Dr on the staff and wore a more ornate gown than the rest, who were only MAs; doctorates were not in those days three a penny. He was the most senior assistant master but had never had a House; perhaps he did not want one, but even that explanation seemed odd in an order of things where being a House Master was a mark of progress and not having one a sign of something going wrong. And he used to invite a few boys to go on Sundays to where he lived on the outskirts of Slough to listen to classical music on a gramophone with a horn so huge that he was supposed to have used his scientific skills to construct it himself. I daresay that Daddy P. had a rewarding time with the Science Specialists but most of his teaching was perforce with pupils for whom science was a secondary kind of learning which lacked the prestige of the Classics. The revived public schools of the nineteenth century and likewise the universities denied to science and nature the status which they accorded to the Classics and literature. From notebooks rediscovered decades later I see that I was competent at absorbing and ordering the basic material of the natural sciences but I was never fired by anything in botany or chemistry or physics.

Yet the Ancients, particularly the Greeks, had been fascinated by what we now call the natural sciences. Their Renaissance heirs, however, paid more heed to the literary heritage than the scientific. Renaissance Man, whose chief claim to fame was knowing something about most things, was in truth the supreme example of the gifted amateur and often little better than a dabbler. The Renaissance combined learning with wealth, particularly in courtly Italian circles, and one effect of this refulgence has been to obscure the achievements of the succeeding seventeenth century which was an even more exciting age of scientific discovery and intellectual innovation, the founding age of the French and English and other Academies (including the Royal Society). The classical education moreover was always more Latin than Greek, and there was less science – in the sense of speculation about the physical world – in Latin than Greek, as the English Franciscan Roger Bacon complained in the thirteenth century when he was trying to get the Oxford curriculum changed to include more

Greek scientific writings. But Latin continued to dominate as the senior partner in the classical duo and a comfortable conformity entrenched the preponderance of humane arts and letters. To the end of the nineteenth century – and particularly in that century – scientific speculation was tainted with religious disquiet and disapproval, so that science in schools tended to be limited to classification (a dull business) while science as an open adventure for young minds had to wait for the age of the man on the moon, the double helix and black holes. I felt no thrill when confronted with the periodic table or the differential calculus, and the names of the great European discoverers from the seventeenth century onwards were unknown to me. In later life I read books about Einstein or Theories of Everything and understood much of what I read but 48 hours later it was gone. Since my memory is good the only reason for this vexing inability to retain what I had read can only be a wholly inadequate data base. I had never acquired that necessary minimum which enables you to go on learning and remember what you learn.

The same was true of mathematics. Dr Hawtrey made maths a regular part of the school's curriculum in the 1850s or tried to, but eighty years later it was for me just boring. It was, so far as I could make out, divided into three parts: calculations (arithmetic – easy but dull), drawing (geometry – in my case messy) and symbols (algebra – intriguing but of obscure import). I had no notion of what lay behind these activities and it was not until many years later that I discovered that mathematicians had ideas as well as slide rules. There was an assumption that you had to be odd to be good at maths, to have a special kind of brain which either you had or you had not and you were unlikely to have. This was nonsense and a self-fulfilling prophecy. Not everybody has it in him to be a Newton or a Gauss but there is no reason why a child who can master Homer well enough to read and enjoy the *Iliad* cannot also master in equivalent degree the aims and workings of maths. The barriers are not intellectual but psychological and conventional. I reckon that my school failed me in this department. I made a bad start and have never been able to catch up. Eton, which claimed to be a nursery for the elite, seemed unaware of the recipe of that great elitist Plato who recommended that the education of the future governors of the state should conclude with ten years of mathematics and nothing else. Plato, it must be said, became bemused by mathematics whence he toppled over into mysticism: he is the supreme example of the marvellous writer with wondrous ideas which stimulate but which there is no reason to believe. I am in consequence shut out of what has been called a Golden Age (Keith Devlin – *Mathematics: The New Golden Age*, a book for the adequately educated layman) and since this age began round about a hundred years before I went to school my school must bear a good share of the blame for my deprivation.

My second grumble is about music. If I have a serious regret in my life it is that I never learned to play the piano as well as I believe I could have.

As a small boy I was reasonably proficient. I began to learn with a teacher who came once or twice a week to our drawing room in Liverpool. I learned the scales, and had some rudimentary training in the pitch of a note. ('Don't bang,' she would say, forgetting that the piano is a percussion instrument.) Music, besides being an art which is no doubt beyond the compass of most people, is also a language to which every child should be introduced. At Eton in my time music was an 'extra' or fringe subject which had to be fitted in at some cost to normal activities. Worse than that, it was a farce. My music lessons amounted to no more than the mechanical transfer of notes from a written page before me to the keyboard also before me but a little lower down. The piece which I was given to transcribe in this way might be one of the easier Beethoven sonatas or some romantic driblet composed by my teacher and entitled, if not obviously related to, sheep at a brook. There was one redeeming grace. Every so often there was a concert in the School Hall and Eton's fame and connections and sense of style saw to it that the concert was excellent. The programmes were unadventurous but right for their audience: a Beethoven or Brahms symphony preceded by the overture to the *Meistersinger* and supplemented by something lighter but in the same mould. The main contrast with today was the absence of Mozart and the rarity of anything of Schubert. Bach, recognised or not, we heard in chapel preluding or rounding off the service. The supremacy of Beethoven was axiomatic but I was duly enthralled by Wagner. I even went so far as to write a paper for a tutorial group in which I maintained that besides his other virtues Wagner was a great melodist, a bold thesis which I illustrated rather obviously with recordings of the last scene in Act I of *Die Walküre* and the quintet from *Die Meistersinger*. I might have instanced too the Wesendonck songs or the youthful adagio for clarinet and strings, but I had not come across them or yet discovered that Wagner wrote anything except operas. I read and half understood intricate books with forbidding titles which, although some of them still sit on my shelves, I would now recommend to nobody. From this time music became one of the most absorbing delights and excitements of my life. Writing about music, however, is a dangerous business, particularly attempts to describe or analyse music's impact. A disheartening proportion of such writing is either extremely banal or extravagantly absurd and the depths are regularly plumbed by those who write about Wagner. He brings out the worst kind of self-indulgent and pretentious gush in his aficionados and his own writings are not much better – volumes of teasing ideas and enticing digressions but in horrid prose and in the service of heavy-handed theorising. Within a few years of his death Thomas Mann, who could wax delirious about his music, was asking pertinently whether anybody took Wagner's theoretical writings seriously, with the implication that neither are they readable nor do they matter to the music-lover – a pardonable but somewhat too hostile verdict.

Wagner was an unrelenting monist who believed that the greatest art is an equal synthesis of all the arts, but he wrote librettos which are vastly inferior to the music which he composed to go with them. He ascribed to a lost Golden Age of Attic tragedy virtues – fusing words with music, performers with audience – which to a large extent he made up to fit his own artistic programme. But he wrote glorious music which has the power to lift you out of your seat. Artistically Wagner is grand but suspect – suspect in his own time and more so in ours, because of the nature of his appeal which combines the most emotional romanticism with a powerful and aggressive egotism (and rather ridiculous stories) to make a mix which belabours the senses as much as it beguiles them and tends to floor as well as charm the listener. Like all the great nineteenth-century composers, of whom he is indubitably one, Wagner lived in a self-consciously romantic culture and also under the shadow of the greatness of Beethoven. Brahms openly avowed the resulting inhibitions and conflicts, took several years before he dared publish a string quartet, and designed with his symphonies only to emulate Beethoven. Other great and lesser composers felt the same constraints: not to feel them would be a mark of inferiority. Wagner, who wrote only one symphony (in his teens) and one quartet, acknowledged Beethoven's genius but found a way round it through his dramatic urges. *The Ring* is a vast rejoinder to Beethoven's Ninth Symphony, sidestepping that triumphant work and so evading comparisons with it. So too in their own way do Mahler's Goethesque eighth symphony and Busoni's vast piano concerto, exhausting symphonic masterpieces which – like Beethoven's last symphony – combine a very full orchestra with human voices. As with painters so with composers it is singularly hard to create a big work which is also a great one.

In my last term at Eton I collected a number of prizes adding up to quite a lot of money which came in the form of credits at the school bookshop. I asked permission to spend some of it on gramophone records and, this unusual request having been referred to the Provost, I was told that I might. I then spent hours deciding what to buy, dividing what I had between plum-coloured labels (four shillings each) and the more expensive red labels with famous soloists such as Kreisler, Cortot and the concert hall stars of those days (six shillings each). I had heard Kreisler play when my mother took me to the Queen's Hall in London for my first hearing of Beethoven's violin concerto, one of those unrepeatable firsts which one never forgets. If the Queen's Hall were still standing today I could point to where I was sitting that night. Today a recording of Kreisler playing the Beethoven concerto is an historical curiosity but for me it had the thrill of first looking into Chapman's Homer. The vogue, as exemplified for example by the programmes of the proms at the Queen's Hall, was strongly for the nineteenth century: Wagner occupied the first half of the programme every Monday, Beethoven every Friday, and Brahms came next, accompanied perhaps by Schubert's Unfinished Symphony. Of the eighteenth century I heard comparatively little and of chamber music practically nothing. When

I got to Oxford and made a new friend who was familiar with Mozart's quartets and quintets I thought him amazingly sophisticated. At Oxford I heard the Lener Quartet play all the Beethoven string quartets in one term and I particularly remember a performance by Schnabel of the Diabelli variations – for the wrong reasons. He was playing in the town hall and as he played a dog began to bark outside. For a time he persevered but after a bit he stopped and quietly left the stage. The dog stopped barking; Schnabel came back and went on where he had left off. What happened to the dog I do not know. Schnabel was the great pianist of my early years and for that he has kept a special place in my memory. I cannot say that he was the greatest pianist I ever heard because I distrust all such comparisons. Even with the help of records they are elusive and deceptive, besides being pointless. Opera buffs are most tempted into such comparisons and go into rhapsodies over a past prima donna who could out-sing and out-charm her modern emulators. I have more sympathy for the elderly ballet buff in the front row of the stalls exclaiming 'Brava, Brava Clementine' with his mind on higher things than her twinkling toes.

Another first was my first voyage through *War and Peace*. I read it in a week sitting in the sun in a deck chair on a piece of lawn known as College Grass, off limits to most boys and all tourists. It was a week in which I had little to do. I was the Head Master's Praepostor. This office was performed each week by two Sixth Formers, one Colleger and one Oppidan, who were excused for that week from attending all school periods except, perversely, early school at 7.30. The functions were light. During the morning the Praepostors collected from the School Office a list of boys who were required to appear that day before the Head Master or Lower Master. Mostly the reason was some wrongdoing but it might be to receive a prize. The Praepostors had to discover where each of these boys was to be found in the last period before midday. On his opening the door of the classroom a hush prevailed and he inquired: 'Please sir, is X in this Division?' On being told that he was, the Praepostor added: 'He is to report to the Head Master after school.' At the appointed hour both Praepostors attended the Head Master in a rather dingy little room, the Colleger inside it and the Oppidan outside the door where he marshalled the queue. Occasionally, if rarely, a boy was there to be flogged. In that event a small procession was formed and moved up a stair to another room where the miscreant removed his trousers, a beadle sat on his head and the Head Master – gowned of course – took a number of shots at his bottom with a twiggy birch. Such beatings were rare. Most beatings took place in the Houses and were inflicted with canes by other boys, not by masters. This delegation of authority was an essential part of the public school system which was supposed to provide education in the business of government at home or in 'the colonies'. It was, however, a small part of school life and there is a moral to be learned from the fact that I spent far more of my week as Praepostor reading Tolstoy than rounding up malefactors or watching their discomforts and disgrace. Reading *War and Peace* for the first time on a piece of grass which was out of bounds to most feet I felt that I was growing up.

Yet another first, an earlier one, comes to mind for quite different reasons: *Macbeth*. It was the holiday task set at the end of my first term at Eton. Inexperienced as I was I took the task too seriously by half. I virtually learned the play by heart and thoroughly absorbed all the notes appended to it in the recommended edition. Not surprisingly, on getting back to school, I won the holiday task prize which was books to the value of, I think, 15s. But I was made to feel that I had perpetrated a misjudgment by failing to perceive the distinction between working hard and working too hard. I took to heart the lesson that there can be too much of even a good thing. Nobody told me this straight out. I simply got a sense of it, a touch on the strings. What was condemned was not being top of the class but trying too hard to get there, not doing my holiday work but giving a disproportionate amount of time to it. It was all right to work but not all right to be a swot. Although there may have been an element of jealousy in this denigration of brainy achievement there was also the sense that the swot was a dreary fellow devoted to a one-track way of life. Even in games, where eminence was more unreservedly applauded, success had to be won without exertion, with ease.

The intellectual spectrum of the public schools was wide, the social spectrum narrow. This was inevitable since the two criteria have no common features. Some of my contemporaries at Eton were very clever – and not all of these were in the College; others were what might politely be called average. The really stupid did not survive, even if they got in, but if you were a duke you had to be exceptionally stupid to be removed. Geographically as well as socially we were a closed society. We lived and worked and played in a space bounded by rules almost as strict as those imposed in a nunnery. Within that space we met only our own kind and not even females of that kind. This was hardly a preparation for the ways of the world, let alone for its government. The idea that the public schools were an ideal training ground for positions of responsibility or power in public life is absurd. What Eton was good at was teaching; but while knowledge and mental agility are prime requisites in public affairs they can be rendered useless or worse by narrow vision and feeble imagination. The worst vice of a narrow system is its inability to see how narrow it is. Boys who were proudly designated to go out and rule the world knew next to nothing about it and just as little about their own country. The public school boy who made a worthy public servant – and there were many – did so in spite of his public school ambience and not because of it.

Most remarked of the limitations of public schools was the absence of females – or, more specifically, females with a femininity likely to appeal to teenage boys. This had, of course, its distorting aspect, but it was offset for the great majority by the fact that it was taken for granted. Critics miss the point that what is taken for granted does not have the impact it is assumed to have when viewed from a different way of life. Not expecting to be aroused goes a long way to sanitising the lack of arousal. The English public school has been celebrated as a breeding ground for homosexuality or, as the French have it, *le vice anglais*, and it certainly provided a convenient environment for probings which were regarded a generation ago as much more unusual than we now know them to be. There was a certain amount of sexual fumbling and fiddling but little else. Boys, even if they pretend otherwise, have crushes just like girls but crushes do not necessarily or even often lead to sex, which was inhibited by sentimental romanticism as well as by training and tabu. Most boys at public school grew up believing themselves to be much less sexed than they were and behaved accordingly. I never heard the word bugger or conceived the possibility of buggery and I did not even learn the true meaning of the word until many years later. Homosexuality of a minor kind was not uncommon, probably among contemporaries rather than between older and younger boys, but it ramped only in one or two Houses where it was rumoured to prevail beyond a normal modicum, whatever that might be supposed to be. Most sex in public schools was by boys bumping into boys on their delayed way to bumping into girls. Heterosexual pursuit, although not entirely impracticable for the more highly motivated, was severely constrained by circumstances and by the ruling ethos, so much so that it did not rank for practical purposes as a major crime in the calendar. There were more serious misdemeanours such as slipping off to the races at Ascot. During Ascot week all timetables were altered and half holidays were curtailed in order to make such ventures hazardous in the extreme. These measures indicated incidentally that, however socially superior the boys might be, few of the masters were in the same class. With the rarest exceptions masters did not venture to Ascot, so that a boy who did contrive to get there did not reckon running into a master as a serious risk. The most notorious sexual scandal in my years occurred when the famous Tallulah Bankhead descended on the nearby village of Datchet on a bed-and-breakfast basis. But the ensuing escapades were treated as breaches of discipline rather than breaches of *mores*. The attendant *frissons* were caused by expulsions from the school rather than by the experience which preceded this most unusual retribution. Breaking bounds was the crime. Sex itself in whatever form was an optional extra, like music or gym.

A school is a place for learning. It has set courses, formal examinations, rewards and punishments, in the midst of which it is easy to forget that a school has also a mood, a climate, axioms. The better English public schools of my time were places which assumed and so instilled certain values. They assumed that moderation is a good thing and fanaticism evil, chauvinism ill-mannered; that open-mindedness is preferable to single-mindedness; that the man who knows he is right is probably wrong. It is easy to forget too that many places of learning throughout the world neither make nor instil these assumptions, thereby adding to the stock of closed minds and intolerant and cruel behaviour.

When my five years at Eton were up I was surprised to discover that leaving was not just sad but something like heartbreaking. Eton had become my world. I had found a place and now I had to leave it and probe another. I was happy at Eton and successful at lessons and at making friends, and instead of being ready to go on to somewhere else I recoiled from it. The unknown did not beckon; it was still alarming. I took the next step with the same trepidation with which I had proceeded from my prep school to Eton. The step itself was the undisputedly natural one of going to the university, which for Etonians of my generation meant Oxford or Cambridge. Other universities were known to exist but Etonians who failed to get into what is now called Oxbridge (as though there were no differences between the two) probably skipped university altogether. I myself tried for a scholarship at Balliol but failed to get one. The two History scholarships that year went to Christopher Hill and Con O'Neill, the one later Master of Balliol and one of the foremost historians of his time, the other a truly eminent ambassador in many capitals: nobody could feel abashed at being pipped to the post by such as they. My headmaster's comment on Balliol's choice was nicely judged. Handing me the leaving present given to all Etonians – the Poems of Thomas Gray most elegantly printed and bound – he said, 'Show them that they have made a mistake.'

Although Oxford was a natural sequel to Eton it was also a bigger change than I anticipated or at the time realised. My Greek background was heavily patriarchal and Eton, although enlightened, was an enlightened hierarchy where masters were masters, boys were only boys and among the boys the difference of a mere year conferred unquestioned superiority. Balliol was profoundly different. It was serious, even strenuous, about a number of things but its general temper was more relaxed and egalitarian than anything I had so far come upon. To my astonishment tutors were called by their Christian names, a practice which never came easily to me although it seemed to me admirable. Some early notions stick firmly, and I have always retained an ingrained respect for age and rank even when not honouring the individuals who have attained them.

Balliol took two things seriously: work and rowing. I worked but did not row or pursue any of the team games which had been the stock in trade of school. I preferred the less highly regarded tennis and golf. My motto was strenuousness in work but not in anything else.

In many ways Oxford repeated the Eton pattern. Just as the seventy Eton Collegers were part of the 1,000 or more Etonians, so the 250 Balliol undergraduates were part of some 2,000 Oxford undergraduates. Since some of my Eton friends went to other Colleges I moved in and out of those Colleges but the focus of my new life was Balliol. The change in scale carried with it a deeper change from the closed world of Etonians to the variety of young men from other public schools and from none. I was nervously aware that Etonians were apt to be unpopular or at least suspect, but at Balliol they were comparatively few. Most Etonians, including the grander ones, went to the grander Colleges like Christ Church and Magdalen and I had no difficulty in fitting in at Balliol. Once more I was in a predominantly male world but the maleness was modified. Like Eton, Balliol was exclusively male but the University was not. There were Colleges for women as well as Colleges for men, although the mingling of the sexes was regulated by rules which closed the gates of all Colleges at 9 p.m. and so confined fornication to the daylight hours. Balliol later became one of the leaders in the dismantling of this transitional regime, as indeed it should since it was the one ancient College founded by a woman. She was the Lady Dervorguilla, widow of John de Balliol. John had been required to lay out some money for the education of poor scholars at Oxford as a penance for an assault on retainers of the Bishop of Durham but he died without doing so. His dutiful and loving widow ensured the safety of his soul by performing what he had neglected to perform. Their son was briefly King of Scotland and her College maintained special links with Scotland.

Balliol, not Oxford, was the focus of my work. The University provided lectures and set final examinations and awarded degrees, but the College provided the tutors, set its own internal written examinations (every term at Balliol) and in a ceremony in the College Hall called Handshaking, at which no hands were shaken, each tutor reported verbally on his pupils to the Master in the presence of other tutors. The Balliol library provided all the books that I needed although I made some use of the University library and, thanks to one of my tutors, the Codrington Library in All Souls. Lectures were less important than tutorials; they were ancillary. A few, but very few, were virtually compulsory for anybody aiming at a good class in his final examinations, but for the most part lectures were a planned ramble through what the University as a whole had to offer. Some courses were useful supplements to core subjects; others looked marginally intriguing. The fun was in picking and choosing, planning an attractive but not too exacting weekly programme. The risk was in picking a boring lecturer, going to two or three of his lectures and then feeling too embarrassed to give up when the poor man's audience dwindled to nearly nothing.

The tutorial system is an astonishing institution. Invented in ancient Greece it had fallen into decay but was re-invented in the nineteenth century in Oxford and Cambridge. Its centrepiece was the weekly written essay read to the tutor either in a *tête-à-tête* or in company with one other pupil. The College engaged foremost scholars and paid them to sit and talk with undergraduates and listen to these essays. I do not think that an undergraduate is treated in this way anywhere else in the world. Some of the newer English universities created after the Second World War tried to repeat this generous pattern. At Sussex, for example, where I taught for a while in the sixties, we had a tutorial system modelled on Oxford, specifically on Balliol, but it was becoming difficult to maintain and the strangulation of the universities which was one of the more malign achievements of the disastrously mediocre Thatcher regime went a long way to destroy it.

I went on with History. My eventual career – the things by which I earned money – lay elsewhere, in writing and publishing and teaching, but my teachers at school and at the university gave me such a delight in History that I have gone on reading and thinking about it all my life and I have in my library more History books than anything else except European and North American fiction. I continued at Balliol a practice which I had begun at Eton of diving into famous History books on the principle that if they were famous there must be something in them for me. Gibbon supremely confirmed this thesis but not only Gibbon. I lapped up Motley's *Rise of the Dutch Republic* (three volumes in the Chandos Classics, 12/6 the set, second hand) and all seven volumes of *The Italian Renaissance* by J.A. Symonds; but sometimes I was disappointed and forced to consider at what point to admit defeat. I bought second hand a handsome set of Prescott's *Conquest of Mexico* and *Conquest of Peru* but found them terribly heavy going and decided that honour was satisfied by getting to the end of one of them but not the other. Thus did I begin to discover that great works can be quite small.

At Balliol I was once again extraordinarily lucky in my teachers, chief among them B.H. Sumner and V.H. Galbraith, the one a silent man, the other not. Both possessed the knack of making the past lively and steering a pupil towards the broad view which is the reward for much mucking around in the details. It was exciting to listen to Galbraith talking about medieval people as though he had known them and their characters, problems and foibles. Sumner's comprehensive and rigorous analysis was a bracing challenge to explore all sides of a question and arrive at a tutorial with an exposition which left him with little to add. What made tutors like these so impressive to impressionable youth was not only their enormous erudition but the intellectual ability by which they converted a mass of knowledge into a coherent and revealing picture. And there was more to it than that. In a tutorial of this kind you learned not only about your essay's subject matter; you learned how to learn. This, a tutor like Sumner would explain, is the problem: first identify it clearly: that done, these are the ways of going about it: and these are the conclusions which you may come to in the light of what we know so far. The limits were as important as the discoveries. The whole was a revelation. Years later when I was teaching at Sussex University I had occasion to note how two or three of my colleagues had a special standing in the eyes of students. Again, it came from extraordinary erudition organised and enunciated with the utmost clarity. This dual mastery gave them authority and admiration, made them special. Authority of this kind among thinking people is the counterpart of charisma among the unthinking which, because it is an expression of the personality rather than the mind, is a two-edged gift as likely to be a force for evil as for good.

The Oxford School of Modern History was established in the nineteenth century. There was from early in the eighteenth a Regius Professor of Modern History – the Chair was created by George I mainly for political reasons – but the Professor was regarded with jealous suspicion by the Colleges as an interloper not to be permitted to encroach on their teaching functions, and until the School was established he was not allowed to do anything beyond giving the few lectures prescribed by the terms of his appointment. The scope of the School was large in time but narrow in area. It covered English History and European History, the latter being predominantly western European. In point of time it stretched from Julius Caesar to Bismarck – overlapping Ancient History which belonged, rightly, with ancient languages and literature in the School of Humane Letters, commonly called Greats. It was firmly grounded in the study of texts from medieval charters to modern diplomatic papers. Few undergraduates, however humble their academic expectations, could make do without Stubbs's *Charters*. I still possess the copy which I bought at the beginning of my course and had interleaved with blank pages on which to make notes about the laws of King Ine of Wessex, the charters of King Stephen, the statutes of Edward I and so on. From the end of the medieval half of the course its geographical scope widened and its basic material was state papers such as the records of the Congress of Vienna and similar nineteenth-century activities which became my special study. History, therefore, was first and foremost documents, more specifically official documents – constitutional, administrative, diplomatic. Unofficial documents – merchants' ledgers, private letters, memoirs – came later and lower down the list; the increasing use of this material is one of the distinguishing marks of historical studies in this century which has developed economic history and given biography a greater academic dignity. So long as official documents were the mainstay of History its main subject was necessarily the state and the main business of historians was getting at documents, absorbing them and making plausible generalisations from them. If the result of this labour was presented in intelligible and elegant prose so much the better. Objects other than documents barely came into the picture in my student years. They belonged to archaeology or art. When at Oxford I read Clapham on Norman architecture, I did so outside my subject and not as an essential part of the history of the eleventh century: a laudable initiative perhaps but irrelevant to getting a good degree.

This concentration on the foothills of history left little time or compulsion for the grander themes of cultural history, history of ideas, history of art; but it was an essential underpinning and, if well handled, opened the vistas. Which is what my tutors did for me. Since those days history has expanded prodigiously. The study of archives and the doings of men of action have been overtaken, sometimes submerged, by economic history, social history, psycho-history and a host of other special aspects – not all of them of equal or, some say, of any value. This proliferation has much enriched History, although it has also roused acrimony within the academies and has led politicians and others on the outside to try to squeeze History back into a dates-and-kings straitjacket. *Histoire événementielle* is only one tributary among many. History is the sum of the tributaries, all of them contributing to *histoire totale*, the necessary if unattainable ideal. The crucial distinction is not between one segment or approach and another but between the quality of one historian and another, and the crown goes to him who comes nearest to *histoire totale*.

The fascination of History is the fascination of the past which is unique to mankind and also, I would maintain, innate in man. The snare of History is to suppose that it may lift the veil from the future as well as the past. Its grey area is the present, the history of our own times which according to some may be a legitimate field of study but does not deserve to be called History.

The past excites antiquarian curiosity. It contains gods and sages whose attitudes and precepts need to be discovered and perhaps heeded. It can be dug out and dug up, engaging pursuits. But History is more than the storehouse of the past. History establishes a continuity, even a causal continuity, between the past and ourselves and so creates a state of mind. It is enveloped by time and is conditioned by our notions of time: in particular by two notions which are comparatively modern. The first is that time is not, as the ancients thought, cyclical but linear; that it does not take us back but on. The second is that time past is immensely long and not a matter of a mere 5,000 years or so, with a beginning and an end. These notions are now so familiar that it is easy to forget how revolutionary they once were and difficult to apprehend the mentality of those who believed otherwise than we do about the nature and extension of time. The nineteenth century again greatly increased the latter and added to man's history a vastly longer past without man but continuously leading to the appearance of man. This continuum, displacing the idea of the past as a sequence of disjunct episodes, is essential to the idea of History because, by showing that one thing leads to another, it makes the past intelligible.

The past fascinates for an opposite reason too. It can never be more than partially recovered or known. Discovering how things were is both History's prime purpose and an impossible ambition: discovery never expels mystery. The search for certainties upon which Ranke rightly insisted has to be supplemented by that most uncertain of exercises, the play of the imagination. But if the historical imagination is to be something more than a cover for subjective fancies or *a priori* prejudice it has to be controlled by rigorous rules of evidence and probability which inevitably leave conclusions open to challenge. History, therefore, is not a search for the truth but a search for enough of the truth to enable the historian to depict panoramas which may or may not stand the test of further searches and the critique of other searchers. Whether or not philosophers may establish a *philosophia perennis*, historians can never present a finally certified picture of the past – except in the merest trivia such as the fact that William the Conqueror died in 1087. The element of the imagination – or fantasy as Vico called it – is as essential to History as is the very existence of time past. History is the interpretation of time past through controlled imagination.

Apart from the pleasure it can give and the interest it can add to life History is a thoroughly good general training. History is the enemy of a static view of humanity. Since it presents life as a continuum it is the enemy of fixed or rigid dogma and so of intolerance and inhumanity; the ideological and the historical view are incompatible. History is also the antithesis of myth. Both exist but they are distinct, and History insists on the distinction. Myths, which are of great interest to historians, are unconstrained by facts. History is based on facts. Facts must be correct; incorrect facts are a contradiction in terms. But History is much more than the facts on which it rests. It is facts plus the generalisation of those facts and deductions from them, and whereas the facts have to be correct the generalisations and deductions do not have to be and cannot be correct. Their function is to be not correct but fruitful, and the conjunction between getting facts right and making plausible use of them is of the essence of History as it is of good education. To focus on the wood rather than the trees is an admirable injunction, but it is as well also to remember that there are no woods without trees and that the trees came first.

In ancient times History's Muse lived on Parnassus, not in the Academy. In medieval times too History was at best knocking on the doors of the Academy. The medieval universities were mostly ecclesiastical foundations and in them theology was queen, albeit not without a consort. The consort was law – or, more properly jurisprudence, the science and generalisation of law. The ground plan of jurisprudence was provided by classical philosophy, and the classics kept thrusting themselves into the realms of higher learning where the theologians tried to blend them with Christian theology. The Renaissance, conventionally the marker of the end of the Middle Ages, was in one sense the acknowledgement of the failure of this enterprise.

The medieval university had precursors in cathedral schools and law schools. A few universities were secular foundations: Bologna, for example, and Corpus Christi College at Cambridge. Medieval higher education therefore was an amalgam. Cathedral schools appeared as early as the time of Constantine the Great and were stimulated by Charlemagne's decree that every abbey must have a school: the Church must teach. What it taught was principally theology and logic which it tried to fuse together into a single compendium where faith and reason, the Church Fathers and the pagan philosophers, would reinforce one another. The church schools dominated learning until around the middle of the thirteenth century but fell into the kind of intellectualism which sets more store by proving something than on discovering something. Their successors the universities, fired by antiquarian as well as theological zeal, laboured to recover classical authors and establish correct classical texts and so established *literae humaniores*, the humanities, as the proper study of mankind. The humanists were the first modern strand in European thought. They exalted disbelief as the beginning of wisdom and learning. Through their work in correcting texts distorted by age or partisanship they proclaimed the need to start from scepticism and proceed by methodical and rational inquiry. Their inquiries were historical in as much as an older text outranks a later one.

European civilisation is dual. Unlike Hinduism or Islam, Christianity failed to construct a civilisation in its own image. We speak, therefore, of a Western, not a Christian, civilisation. The Greco-Roman tradition was never submerged and even in the heyday of the Christian Church's dominion pagan Greek and Latin authors continued to be venerated in the class room. Alcuin of York, Charlemagne's mentor and head of the most prestigious abbey in France, found it hard at times to venerate Virgil less than Jesus. Esteem has material value too: one medieval scholar who lost nearly all he possessed when his house burned down was able to rebuild the house by selling two small volumes of Cicero which he had saved. Petrarch's father, when he found his son reading Classical books instead of getting on with his homework, destroyed most of his ancient texts but not Cicero or Virgil: they were inviolate. The Middle Ages submitted to classical masters and ideas and depended on Latin for the practical business of communication. Although Latin died as a generally spoken language about the sixth century it was western Europe's only *lingua franca* and, for a long time, its only written language. It was used of necessity and not from any archaising propensity or any sentimental attachment to a classical Golden Age. It was a powerful factor in preserving the secular and rational elements in a culture which might otherwise have become predominantly theological, dogmatic and authoritarian.

Practicalities ruled too in the law schools, some of which ante-dated the cathedral schools. The lawyers of Ravenna (once an imperial capital) were to provide the secular ruler with a non-clerical and non-divine basis for his rule. To do this they had to reach back to pre-Christian times and to classical ideas and texts. Which is not to say that their teaching was anti-Christian, for few people in the Middle Ages or the Renaissance were anti-Christian even when they were anti-clerical. But they more or less tacitly established the proposition that Christianity was not enough and they did more than any other class to promote the claims of the king and the secular state against the divine imperialism of the Papacy.

From its beginning in the Middle Ages the university has been by its nature open to all the winds that blow. After Roman law came Aristotle, as more and more of his works became opportunely available (at first in Latin) and the corpus of Latin and Greek literature, the mentors and delight of the humanists for whom the centre of intellectual inquiry was not god or heaven and hell but the physical world and man. As the humanities became the focus of education, so theology began its slow decline into a marginal speciality. The mechanic arts too claimed a place: the science of engineering, including classical engineering, was on a par with literary and philosophical pursuits. Cathedrals were not transferred from the drawing board to reality simply by men of taste and devoutness, nor were the material needs of a swelling and urbanised population – waterways, underground mining, for example – met by men unversed in applied sciences and mathematics. But as the Middle Ages melted into the High Renaissance the moguls of taste and culture in the Italian city states gave a special prestige to literature and philosophy and relegated the scientific and technological aspects of education to an inferior position which, in some countries including England, they were still occupying in my childhood.

With hindsight I can see that 1931 was a strange year to go to Oxford. It was a time of palpable change, marked by economic crisis and social trembling. In the twenties the vogue at Oxford and elsewhere had been introspective, aesthetic and seclusive. The economic crisis killed that vogue. The wider world and its inhabitants forced themselves on the attention of people who, until then, had imagined that they could get on very well without, and largely in ignorance of, the distractions and conundrums that go with looking outward. That is not to say that Oxford undergraduates suddenly became politically active. Most did not. The odd event, such as a debate in the Union, might get into the London newspapers but if the readers of those newspapers proceeded to make deductions about life at Oxford they were deceiving themselves. Nevertheless the context had changed and an undergraduate from the thirties, reading in later life memoirs about Oxford life in the twenties, finds himself in a strangely unfamiliar world. Whether he condemns that life or wishes he had been in time to partake of it, is another matter.

My education at Eton and Balliol served me well up to a point, and if that sounds a trifle grudging it is not meant to be. If and so far as my education fell short, the failure was at least in me myself and my circumstances as in my teachers. I was anxious about doing well – to gratify my parents, satisfy my teachers and stand well with my fellows in that way of life to which my wits had called me. I was, therefore, disposed to concentrate on what I knew I could do well, which was collecting, remembering and ordering facts and, beyond this basic if prosaic stage, expressing facts and conclusions clearly and convincingly in speech and writing – more in writing than speech which I was still too timid to essay beyond a narrow circle. None of this is to be belittled and by strengthening my talents in these directions my formal education strengthened also the base for further intellectual development, implanting in me an urge to spread my wings instead of remaining content with Candide's advice to cultivate my own garden. But it did not go much further and, looking back, I am surprised and somewhat mortified to recollect how weak I was in handling ideas. History, the principal vehicle of my education, still meant the recovery of facts.

This is the perennial pitfall of an academic education. It sets a premium on knowing what the great men of the past thought about this or that, while insisting less on what you yourself think. Intelligent persons of my generation who missed university – which means by and large intelligent women – often bemoan what they missed without realising that there has been some gain. They may not have learned what Plato or Aristotle wrote, but they have not been deflected by those great names from thinking for themselves. There is even a case for having no formal education at all. That case is made – and unmade – by the example of Goethe, the grandest European after Dante, who was sent to school for one year only and that because the family home was being done up. But Goethe's innate talents were even more extraordinary than his up-bringing and few parents are bold enough to prepare their offspring for life without schooling and fewer will be justified in so hazardous, not to say reckless, a course.

Here, from a later day, is a cautionary tale. Two pupils, freshmen in a new university, are given an essay subject and a reading list. Pupil A wanders off, gets himself a coffee and then repairs to the library where he finds that pupil B has been before him and carried off all the prescribed books. Pupil A does the best he can and turns in a three-page essay. Pupil B writes a thirty-page essay in which he gives a precis of each of the books. At their next tutorial the tutor addresses pupil A: Well done; you have some good points but you have missed ... etc. etc. To pupil B he says: I have not read your essay and I do not intend to. I see that it tells me what is in these books, but I know what is in them and do not want to be told again. Come back next week with another essay telling me what you think and meanwhile do not look at any books. Pupil B is shattered by this gruff reward for his labours, but he has learned promptly, if brutally, what education is.

The School of Modern History at Oxford included a paper on Political Theory, sometimes and forbiddingly called in those days Political Philosophy. As my finals approached I still had no idea what this phrase meant and I feared that I would make a spectacular ass of myself in the relevant paper. The subject, or rather its name, created a blank in my mind. I could not tackle a subject if I did not know what it meant. In desperation I told one of my tutors that I seemed to be heading for a disaster which would undo all my work in the rest of the curriculum. He gave me in a brisk single sentence a simple translation of the term Political Theory and gave me one book to read in my last vacation before my exams. I read half of it in the train between London and Athens, the other half on the way back, did well enough in the examination and have never since parted with that excellent volume. It was an introduction to a history of ideas, an eleventh-hour introduction in terms of my degree but also a springboard since anybody who fails to see that the essence of history is the history of ideas will soon get bored with history. The source of my perplexities over Political Philosophy was simple. I had started with Rousseau's *Social Contract* and could not make head or tail of its central postulate, the General Will. I did not realise that I could not make sense of it because it makes no sense. There is no such thing as the General Will and nothing is to be gained by supposing that there is.

I learned a lot of history at Oxford and other things too: how to temper specialisation with generality. I learned how to handle knowledge and I absorbed attitudes and ways of living. I learned to divide my time between work and play without fretting over either; how to judge standards and how to confront ideas. I was not unaware of these needs before I went to Oxford but they were greatly developed by the way things were at Oxford. Above all I learned that while some situations are black-and-white most are not, that to pretend that they are is deceitful and lazy, that life and its choices are – to use Montaigne's expressive word *ondoyant* – fluid rather than combative. Finally, I learned that learning is not merely cumulative: that, as Lord Acton warned, there is such a thing as 'the vanity of pointless learning'. (He should know. Although he apparently had in mind George Eliot's Mr Casaubon he could have reflected on his own fate. He knew so much that he never got around to writing his great work.)

At Oxford in the thirties the examination for an Honours degree consisted of a dozen written papers, endured morning and afternoon for a week in formal academic dress and capped, after several weeks, by a *viva voce* encounter, equally formal, with one's examiners. The *viva* was compulsory, even for candidates whose class was obvious from their written work. It was also in theory public. When I turned up for my *viva* there was a small audience consisting of an elderly clergyman with two girls who had presumably been brought to see and hear what true scholarship was like. Preceding me before the examiners was a young man whose journey back to Oxford for this ordeal had plainly been less than necessary. 'Mr So-and-So,' said one of the examiners, 'into what sea does the River Elbe flow?' After a pause the candidate replied: 'The Baltic.' 'Thank you, Mr So-and-So,' said the examiner in tones denoting that the *viva* was over. I was greatly encouraged by this simple passage of arms, but misleadingly.

My examiners were five, four Oxford dons and one from Cambridge. The chairman was J.C. Masterman, then of Christ Church, later a wartime intelligence officer, and later still Provost of Worcester. He lectured in Christ Church Hall twice a week instead of the more usual once and he could be relied upon to make a joke at twenty minutes after the hour and twenty minutes to it. His Cambridge colleague was the even more distinguished Herbert Butterfield, later Master of Peterhouse. I am startled to discover that of the three others I can recall only two. They were Jolliffe of Keble and Boase of Hertford. Jolliffe had recently published a book about the strange system of landholding in medieval Kent which, knowing that he would be one of my examiners, I had read with special care. Time wasted: he never addressed a single word to me throughout a long *viva* and, as far as I could see, spent the time drawing pigs on his blotting paper. Boase, another future Head of a House (Magdalen), whose biography of Pope Boniface VIII I read with equally unrewarded assiduity, I got to know years later when we were colleagues at Bletchley Park during the war. He lodged not far away in a comfortable country house to which he brought for safety a number of treasures from the Courtauld Institute, of which he was then the Director. His landlady, the owner of the house, was an elderly devotee of the Anglican Church who was reputed to keep a card index of curates under her bed, an unverifiable assertion. From Tom Boase I learned what my examiners had thought of me.

My *viva* was a long one in two parts. As the lunch hour approached I was dismayed to hear Masterman say that they would like me to come back for a further session after lunch. I took myself back to Balliol where Humphrey Sumner gave me a suitably modest lunch with barley water to drink. Afterwards Tom Boase asked Sumner what he had given me, since my form after lunch showed a marked decline. But they gave me a First all the same. Tom Boase told me that they did so because I seemed to know so much that they could not decently do otherwise. In other words, while a First may denote brilliance, it may equally well be a reward for knowledge. There is a third possible ingredient – bluff. Far may it be from me to suggest that bluff may command a First, but bluff may help. The History Finals included a number of optional language papers. I offered French and German, which I knew pretty well, and I also offered Italian, which I knew hardly at all, on the principle that there was nothing to lose and perhaps a little to gain. At the very beginning of the *viva* Masterman reeled off some Italian poetry and asked: 'To whom was the poet referring?' I had barely understood what the lines meant and had no idea to whom they referred, but not wanting to begin by looking a fool and knowing Masterman's special interests I took a chance and replied confidently: 'Napoleon.' This was correct, and after that Masterman took no further part in the proceedings which were conducted almost entirely as a duel between Butterfield and myself.

In those days results came out some time after the *viva*. On leaving the Examination Schools in the High Street, one gave a shilling to a janitor who undertook to send a telegram as soon as the results were posted at the Schools. The telegram came early in August. I had known that I could not do worse than a Second but a First came into that tantalising category of the possible but improbable. There was as it happened nobody at home when I got the telegram and not knowing what to do I picked up the telephone to tell my mother who was out at a tea party. This was success pure and simple and I did not suppose that I would ever again know anything like it.

4

Around in the Thirties

In 1934 I left Oxford with a BA (Hons.) First Class. I was now educated. Nobody in those days aspired to a second degree unless he were going into the Church or into teaching and in any case an Oxford MA, if you wanted one, could be bought for £5. Oxford was a place for teaching undergraduates and those seeking second degrees were few and unregarded.

The next few years were an interlude. The imperatives of formal education and its institutions disappeared. They had provided a framework whose constraints might be resented but whose certainties were comfortable. In their place were the problems of choosing a career and making good in it and the feeling that the days of living at home were – imprecisely – numbered. These years ended with two events: the outbreak of war which disrupted every person's life for nearly five years and marriage which remodelled mine for more than fifty.

By this time we had been living in London for some years. When my father was sent to Liverpool in 1913 he was one of three managers who ran the firm there and he became, while still a comparatively young man, the senior manager. In 1928 he was translated to London and my parents set about the exciting business of finding a new home. We stayed first with my grandmother in Porchester Terrace and then rented a house in Portman Square, not such a grand house but a grander address: the difference between W2 and W1 meant something. My father's move had social as well as career implications and he relished both. He was extremely serious about his work but he also loved company and parties. Years later, when he was in his eighties, he told my wife that his idea of bliss was going to two cocktail parties in an evening. He was attracted by a house just off Park Lane which overlooked Dorchester House and its grounds, but the price was high – £80,000 for the freehold, I recall – and his sound sense of the value of money made him recoil. Although he hankered after a good address he was not the man to pay for it over the odds and he was never showy. His hesitations on this occasion were just as well since Dorchester House was pulled down soon afterwards and a great lump of an hotel was built on its site. My parents eventually chose 23 (now 24) Hyde Park Gardens, W2, the end house in a row overlooking the park across Bayswater Road from which it was distanced by its own gardens, carefully tended but mostly ignored by the house-owners. This was not a standard London house with L-shaped rooms lapping round the staircase. It was a spacious four-square house with a big central hall going up through two floors. There were two rooms on each of these floors and one of these was turned over to my elder sister and myself, quarters of our own where we entertained our friends, played the gramophone and had our daytime being. We were waited on hand and foot by a staff of seven or eight which now included a butler and footman. The butler, being Irish, was amazingly adept at getting his tongue round the strange Greek names which he had to announce. The footman, less accomplished, was a refugee from the economic devastation of the northern coalfields and so unused to the ways of London's rich that he occasionally handed round food without first handing round the plates to put it on. People say that this way of living has disappeared. I do not believe it. Nowadays it is lived by people whom we do not happen to know.

It may seem strange that as my formal education drew to an end nobody suggested that I should go into the family firm. I could easily have done so, thus solving at a stroke the tiresome question that older people were constantly putting to me in my teens: 'What are you going to be?' The verb, I remember, was always 'be', not 'do'. My record at school and the university was more than good enough, and I was founder's kin on my mother's side and the son of a senior manager. Going into Ralli Bros. would have meant going to India for an indefinite number of years but there was nothing daunting about that. My favourite uncle had spent nearly all his life there and seemed to have had a thoroughly good time. Yet the idea hardly crossed my mind. It was assumed that I would do something different and this assumption is one of the more telling markers of the transition of the Chiot community, the transition from looking to one another for virtually everything from cradle to grave and becoming Englishmen – or imitation Englishmen – who would prefer to make their way in vocations open to all Englishmen. If the outstanding instrument of this change was the educational system to which for want of another I had been committed since my tenth year, there was also the cast of mind of my parents' generation. They saw me living a life in the larger community. Assimilation was an achievement, not a betrayal.

There was, too, the outlook which I had imbibed from that community itself. It did not have a high regard for 'business'. This disfavour applied less to industry than to finance, less to making things than to simply making money. 'The City', however, was suspected of being a nepotistic enclave and rather too happy a hunting ground for shady characters and downright crooks, if not on the scale of fifty years later. Besides, as my father (who became a director of Ralli Bros. on the incorporation of the partnership in 1931) must have realised, its palmier days were over. The thirties were not kind to commercial enterprises and in India the profits of Ralli Bros. were being pared by the growth of Indian manufacturers at the expense of imports of goods from, for example, Lancashire while the firm was also losing some of its pre-eminent market share to competitors. In the thirties its profits never reached one per cent of turnover and turnover remained virtually static at £19 million a year. This trend was particularly alarming for a firm whose basic maxim was: small profits on expanding turnover. A small boom around 1937 faded quickly and throughout the decade an ordinary dividend was paid once only and then out of an unexpected windfall. A special report presented to the President a few months before war broke out indicated that the business was sound and its capital intact but its financial structure was rigid and costly, its staff in India no longer as sharp as might be desired, its overheads excessive and its directors in London too numerous and overpaid. This last conclusion seems harsh by modern standards since fifteen of them shared £32,000 at the beginning of the decade and £24,000 at its end. The upshot of this report was that the successors of the original Ralli Bros. knew their business as merchants but were, or had become, surprisingly naive as financiers. Its recommendations did not really hit this nail on the head. They included recruiting more British staff of the university and public school type. But I was not to be one of them. I suspect that from about the turn of the century the partners had been good at conducting but no longer good at creating business.

My parents' first choice for me turned out to be one which was not open – the diplomatic service. The rules said that British diplomats had to be British subjects by birth and the sons of natural-born British subjects. While I myself and my mother satisfied these requirements, paradoxically because we had both been born in India, my father did not because he had been born in France and was a British subject only by later naturalisation. Some half-hearted attempts were made to see if there was a way round the rules but they produced the advice – from Anthony Eden, whom I was taken to see – that even if there were I would never get anywhere in the service with a name like mine. When one of my uncles asked me if I had ever thought of changing my name I was shocked. When later in life I observed the names of American diplomats I had cause to reflect on one of the differences between that country and this.

This discomfiture, which occurred while I was still at Oxford, was more of a disappointment to my father than to me. He was proud of me and keen to see me shine in the most prestigious possible profession. He was quintessentially a family man. What mattered most to him was the family and for the family only the best was good enough, although within the family what was best was not always agreed. After further thought and consultation about equally distinguished and agreeable occupations it was decided that I should read for the Bar. So I started 'eating dinners' at the Inner Temple in London while I was yet an undergraduate at Oxford. Eating dinners was a vestigial formality. Having joined one of the four Inns of Court by paying the prescribed fee one had to 'keep terms'. In a university keeping terms, a prerequisite for getting a degree, meant spending the requisite number of nights per term in College or approved lodgings; keeping terms at the Inn meant no more than turning up three or four times in the term to eat the evening meal. There was a glass of sherry before a fairly modest repast which was served in the Inn's Hall, with occasional glances at half a dozen seniors eating their meal at a high table on the dais. These were Benchers of the Inn, judges and the like, the equivalents of the Fellows of a College, presumably mostly bachelors with nowhere better to go for dinner. The number of legal terms was four in the year in place of the three university terms, and undergraduates were required to eat only half as many dinners – three per term – as others. The process, therefore, was not time-consuming; neither did it instil any particle of legal knowledge.

At the end of these years and after passing a number of examinations I was ceremonially called to the Bar by the Inner Temple. I knew very little law and nothing at all about legal practice. The examinations were numerous but rudimentary; it was possible to learn (at any rate in those days) all that was required by buying a set of books called Nutshells – Tort in a Nutshell, Roman Law in a Nutshell. I completed the process in a year after leaving Oxford and emerged from the grind knowing very little law but at least knowing what I needed to learn more about – the law of Contract, Torts, Real Property, Equity and so on. Repairing the ignorance took place in two stages, first as a paying pupil in active chambers and then as a junior member of chambers picking up minor briefs in minor courts which more senior members disdained or the clerk in the chambers – the key figure – wangled out of the solicitors whose clerks it was his business to know and reassure about the astounding brilliance of the latest recruits to the chambers. An added obstacle to progress in Chancery chambers, to which my career was directed, was the fact that a court practice meant the High Court or nothing: there were no subsidiaries like petty sessions or police courts in which to cut one's teeth. So climbing the Chancery pole demanded more stamina and was more fiercely contested. I began as a pupil to an eminent conveyancer called Hubert Rose who did an immense amount of work for the Public Trustee among other clients and was the sort of quiet unglamorous figure that a backroom lawyer was supposed to be. From him I learned how to concoct appropriate documents by looking up the right models in two fat volumes called K and E (Key and Elphinstone) and adjusting them to the circumstances of the case before me. It was a bit like cooking, a false ingredient could ruin the whole thing. After six months of this noviciate I found a place in another set of chambers where I was a pupil of Jack Reid, a more extrovert character with a wider practice. These chambers specialised in company law besides having a general Equity practice. It was a good amalgam, since company law derived almost entirely from statute and equity from precedent and theoretical jurisprudence. At the head was Cecil Willie Turner, one of the great pundits of company law. His table was enviably littered with briefs.

He seldom went into court, except on Mondays when companies were wound up in droves. His practice was behind the scenes, sitting at his desk where he tackled one brief after another and wrote on the backs of them terse answers and advice in longhand. He too was a retiring man of whom I saw little, always courteous, always busy, but undramatic and the reverse of the public's idea of a highly successful man of the law. Jack Reid was jollier and less pacific, quick-witted, conscientious towards his pupils but easily irritated by fools – he had lost a leg in the war, which may have accounted for a lack of forbearance for lesser folk. He ended up as a County Court judge – Your Honour but not M'Lud – although he was abler than many High Court judges. There were then only six judges in the Chancery Division of the High Court, and becoming one of them was impeded not only by their small number but additionally by the fact that there was no retiring age. The senior judge in the Division in my time had sat there for thirty years and passed 80 before he retired.

My years at the Bar were a curious combination of working hard and having little to show for it. I worked on Jack Reid's cases, mostly in the library of Lincoln's Inn, of which I had become a member on going into Chancery chambers. This move from the Inner Temple was more or less compulsory since Lincoln's Inn was the focus of Chancery activities, whereas the other three Inns consisted almost exclusively of chambers devoted to other branches of the law. (Lincoln's Inn is so called because it was once the medieval town house and garden of the Bishop of Lincoln, once England's most extensive diocese.) Jack Reid had more than enough work to keep him regularly busy but the prospect for younger members of the chambers was hard work irregularly. I liked the work and did not mind how hard it might be, but the uncertainty was something new and vaguely worrying. The worry was not financial since my parents gave me a decent allowance, but it was disturbing not to be earning money or to be able to discern when or whether I would have an established practice of my own. I was not foxed by the nature of the work which I knew I could master but I realised that getting briefs had as much to do with connections – connections, that is, with solicitors who were the sole source of a barrister's work – as with native ability or application. I knew I could do the work. What I did not know was whether anybody would ask me to. I felt a bit stranded, not in the sense of being washed up but in the opposite sense of not knowing how to push off.

But these worries were marginal and intermittent. Work and prospects had their place in life but it was a well-defined place which left room for plenty of other things. The four legal terms did not extend over the whole year and even in term time the legal week excluded weekends and everything after 5 pm. There were holidays and there was life in London with friends. These were the better years of the thirties, the Depression fading and the war still to come. By the time I left Oxford I could see that life promised well, although it was not without its hazards. I was an eligible young man – such was the current, rather dreadful classification – inasmuch as my financial prospects were sound, I was good-mannered with mothers and entirely dependable with daughters. But socially I was marginal and I had not yet outgrown the edginess of having an awkward name and too exotic a background. I had to watch my step, or thought I had to, but I would never have let on to anybody that that was how it seemed to me. Meanwhile, there was a good time to be had – not the frenetic social round of the postwar twenties but a carefree and guilt-free social circus, enjoyable, replete and as serious or as light as you might choose at any moment to mix its varied ingredients. The London season was, as has often been remarked, a marriage market, but for the young it was also fun. As a marriage market it worked less and less well as parental control diminished and parents, so far from making matches, fell back on creating the situations in which they hoped the young would make the matches the parents desired. The young, released from the disciplines of regular education, enjoyed themselves, going to dances and parties in the evenings and gossiping about them on the telephone the next morning. The telephone gave the party-going an afterglow which it had lacked before the dissemination of that insidious instrument. While primarily designed for girls the season needed boys and there were consultations among mothers about roping in the respectable and desirable. Some were roped in automatically because they belonged to the right families but the pool had to be widened by suitable increments. Suitable meant boys with the right manners and the right income, although the income might be prospective. I qualified on both grounds but the season was not for me such good fun as it might have been. This was a narrowly self-conscious world, I was not sure that I really belonged in it and there is nothing more uncomfortable than being on the fringes. I was shy, bad at conversation with mere acquaintances, and not at all sure how girls expected to be treated or what they liked to talk about. There was, however, one great compensation. I loved dancing and was good at it and many girls danced well because dancing had a prominent place in their jejune preparation for the world. Just as the Victorian young lady had learned to play her pieces on the piano, so her successor had been taught to dance. What I needed at this stage was a girl who could dance and either did all the talking or did not mind if we danced without talking all the time. Happily such were to be found. And in any case this social stage, half way between the chrysalis and the butterfly, did not last long and was followed by – or perhaps overlapped with – the more intimate and less intimidating world of smaller parties and *têtes-à-tête*: a West End restaurant with a dance floor, a theatre, an evening at Glyndebourne with the luxury of car with a chauffeur (we had a Rolls by now). There were concerts of all kinds to go to either with my mother or by myself or with a judiciously chosen companion and there was the discovery of ballet. I came too late to see Diaghilev's famous company or any of his most famous ballerinas, but much of his repertoire was revived by de Basil's Ballets Russes de Monte Carlo which had acquired Diaghilev's sets and costumes.

I became a balletomane, first at the old Alhambra on the east side of Leicester Square – opposite London's leading billiard saloon and across the way from Le Perroquet where Signor Bellometti would present a flower from his own garden in Sussex to the girl whom you brought to his restaurant – and later at the Covent Garden Opera House. The classical ballet as it developed from about 1830 to 1930 was an aesthetic delight and intellectually undemanding. It combined perfection in a small compass with a kaleidoscopic but tightly integrated variety. Its essence was dance and, with dance, music but also stage scenery and costume and the telling of a story. The dance was strictly and artificially restricted but the artistry lay in using the rules and conventions, the stylised steps and gestures, to make works which were more than exercises – as the Art of Fugue or the Diabelli Variations are more than exercises – and the best classical ballets provide the ideal meeting place for classicism and romanticism. *Les Sylphides* is a symbiosis of these two aesthetic attitudes and a warning not to draw a hard-and-fast line between them. Classical ballet developed from the relatively boring works of the mid-nineteenth century through the partnership of Marius Petipa and Tchaikovsky and then the genius of Michel Fokine and ultimately the cooperative galaxies of the Diaghilev era when artistic seriousness, aesthetic daring and lightheartedness were brought together by Stravinsky, Bakst, Benois, Nijinsky, Massine, Milhaud, Falla, Picassa, Cocteau, Derain, Gontcharova. I became less enamoured of ballet when gymnastics were added to the brew.

Evenings at the ballet and other diversions were by later standards unbelievably decorous. To a generation to whom kissing has become so universal as to be meaningless it will seem absurd that I never kissed a girl except my sisters and close cousins until I got engaged to be married. Not everybody was like that, nor do I commend so austere a pattern, which was less a form of self-discipline than a substitute for it which nourished ignorance, hypocrisy and deceit. But it was the norm and I was normal. An evening for two would end with my taking my friend by taxi to where she lived, pausing until her street door had safely closed behind her and then back to our handsome house in Hyde Park Gardens (where later numerous Tollands were located by Mr Anthony Powell). A special delight were events which came only once a year: Wimbledon where my grandmother had perennial Centre Court seats and, from the mid-thirties, opera at Glyndebourne with its combination of marvellous singing and supper on the grass that made you tingle before you got there. The calendar mattered more in those days, particularly in the matter of food – asparagus, strawberries – which appeared at a certain point and for a short time, not all the year round.

Beyond London were country houses where parents worked hard – the servants of course harder – to give their children and their friends a good time focussed, in the summer, on weekends with tennis and the like and, in winter, on the Hunt Balls which were jollier versions of London dances and took place in splendid houses. But above all there were holidays which, increasingly for me, meant going abroad. Abroad was a distinct place and going to it was magic.

The magic had begun a decade earlier – in 1926. I had just won my Eton scholarship and the gods were smiling on me, for at that very moment an epidemic broke out at my prep school and served as a happy pretext for my premature removal from that odious establishment. Unexpectedly summoned to see the headmaster and be told I was to leave the next day, I listened to his stilted hopes that I might remember my time there with gratitude but could think of nothing beyond my delight at getting away so soon and for ever.

My first taste of abroad was Tuscany, which has never lost its intoxication, but the purpose of my first foreign excursions was not to see things but to see people – relatives. Family came before scenery or art, duty before pleasure, although all these could be combined. In 1926 we were off to see my grandmother, my father's mother, who lived and wandered with her married daughter and her husband and three daughters. He was a Greek admiral, marvellously handsome, as silent as any English naval prototype, erect, bearded, meticulously dressed, courteous to adults and kindly to adolescents. He was said to have been the first naval officer ever to command a submarine in battle – presumably in those Balkan Wars which were in progress at the date of my birth. He was a man of the most absolute personal probity which, since he had been commissioned in the Royal Hellenic Navy, compelled him to unquestioning loyalty to three Greek monarchs of the house of Schleswig-Holstein-Sonderburg-Glucksburg, two of whom he followed on various bouts of exile in Swiss and Italian cities. With him went his family but they were now about to return to Athens with the current king and we were going to join them in Italy for an extended holiday before they did so. We met on the Tuscan coast at Forte dei Marmi, then a tiny resort with a single hotel: the Marmi of its name were the marble mountains of Carrara a few miles back from the coastline.

The children in the party were six, aged between 21 and seven. I was roughly in the middle and the only boy. Although I was not much aware of it, I was probably the kingpin in this group. I had just won a prestigious scholarship and I was what grown-ups call well-mannered; I was always popular with older relatives, particularly older female ones. My uncle, the admiral, and his eldest daughter – with whom I made an enduring relationship of special affection – both treated me as a semi-grown-up, which nobody had done before. On the beach, when I had had enough of bathing or canoeing, I listened to adult conversation which I only half understood. These were the early days of fascism and the acquaintances whom we picked up at the hotel included a flamboyant Anglo-Irishman called Barnes who was an enthusiast for Mussolini and wrote the principal eulogy of him in English. Barnes had, so he said, declined the Albanian crown (he was not the only one), a circumstance which gave him a mundane halo and a claim to be heard on the affairs of the world as he sat holding forth energetically and with equal energy scooping up sand into sand-castles with his long arms. Sometimes he would pause to pay attention to us children, a virtue which may perhaps count for a little for him in the hell where fascists roast.

From Forte dei Marmi we went to Pisa to see the Leaning Tower which had not yet leaned so far that visitors were prevented from climbing up it. It was much whiter than I had imagined in those days before the ubiqui-tous colour brochure and so I got a delicious shock from seeing it glistening alongside the white cathedral, white baptistery and white Campo Santo (the last terribly battered in the Second World War). I had never seen buildings like these. It was the day of the feast of the Assumption of the Virgin and while we were in the cathedral a grand procession of clerics, including the cardinal-archbishop, pressed us aside as its display of pur-ples and violets, birettas and lace, asserted the holiness of a place which still belonged to worshippers rather than tourists. The cardinal was said to be *papabile*, which shocked me as he looked like a doddering dumpling. We moved on to Siena and the Palio. Because we had failed to find rooms in Siena we stayed in San Gimignano, the City of a Hundred Towers. It was hardly a city and most of its towers had fallen down, but no matter. I insisted on looking into all the churches I could find and bought Alinari prints of the principal monuments. I cannot ever enter the main square in San Gimignano without a glance at the hotel where we spent two en-chanted days and nights – and I got into a fearful row with my father because I had brought with me no spare shirt. I already believed in travelling light, as I still do. Taking three of a thing when two will do is a kind of intellectual offence, like walking up a moving escalator.

In Siena we had booked seats in a building overlooking the steeply sloping, oval piazza, but before taking our places we managed through some connection to squeeze into one of the parochial churches where, before the race for the *palio*, the horse carrying the colours of that parish was to be blessed. It was a small church, already packed tight before the horse arrived, and I noted with envy a man so tall that he had a perfect view of the proceedings. I was told that he was the king's cousin, the Duke of Aosta. When the horse arrived and was urged up the steps outside there was great alarm inside since there was next to no room for manoeuvre. The horse was nervous and so was the waiting priest, whose hand shook so much that the holy water sprinkled over the horse spontaneously. The ceremony performed, there was more commotion as the horse was made to turn round and make its way back to more familiar surroundings.

Nowadays a boy of twelve could well know something about the Palio from television but I had never heard of the race itself or the fantastical procession which precedes it – the extraordinary gyrations of banners thrown in the air by men in brilliant costumes as the parish contingents slowly circle the piazza; the sudden and fearsome whistling of the groundlings (the Italian version of booing) when the rich and unpopular parish of the oca or goose debouched into the piazza; the chaotic assembly of the horses at the start; the loosing of the race before they had got into any sort of line; the perilous race over the cobbled circuit and its sharp corners for a prize which goes to the first horse to get round twice with or without its rider; and finally the charge of police to the finishing post to protect the winner from being lynched. In 1926 the winning horse belonged to the parish of the snail and as we drove back in the dark to San Gimignano we had to shout out of the car, 'Carracciola, carracciola', in response to cries of 'Chi ha vinta? Chi ha vinta?'

Although we spent most of the summer on the Tuscan beach we made a quick dash to Florence to see the main sights and I was amazed to find that the streets had names which I knew from books about Renaissance Italy – Tornabuoni and so forth. They gave the new a dash of familiarity, like an *omelette surprise*. I came back to England with three things: a leather-bound book called *The Wonders of Italy*, with 2,939 illustrations (I still have it); a romantic attachment to platform 1 at Victoria Station, gateway to abroad; and a passion for foreign travel, particularly to the Mediterranean for its blue sea and white roads, its history and its sun. I would never thereafter be content to stay in England from one year's end to the other. There are two kinds of travellers. True travellers, Baudelaire said, set out for the sake of setting out: *partent pour partir*. The grand object of travel, Johnson said, is to see the Mediterranean. I am both kinds of traveller.

This holiday abroad was followed by a string of equally exciting visits to Greece. My grandmother was getting old – she had been born in 1847 – and so we made a point of going to Athens to see her in the Easter holidays (not too hot). We went in 1928 and 1929, 1931 and 1932, but not in 1930 because in that year my father's elder brother was there and they were in one of the recurrent states of feud which punctuated their relationship. They were the elders in a family of six, very close to one another at different stages of their lives and always generous to the rest of the family, beginning with their mother. But they were prone to the sort of quarrels which blow up in even the closest families. They used regularly to invite two of their nieces, daughters of their only sister, to come to England in the summer, dividing their time between the two houses which the two uncles rented for the summer. This particular quarrel flared up over the precise date at which the nieces should move – or should have moved – from the one house to the other. It generated huge indignation and bitterness and went on for years, during which the brothers refused to meet. Each felt mortally cheated by the other.

We went to Greece by train as far as Venice or Trieste and then by sea. The thrills of Victoria's platform 1 lasted as far as Dover; the crossing to

Calais was less appealing; the thrills began again on the French side where, after leaving the boat, one wound one's way among the blue trains lined up by the quay to find the one marked Paris-Dijon-Milan-Venice-Nish-Salonica-Athens. I noted that foreigners did not build proper platforms for their trains but provided them with excellent big windows to look out of. When we reached Paris we went through a ceremony which testified to the strength of family connections. At the Gare du Nord most of the passengers got out, but there was in those days a connection round Paris called the *ceinture* which carried one or two coaches in a slow trundle to the Gare de Lyons where they would be hitched to the Orient Express for the next stages of the journey. At the Gare du Nord we were met by a cousin of my mother called Augusto Gilbert de Voisins. He was her first cousin but they had met very little in their lives, certainly not in recent years and not even, I think, earlier on. He and his wife, Louise, lived at Arcachon which is about as far as you can get from Paris without leaving France. Nevertheless the relationship pulled. This couple had various claims to fame. Augusto was the last in his line in an extensive family which, coming to Paris from Burgundy in the fifteenth century, made name and fortune as lawyers and servants of the Crown. They epitomised the opportunities open to men of the pen, the *noblesse de la robe*, rather than the sword. By the time of the French Revolution they were rich but not equally sure-footed in the turbulences of politics. One of them, although a friend of Rousseau, was guillotined after shilly-shallying between the *emigrés* and the new regime. His son was no more decisive but luckier. He was made a peer of France by Napoleon when the *parvenu* emperor was sucking up to the old nobility. He abandoned Napoleon in 1814, which was ungrateful, but rallied to him after his return from Elba, which was unwise. He was out of favour with the restored Bourbons but recovered it when the revolution of 1830 brought to the throne Louis Philippe whose father, the decapitated Philippe Egalité, had been one of his schoolfellows. Through all these vicissitudes the family wealth remained intact or better. In the next generation Jean-Pierre, diplomat, made an impulsive and spectacular marriage. At the ballet one evening in a small town in the north-eastern corner of Spain he was so struck by the principal dancer that the next morning he sought out her father and asked for her hand in marriage. She was Marie Taglioni, half-Italian half-Swedish and about to become the most famous ballerina of the nineteenth century. Of their children one married a Russian prince and another a Greek heiress who was my grandmother's sister – which brings us back to the Gare du Nord and Augusto their son.

As a rich young man he was keen on travelling and collecting and mad about circuses. He did Buffalo Bill acts himself before becoming a prolific novelist and poet. His best-known novel was about the Gold Rush to California, but more of them were set in China, for which he had a special interest and love. His entire *oeuvre* was *couronné* by the French Academy, but I fear that his books are not easy reading for the modern taste. They are to be found in the London Library where they look sadly undisturbed. Through his wife, Louise, he was connected with the reigning worlds of Parisian letters. She was a daughter of Cuban-French poet Jose Maria de Heredia, the leading light with Leconte de Lisle in the circle of poets called *parnassiens* – who were more concerned with the craft of poetry, particularly the sonnet, than with the romantic emotions. She married first Pierre Louys (his name was really Louis) who wrote a celebrated erotic novel and a sequence of 150 erotic poems, *Les Chansons de Bilitis*, which he pretended were translations from Greek. His friend Claude Debussy was inspired by them, if only moderately since most of the pieces he wrote with them in mind he left unfinished; some of these were completed half a century later by Pierre Boulez. Pierre Louys was a disastrous husband and Louise left him for Augusto whom she married first in a civil ceremony and then after the death of Louys in church. Her sister married the Symbolist poet Henri de Regnier and herself wrote poetry under the name Gerard d'Houville. Augusto and Louise must have been interesting people but to my sister and me they were a couple of elderly and rather melancholy relatives (they were around 50 or not much more) and we preferred to stand in the corridor watching Parisian suburbs go by while our parents exchanged family reminiscences and news in the compartment. At the Gare de Lyon they got out, waited on the platform until our train left and then made their way back to Arcachon.

In Trieste a different and more lively set of relatives awaited us. These were a clutch of Rallis who lived gregariously in a house called the Casa Ralli, which was so big that only one branch of the clan occupied an entire floor. He was the current Baron Ralli, another cousin of my mother. His grandfather, a refugee from the 1822 massacre, had been born in Chios but died in Trieste at the age of 88 after siring fifteen children. He had been made a baron by the emperor Francis Joseph and so all his male descendants were called Baron This or Baron That, by their Christian names. They were small, friendly, vivacious and courteous: formal without being stiff, loquacious without being rowdy. They made a great fuss of us but we stopped with them only one night before embarking on the 48-hour sea journey to Piraeus via Brindisi on a ship labelled *celerissimo* (very fast) to distinguish it from the *celere* (just fast, i.e. slow). They were doggedly anti-Italian, regarded the transfer of Trieste from the Austro-Hungarian empire to Italy after the First World War as a catastrophe, and they were said to have portraits of the old emperor and his family hanging on their walls but back to front in order not to get into trouble: an allegorical tale, I fancy, rather than a fact.

On the first of these visits to Athens we stayed in a small hotel which was a converted palace. It had been the home of Prince Nicholas and his Russian wife (parents of Princess Marina, Duchess of Kent). I remember it chiefly because I woke up one night to find the drawers rattling and the doors of the wardrobe flying open. Not far away Corinth, which we had visited the day before, was being flattened by an earthquake and as we steamed home next week we could see from our ship tents being put up to house the homeless population. In later years we stayed at the much bigger Grande Bretagne on the main square from which we could from our balcony see the Good Friday processions with the empty catafalques being carried round the city, followed by gorgeous hordes of bishops and preceded by brass bands playing Chopin's funeral march over and over again – a moving sight even if the bishops did look rather too self-important. Although written for the piano the funeral march is not demeaned by its transposition to the brass band. The last time I saw this Easter ritual was some sixty years later in Cephallonia where the archbishop was an imposing figure about six-foot-six without his hat and attended by acolytes including a small African boy – a strange sight in an Ionian island but one reminiscent of a long tradition of trade between the Ionian islands and Africa.

Much of our time in Athens was devoured by calls on innumerable cousins on my father's side, friendly, delighted to see us, but a great nuisance because they quickly reverted to animated conversation in a language which we could not follow and because our visits to them prevented us from spending more time sight-seeing outside Athens. We visited the Acropolis by day and by moonlight and other sites in the city but beyond Athens we were rationed to one trip a year. This took the form of a carefully organised excursion of several days in a couple of hired cars, holding selected cousins as well as ourselves and driven by maniacs who liked racing trains to level crossings and outspeeding the fierce dogs which considered themselves in duty bound to rush towards us from their sentinel posts on neighbouring hills. So did I get my first taste of the road to Delphi, of Mycenae and Olympia and the central Peloponnese, the precursors of many marvellous holidays which my wife and I would take after the war in mainland and maritime Greece in search of ruins, flowers, sun and sea.

In these previous years the one journey of substance which I took without my family was a circuitous trip with a Balliol friend whom I had gone to visit in Rome. He was George Allison. His father ran a restaurant somewhere in Yorkshire where the keen eye of Kenneth Bell, Fellow of Balliol and personification of its peculiar amalgam of scholarship and heartiness, had picked on young George as the sort of boy who ought to go to Balliol. George was killed in the war but not before displaying a measured talent for knocking up against all sorts of people, including well-placed ones whom he beguiled with innocently exaggerated indications of his personal connections. At this time he was an honorary, that is to say unpaid, attaché to the British Ambassador in Rome and was occupying a small tower overlooking Trajan's forum. I joined him there as his stint at the embassy was ending and we wandered home in his ageing two-seater Morris through Switzerland to Budapest, Prague and Germany. Before leaving Italy we bought a large crate of peaches and practically lived on them until the last of those that remained were too bruised to be appetising. Somehow or other we took in Monte Carlo in what must have been a singularly circuitous route. There I visited a casino for the first and last time in my life. I came out with exactly the same amount of money I had on going in – a pointless procedure therefore. Budapest provided another first – and last: I was arrested there. I was taking photographs when a soldier came up and told me that I was not allowed to. I said I was sorry but defended myself by adding that I understood no Hungarian. He retorted that he had been speaking not Hungarian but German. Nettled, I gave him the lie by saying that I knew German and what he had been talking was not German. He then seized my camera and proposed to seize me too but eventually we compromised. He extracted the film but let me have the camera back and go on my way.

Other foreign forays had a more instructional object. For several years in a row I went in the summer to Germany to improve my German in a family which specialised in that sort of extracurricular topping up. Dr Blassneck and his wife were a friendly, donnish couple who lived in a suburb of Cologne called Kirschweg. It was far enough outside the city to be countrified but connected with it by a tram which got to the centre in about fifteen minutes. My visits to the Blassnecks began before the Nazis' electoral triumph of January 1933 and one of these visits coincided with one of the last elections before that calamity. I remember sitting round a radio listening to results coming in and marking them on pie-charts to see who was going up and who down. It was clear that the Doctor and his wife did not vote Nazi; they probably voted for one of the centre parties, either the Roman Catholic Zentrum or perhaps the Social Democrats. Their daughter, however, a pale girl in her late teens with flaxen pigtails and little sexual allure, had recently joined the *Hitlermädl*, the female side of the Nazi youth brigades. She was probably a worry to her parents.

We pupils were four or five. Besides Dr B. and Mrs B. we had lessons from a younger man who came in for a number of hours a day. Since this was summer we sat under the trees in the garden. The atmosphere was serious and punctilious but relaxed when compared with the stuffy classrooms to which we had been accustomed at our schools. Mostly we read and translated *viva voce* texts ranging from Schiller or Lessing to modern books which added conversational German to the literary poetry of the great *Kulturträger*. The only modern book which floats back into my mind was called *Die Biene Maja* – a Bee called Maja. Dr B. was one of those bald men whose baldness was preternaturally polished and shiny. This had a strange disadvantage for him in some weathers, when swarms of very small beetles called *Maikäfer* were attracted to his bald pate and tickled it, so that he was perpetually moving one arm up to smite himself on the head and extinguish these distracting pests. His expression never betrayed impatience with the insects; he looked like one of those mechanical toys which ceaselessly perform regular but jerky movements. Twice a week Dr B. would set off for the city with a *Mappe* or briefcase of the kind used for carrying sheet music. Where he went we never knew nor was it our business, but we were intrigued by an identical bulge which always marked the briefcase and one day, our curiosity overcoming our good manners, we took a peep inside: the bulge was caused by a couple of bananas. Years later I learned that Frau B. committed suicide by setting her bedding alight while sleeping one night in the garden. Dr B. discovered her half-dead and dying. What became of him I do not know. They were good people, not perhaps very exciting, professionals doing a professional job, inconspicuous members of a decent section of a civilised and hardworking people. Multiply their fate by thousands or tens of thousands and you have the horror and the tragedy of Nazi Germany. The last time I stayed with the Blassnecks he gave me as a parting present a pocket encyclopedia called Knaurs *Konversationslexikon,* a handy little volume with 15,000 entries, 2,600 illustrations and many tables, maps and city plans. I have always kept it – and not only because it is useful.

Visiting Germany in the early thirties should have made me a committed student of the ideological conflicts and hideous brutalities which were scarring Europe at that time. Countless memoirs of the period tell how clever and alert people were caught up in those agonising preoccupations, but I was not among them. I was almost totally a stranger to political discussion – at home because there was none, at Oxford by choice or simple, negative abstention. Public affairs, whether domestic or foreign, interested without involving me. I followed them by reading *The Times* and thought that reading *The Times* was enough. When I arrived at Balliol for my first term I was quickly visited by emissaries of the university's Conservative, Liberal, Labour and Communist Associations and joined the lot – half a crown for life membership, an easy way of sidestepping further attentions. In my three years at Oxford I never discovered where the famous Union was.

Yet somehow or other political germs were there. Just as surely and just as secretively as I discarded God at Eton, so I knew that I was not a Conservative. My first brush with politics occurred even earlier, as far back as the General Strike of 1926. It was a very light brush but it planted a small seed of revulsion. Although the General Strike lasted only one week it was a week when I was due to go back to my school in Kent from Liverpool. But there were no trains. So it was decided that my mother and I would go by car, breaking the journey in London where we stayed the night at Claridge's. That we should be driven by this climactic social upheaval to stay in London's most expensive hotel made me think that there was something to think about, although for the time being I got no further than that.

At home all around me were Conservatives. Liberals were regarded as sadly eccentric or mildly dangerous, Labour as beyond the pale. But mostly politics were ignored. My family and their friends were Conservatives as a matter of course. When a cousin of mine stood as a Liberal in a general election this aberration was put down to being female. Another female cousin contested a by-election in which there were four candidates, all of them including herself Conservatives. These Conservatives were not wicked people, far from it, and yet I became more and more profoundly imbued with a deep and hard hostility to Conservatism and its main public representatives who were at that time Stanley Baldwin and Neville Chamberlain with a supporting cast of minor eminences. My main reasons were two.

There was, first, their anti-semitism. This did far more than fascism to politicise my adolescent emotions. Today, since the Second World War, anti-semitism has an entirely different resonance to the anti-semitism of the thirties in England when the wartime atrocities against the Jews were undreamt of and unimaginable. None of the people whom I knew would have done or condoned the slightest physical harm to a Jew. Fascist and Nazi anti-semitic behaviour would have revolted them in the twenties if they had stopped to think about it, and it was still in the thirties disbelieved in spite of the evidence because it seemed humanly impossible. Yet they made snide remarks and nasty little jokes about Jews as a matter of course and with an insouciance which, in the changed perceptions of today, would rank as the most appalling bad taste, to say the very least. I was not bold enough to protest against these sneers and quips but they rankled. Anti-semitism is by no means confined to Conservatives but it was characteristic of Conservatives and widespread among them and although far removed in its expression and consequences from the rabid anti-semitism of the Nazis and their like, it cannot escape kinship with it. Even when not extreme, anti-semitism is profound. It may seem comparatively innocuous when it goes no further than accusing Jews of being too skilled for their own good at playing the violin or making money, but such superficial pleasantries conceal profoundly malignant and profoundly ingrained prejudices. Even the sickening manifestations brought to the surface during the Second World War have not exorcised it and since that dire experience Israel's leaders, by making even the most liberal Gentiles anti-Israeli, have helped to rekindle anti-semitism and allow it to poke its nose out of the woodwork once more – a sick paradox. For anti-semitism is a dual and durable vice. Its prevalence and virulence owe much to the conjunction of two distinct strands. Its roots are religious – the anti-Judaism fostered by Christian churches and leaders for 2,000 years – but its sting in the last 200 years has been provided by the secular and pseudo-scientific racism which developed in reaction to the latitudinarianism of the eighteenth-century Enlightenment. The Nazis jolted all but the most benighted anti-semites into recognising the vileness of their feelings, but Hitler scored a posthumous victory when people began to classify anti-semitism as the Nazi variety (execrable) and other forms (not so bad). It needs to be said that what is vile is not one species but the entire genus. The same goes for racism. South African apartheid may be extremely dreadful but no form of racism is venial.

The anti-Conservative convictions of my adolescence were further strengthened by something else. The quintessential political issue in every democracy is the contest between the haves and have-nots. That this contest does not become, or rarely becomes, violent is due to the fact that the dividing lines are fudged. A section of the upper classes and of the professional (not so much the financial or commercial) classes side with the have-nots in varying degrees, while the have-nots include substantial numbers of men and women who are conservative by temperament even when they believe that the dominant classes treat them unfairly. In the thirties there was more than unfairness. The Depression threw a lurid light on the gap between the haves and have-nots, on the pains of the latter and on the readiness of the haves to be panicked into selfishness. Nobody much believed in equality but, putting fact before theory, it was apparent that inequality was indecently extreme and widespread. The charge against Conservatives was and is (Thatcher acutely revived it) that they display a discreditable ability to bear with equanimity the misfortunes of others: in other words that they are humbugs. In the thirties Conservatives did not go so far as to use the word 'caring' as the term of ridicule that it became in the Thatcherite vocabulary but they were quick then as later to write off social problems by labelling the poor indiscriminately as undeserving scroungers, by looking the other way, by looking at facts otherwise than in the face. The Conservative recipe for poverty is to make the rich richer so that there shall be more over for the poor, but in practice the rich or most of them do not make this equation work and the poor stay poor: the Conservative model of a free-market society is a delusion. The notion of surplus wealth trickling down to where it is needed is little more than an excuse. In later years I became even more firmly anti-Conservative as Conservative leaders – Maudling, Barber and above all and once again Thatcher – showed that there is nobody like a Conservative for doing real damage to the economy.

It has been common to level two other charges against the Conservatives of the thirties: that they were stupid and that they were fascist. Both are wide of the mark. Much may be forgiven the stupid; that Conservatives are not stupid makes their offences the graver. Nor were they by and large fascist, for which they lacked the energy. They lacked too an essential ingredient of fascism which is mass class indignation. Unlike those in Italy, Germany and elsewhere in Europe who were attracted by fascism British Conservatives had nothing to be indignant or angry about. Their lot was a comfortable one. Fascism on the other hand, beginning with Italian fascism which was the prototype of the species, was bred and prospered in disgruntlement. It appealed first and always to sections of the lower middle class who rejected the political and financial alliance between the middle and upper classes and resented the way the upper middle class aped the social manners of the aristocracy and looked down on their lower middle class neighbours. For all their international links and foreign pretensions and ambitions fascist movements were essentially home-grown and rooted in domestic bile, including fear of the multitudinous proletariat and fear in the other direction of the expanding industrial capitalism which menaced the small producer and proprietor. Both Mussolini in Italy and some of the early Nazis in Germany appealed to these emotions, although Hitler himself was more obsessed by his two appallingly crazy imperatives of the need of the Germans for more *Lebensraum* and the need to purge Europe of Jews. (He knew how to set about the first but had until his conquest of Poland no plan for compassing the second except a half-baked scheme for sending Germany's Jews to Madagascar.) Poujadism in France in the fifties was a product of the same social and economic tensions in Europe, and there were similar strains of social disease in Thatcherism.

Communist and other left-wing critics were not so very wrong about western societies. They were, however, very wrong indeed about Soviet society. They criticised the class-ridden societies which they knew, without realising or acknowledging that the Soviet Union was a clique-ridden society and that a clique-ridden society is infinitely more evil than a class-ridden one. In this matter the thirties were different from the twenties. In the twenties Moscow stood for revolution and hope, but for most people in the thirties this was no longer so and by the late thirties Moscow stood for rigged trials, tumbrils and precious little hope.

The first general election in which I had a vote came in 1935. I suppose I voted but I do not remember doing so. I cannot have voted Conservative. I doubt whether there was a Labour candidate in South Paddington where we then lived and I doubt whether I would have voted for him if there had been one. So presumably I voted Liberal or not at all. At the next general election, ten years later at the end of the war in Europe, I was a Liberal candidate, coming third in the poll but saving my pride by putting up the Liberal vote. From 1950 I have steadily voted Labour. I have never agreed with the entirety of a Labour programme but when it comes to choosing between Labour and Conservative I need no more than a minute's reflection. I place myself on Labour's left on some things, on the right on more. What I hate most in politics (and elsewhere) is mediocrity and I have seen a great deal more of it in Conservative bigwigs than in Labour's, even before Thatcher elevated strident mediocrity into a system of government.

The thirties have got a bad name and they deserve it. They were dominated by Conservatives whose overall reactions to the two big issues of the Depression and fascism were dismal. For the hardships of the poor they did too little and seemed to care too little. For fascist leaders they evinced both repulsion and admiration but on balance far too much of the latter. On neither issue were they wholeheartedly on the wrong side, but on both they leaned in the wrong direction too evidently, too far and for too long. Half a century on their apologists have done little to retrieve their reputations. What placed me on the left in the thirties were domestic rather than foreign issues, practical politics rather than ideologies. So I was not compulsively caught up in what has become in retrospect the outstanding mark of that decade: the clash of ideologies, fascist and communist, and the bitter conflict over the 'appeasement' of the fascist dictators. What people at large thought about Mussolini and Hitler has come to be treated as a question of ideology. That it was, but it was also something simpler. Whatever the ideological content of fascism as a bundle of right-wing attitudes, the fascist leaders were easily recognisable as bullies. Millions of people who did not care a fig about political ideas were shocked and outraged by the behaviour of men who reached the highest positions in civilised states and then ran them with malice and torture. Fascist leaders such as Mussolini and Hitler were more obnoxious than Stalin because they were nearer geographically and because Russia, besides being half-hidden by its remoteness (particularly Siberia), had long been regarded in western Europe as a country of which, whether communist or tsarist, little in the way of decency was to be expected. So the extremes of indecency in Stalin's Russia were minimised, even excused. The intensity of feeling about foreign affairs in Britain in the thirties, and the bitter accusations made against the would-be appeasers of Hitler and Mussolini, arose from the perception of such men as retrograde perverts. What stung was more moral than political.

Supporters – open or covert, brazen or apologetic – of foreign fascism were despised, even hated, not so much because they too were right-wing but because they allowed their right-wing inclinations to push them into applauding the minor virtues of Mussolini and Co. at the expense of turning a blind eye to their major vices. This sneaking partiality was seen as disgusting hypocrisy, which it was. It excused or evaded appalling maltreatment of socialists, Jews and other unpopular groups by concentrating on trivialities such as making trains run on time. It insisted that alleged malpractices were grossly exaggerated by ill-intentioned pressure groups and that what happened inside other countries was not our business. This state of affairs could have persisted indefinitely and would probably have done so but for one distinct provocation. Mussolini's aggression was directed not to Europe but to Africa where Britain, France and others were already well provided. Hitler on the other hand was prepared to make war in Europe.

Fascist and Nazi brutality coincided with German expansionism. The latter, and only the latter, became the cause of the war which led to the slaughter of six million Jews and the subjugation of central and eastern Europe to foreign dominion – not, as it happened, German dominion but Russian. Without the war Europe's Jews, including perhaps even the German Jews, would not have been killed wholesale and central and eastern Europe would not have been annexed to the Soviet Union for forty years and wrecked by it. The war defeated Hitler's expansionist plans at the cost – among much else – of consummating his anti-Jewish fantasies and enabling him to turn his vague vapourings into atrocious fact.

The war which could be won only at such terrible cost was fought not because Nazism was evil but because Hitler's Germany became both strong and frightening: it had to be stopped and dismantled. The crucial question is not how Germany became so strong after its defeat in 1918 but why the Germany which did so was an aggressive Nazi Germany whose central aim was the conquest of large chunks of central and eastern Europe. The answers to this question are in the history books. At the time – the thirties – questions which became clearer much later were debated in terms of appeasement which, more and more, was taken to be an abject abandonment of principle and also of sound sense. The appeasers, chief among them successive Prime Ministers and their senior colleagues, were reviled as few politicians had been reviled in Britain for a century or more – Lloyd George perhaps excepted. Attempts to exonerate them have by and large been unsuccessful but time has refashioned the charges against them. In the thirties they were to many of us villains; Chamberlain was hated. In retrospect they should be judged to have made disastrous mistakes not because they were wicked but because they were not up to the job.

Appeasement, which means giving somebody what he wants or part of what he wants, is not necessarily a sin or a crime. But it may be a great mistake. By 1938 at the latest giving in to Hitler was idiotic. It was prompted by two things in particular: the view, partly but by no means entirely correct, that the Treaty of Versailles in 1919 had been unduly harsh and in some places unjust and that therefore something was owed to Germany; and secondly, the fear of war, an honourable rather than a cowardly emotion. Chamberlain and his colleagues loathed war and loathed the thought of sending young people to die in a war for which they themselves were past military age. But having credited them with these honourable feelings it must still be said that the effective capitulation to Hitler over Czechoslovakia at Munich in 1938 was not only dishonourable conduct but also a ghastly blunder. The Munich compromise postponed war for a year and substituted for a war (in 1938) on terms severely adverse to Germany a war (in 1939) which Hitler nearly won. War in 1938, as I have argued at greater length in my *Total War*, involved a duel between Germany and Czechoslovakia in which the two sides were roughly equal in all departments except reserves of manpower; a commitment therefore of virtually all German forces to the eastern front and an open door for French forces in the west; and no prospect of a German conquest of Belgium or northern France, without which no air or other attacks could be made on Britain. War in 1939 on the other hand, after the dismemberment and occupation of Czechoslovakia, gave Hitler half Poland in two weeks, released his forces for the separate conquests of Denmark, Norway, the

Netherlands, Belgium, France and all south-east Europe; and enabled him to bombard Britain and come within an ace of taking Moscow or Leningrad. If, for the victorious survivors, it all came right in the end, it was no thanks to those who pursued a policy to the brink of total catastrophe.

We have become used to thinking of the thirties as a terribly shocking time when terrible things happened in places – Europe, in particular – where barbaric behaviour was thought to have been relegated to history. But the real shock was not that behaviour during the decade but the war which came at the end of it. People, unhappily, are not so easily shocked by things happening as by things past. The crimes of the thirties included not only what was done then but also overlooking those doings until they could be handed over to historians. Looking back at the thirties one sees the need to distinguish between what they felt like at the time and what they did to one more lastingly and subconsciously. I was well aware of the slump and unemployment, of fascism and the Nazis, but they did not directly affect the way I lived. There is a huge difference between knowing about unemployment and fearing it for oneself, and never did it occur to me that I might myself not get a job. So it is easy to conclude that these sores impinged on me, but not much. Yet that would be an inadequate conclusion, for by living through such times one became imbued with the inescapability of the wider world, from which a moral sense forbade one to avert one's gaze.

As the thirties were ending and peace too, some people proclaimed their conviction that there would be no war and others with equal confidence that there would, but most said half-heartedly that war would not come while believing that it would. I was among these. Hope dictated one's utterances, reason denied them. Life at the Bar went on diligently but tentatively. I was beginning to get a little work but not to see much of a future. Since I had been told that my origins stood in the way of getting anywhere in the diplomatic service I presumed that the Bar was unlikely to be much more welcoming and the Bench unattainable. Perhaps this was an unduly pessimistic view. Looking back I suppose that with a little more persistence I might have gone on to the honour that goes with being a judge, and the licence that goes with being a retired judge. I was truly interested in law – and have remained so – but I did not see myself fitting into that rather special setting and I had little faith in my forensic talents. The prospect of standing up in court to make a speech or examine a witness before an awesome figure in wig and robe alarmed me. I was not unhappy but I was unsure. At work and away from it I was enjoying life in the present but was alive to the need to watch my step, to be wary. I felt myself among people who prized conventions and gradations which perhaps I had not fully mastered and who took for granted divisions whose verges ran perilously close to where I stood. I doubt whether any of this showed, for I took pains not to let it, and within myself it did not matter most of the time. But it was a cautionary restraint and it kept me from spreading my wings and made me hesitant in responding quickly to friendliness or to newcomers. I made good friends but not many, and I regarded girls as a distinct species. *Savoir faire* was not among my accomplishments. I was conscious of an ambiguous footing and of possible areas of hazardous ignorance. This feeling of ignorance was sharpened by the first slice of my war service when I was briefly propelled into the entirely unfamiliar world of RAF stations and officers' messes. One revelation that has stuck in my mind, perhaps because of its piquant vulgarity, may illustrate this apprehension of betraying a risible innocence. In the course of general chat in the mess somebody casually dropped the remark: 'Red hat, no knickers.' I was shocked – less by the indelicacy of this neat and useful aphorism than by the fact that for everybody else it seemed to be a truism. If they all knew, how come I did not? To be caught out in a lack of worldly wisdom is worrying.

But for me the thirties ended with something far more transposing than the war. In 1938 I got married. Our marriage coincided with the Munich conference which curtailed our honeymoon in Italy and sent us scurrying back as far as Paris where we saw Edouard Daladier parading down the Champs Elysées, much relieved to be received with rapture instead, as he had feared, of being roughed up on landing at Le Bourget. My marriage was to give my life an entirely new base, making everything outside marriage secondary, marginalising my doubts about where I stood, and making setbacks unimportant. My *terra* became *firma*. What my life would have been otherwise is no small question.

5

War at Bletchley Park

When war came in 1939 I had been married just a year and was in no mood for gallantry and death. So I welcomed the official line which told people not to rush off and volunteer but wait in an orderly way until needed. The first few months of phoney war confirmed the sense of this prescription, but by the spring of 1940 it was obvious that all the optimistic forecasts about the length and nature of the war were wrong and that the Germans were turning it into a sequence of walk-overs.

For most of this time I was a temporary civil servant, recruited into the Ministry of Economic Warfare which had been created to stop the war by stopping the Germans from importing essentials for their war effort. The Ministry issued what were called Navicerts. Without a Navicert goods were liable to be seized. Ships' manifests were submitted in advance to the Ministry and it studied them, looking for prohibited items, suspect importers, or suggestions that things were not what on paper they were made out to be. We used local telephone directories to check the addresses and activities of consignees in neutral countries and to check whether the consignee was the sort of outfit which might be expected to import, in the normal course of business, what was declared to be in the consignment. If he was a hairdresser in Helsinki importing a load of chemicals he would not get them. It was hit and miss – like, for that matter, most bombing at that date – but contributed something to our war effort. It was not, however, a war winner.

When Hitler turned west sitting in an office in Berkeley Square no longer seemed good enough. Not to volunteer seemed shameful and a virtuous resolve to join the fighting was strengthened by the calculation that a volunteer who did not wait to be conscripted would go straight into the officer ranks where people like me were supposed properly to belong. So I sent my application to the War Office.

Summoned to Whitehall I was passed from one section to another, examined and rejected. The reason was an accident in which I had suffered a broken head a few years earlier but the verdict, which I caught sight of at the foot of a piece of paper, struck me as crass. It read: 'No good, not even for Intelligence.' Offended by this judgment and encouraged by a secretary at the Ministry of Economic Warfare who turned out to be the daughter of the Director of Intelligence at the Air Ministry, I wrote to offer myself to the RAF. I was interviewed a few days later in a pokey office in Ryder Street round the corner from the Ritz by a wine merchant who had given up his business in Portugal to help with the war and had been put into uniform and told to recruit Intelligence officers, of whom the Air Ministry had hardly any. Since my accident was deemed to make me unfit for flying duties the Intelligence branch was entitled to commission me as an Intelligence officer and did. A week later I was in Northumberland where I remained for the next few months, first at an HQ on the edge of Newcastle and then on two Fighter Command airfields where my duties included instructing pilots how to distinguish German from British aircraft and taking down their accounts of their engagements as soon as they landed from battle. I was then posted to Fighter Command's principal HQ in a north London suburb, but within a week or so I was summoned to another interview in a cell-like office below ground in Horseferry Road, not far from the Houses of Parliament. Behind a solitary table sat an RAF officer who clearly did not believe in wasting time. He was called Oscar Oeser and he was an Australian psychologist (after the war a Professor of Psychology in Melbourne). At that moment I knew neither his name nor anything else about him, but I was soon to know him as a colleague. He handed me a piece of paper: 'Your records says that you know German. What does this say?' I read and translated with all the *sang froid* which I could muster from my public school training. It was about parachuting and I imagined myself on the way to enemy territory, capture or worse. Such fleeting fantasies were soon dispelled. I was directed to yet another and dingier office near St James's Park which was the HQ of the Secret Service although I did not know this when I arrived there. It seemed to cultivate a dilapidated image, an indifference to amenities where all that mattered was brains. I was told that I had been chosen for specially secret work ('Your name will be on a list given to Churchill') and I was given a one-way ticket to Bletchley. I knew nothing about Bletchley except that Zuleika Dobson had ended up in a siding there on her way to Cambridge after proving too hot for Oxford. I was in for the surprise of my life.

Bletchley Park – commonly known as BP or the Park or, a little more spicily, Station X – was the seat of the Government Codes and Ciphers School. It consisted of a medium-sized mansion built around 1900 in modest grounds on the edge of an unappealing railway junction fifty miles from London and bought in the thirties to house in the event of war a handful of code-breakers who might there continue their unobtrusive labours. Why Bletchley was chosen nobody seems to know. I suspect the main reason was that the house and its grounds happened to come on the market at the right time and were about the right distance from London and easily reached on the main LMS railway line or the A5. The notion that it was chosen because it lay also on the line between Oxford and Cambridge is clearly a myth since nobody then knew that its few dozen intended inmates would swell to thousands, drawn in the early days of the war from Oxford and Cambridge colleges. Soon the mansion bulged, huts proliferated in the grounds, these were pulled down and replaced, and all around within a radius of thirty miles men, women and teenagers were billeted in towns and villages whence and whither they were bussed every day for the shifts which they worked round the clock.

I spent my first week or two in a village pub called 'The Boot' and the next two years in digs in Bletchley within walking distance of the Park. Then, joined by my wife and children, we rented a cottage from which we were almost immediately evicted by the owners who suddenly discovered they wanted to live there themselves. We moved to another pub where we were so uncomfortable and unwelcome that we bought a house at a few hours' notice and lived there for the next 39 years. So long as the war lasted we had billettees, generally seven or eight of them, in various nooks and crannies. Nearly all of them worked at the Park and I ensured that enough of them could play musical instruments to provide us with string quartets. The staple fare was Haydn quartets and Purcell fantasies under the professional rule of the violinist André Mangeot who, although not an inmate of the Park, had landed up in the area for the duration and became one of our lodgers. As an alternative to chamber music an American form of charades was organised by Bob and Elisabeth Slusser in what later became our dining room where, in quieter hours, Bob could be found immersed in a late Beethoven quartet or in *Finnegans Wake* or, some said, in both at once.

GC & CS had been established in 1919 as a small specialised body to continue work done in Room 40 in the Admiralty during the First World War. In 1922 it was taken over by the Foreign Office, became closely associated with the SIS and in 1925 moved with the SIS into the quarters in London which I visited for about an hour in 1941. The SIS was what the man in the street calls the Secret Service. This famous and awesome phrase had no official justification and could be found in no official table of organisation. The correct name for secret activities not run by the regular Departments of State (the Foreign Office, Admiralty, War Office, Air Ministry) was Special Intelligence Services – a name neither inaccurate nor inappropriate since the SIS did succeed in keeping its affairs secret. It was distinct from all other Intelligence agencies, had its own funds, has never had its full history written for publication, and is subject to no statutory opening of its archives even after hundreds of years. So there is no way of telling whether its achievements have matched its reputation.

The principal task of the SIS was the finding and running of what it called agents and other people call spies. At its head was a naval or army officer referred to simply as C, although this camouflage had limited effect. During the war, so the story ran, it was customary to track C down to his club by asking for him by name, whereupon the club porter would reply: 'I will see if the Chief is in the club, sir.' The SIS was small, dealt with a small amount of Intelligence and was incapable of handling any major new source. But it was alive to the potentialities of new sources – and to the desirability of getting them under its own wing. To do so would expand its own prestige and budget: and it also made sense. Between the wars cryptographic Intelligence was an intriguing new source, if still unproven, and by adroit cooperation with the Foreign Office and the Service Departments the SIS yoked cryptographic Intelligence with the entirely different business of espionage and in doing so created, more or less inadvertently, the inter-service agency which was to become the brightest jewel in its discreet crown.

Like the SIS, GC & CS too was small, even minuscule. Established with 25 officers (plus clerical staff), it had in the early thirties only 31 officers. It had no out-stations of its own to intercept the traffic which it was charged to decipher. These stations belonged to the three Service Departments. It worked mainly on diplomatic traffic but wars – notably the Italian invasion of Ethiopia and the Spanish Civil War – enabled it to have a go at naval and military ciphers and it read a fair amount of Italian naval traffic (and also in these years Japanese). It began to plan seriously for war in 1937 and the purchase of Bletchley Park a year later was part of these plans.

GC & CS and the SIS were not the only parts of the Intelligence industry. Much the largest collector of information about foreign countries was the Foreign Office and Diplomatic Service. This service had become one of the best organised and most professional in the world, notwithstanding the fact that until the present century it was staffed mainly by amateurs, intelligent or not so intelligent. The purpose of the service was to be in permanent contact with other countries, partly to deal with them and partly to know them. The job was on the whole well done. But the same cannot be said about Intelligence in the three Service Departments which had the more specialised task of learning about the size, equipment, organisation and doctrines of foreign armed forces. British Military Intelligence came into being shortly after the Franco-Prussian War when astonishment over the defeat of France by Prussia led to the conclusion that a bit more information about the Prussian army might be a good thing. A Naval Intelligence Section was formed in the Admiralty a little later. But these were not distinct Intelligence services in the sense that their members were specialists in Intelligence. They were on the contrary quite the reverse. They were staffed, on a temporary basis, by officers who had chosen careers in which heroism and drill were far more highly esteemed than knowledge, and a posting to an Intelligence section in London or as an attaché in an embassy abroad was nearly always uncoveted and bad for promotion. The results therefore were poor. The Air Ministry, created after the First World War, suffered the same infirmity. To make matters worse the three Departments preferred to hold themselves separate and, when forced into consultation, cooperated in a spirit of rivalry rather than solidarity.

There were other Intelligence services too. Both the Treasury and the Bank of England collected information for economic and business purposes. Their products were complementary. The Treasury would provide government economic missions or travelling businessmen with briefs on a country's resources, finances, industrial and commercial performance and so on. The Bank, which was in those days a private company uninhibited by official scruples, would add information about the skeletons in the cupboards of Finance Ministers and tycoons, explain who was whose mistress, and provide other similarly useful titbits. I have been told that after being nationalised the Bank felt obliged to stop making itself useful in this way. But I wonder.

In spite of this complexity GC & CS had in its own field a monopoly. Nobody else was doing that sort of work, and this is the first important point to make in assessing BP's success. It did not have to waste time fighting anybody. The second is that it was converted from a purely cryptographic establishment into a full working partnership between cryptographers and Intelligence. As BP grew in size it grew also in scope. This comprehensiveness was a vastly important factor in its success. So far as I can make out it was unpremeditated. Combining all grades of cipher in all languages with Intelligence appraisal brought intellectual and technical benefits. It concentrated talent in one place and it increased the possibilities of breaking one cipher by reference to another. Although it is against all the rules to transmit verbatim in a higher grade a cipher text already transmitted in a lower grade (or *vice versa*), rules are broken from time to time. Weather reports, for example, sent by U-boats using a high-grade Enigma cipher were not infrequently retransmitted in a lower-grade cipher which was broken comparatively easily.

The basic problem in making a cipher secure is to achieve randomness in successive settings, but left to themselves human beings, and machines created by human beings, quickly stop being random and fall into some pattern or quirk which may then be spotted and used to break the cipher – for example, a Luftwaffe operator during the war keyed in his signals with his girl friend's initials instead of choosing three letters at random and did so over and over again. This lapse was both innocent and serious. Another was more gruesome. German cryptographers responsible for ensuring randomness in the keying of Enigma traffic thought they had hit on a bright solution. Every day the concentration camps rendered returns giving the numbers of prisoners who had been delivered to the camp that day, the number who had died or been killed, and the number of surviving inmates at the end of the day. These were truly random figures. They were reported in a low-grade cipher and the recipients passed them on to their Enigma colleagues who used them in determining the settings of their machines. BP was reading that low-grade cipher and somebody realised that the concentration camp returns were being used in Enigma settings.

So these sad and grisly statistics of human misery and indignity played a part of which the piteous victims never dreamed.

BP was comprehensive in another way too. It was inter-service and non-service. This was more remarkable in the thirties and forties than it may seem today. When GC & CS was first transferred from the Admiralty to the Foreign Office the switch had bad as well as good effects. It down-graded service Intelligence in favour of diplomatic Intelligence but it also paved the way for inter-service collaboration of a kind unparalleled elsewhere in the world. This collaboration was not achieved painlessly or even completely but by the time war came in 1939 it was institutionalised, more cordial than, for example, in the USA, and immensely more effective than in Germany where six or seven different cryptographic establishments fought one another almost as venomously as they fought the enemy. Finally, BP's comprehensiveness was consummated when Intelligence was grafted on to cryptography and these two partners were set to work in the same compound. Producers and consumers were cheek by jowl and the constant, easy and fruitful interchange between the two – mostly by word of mouth between people who saw one another every day – was a major element in their joint achievement.

There was one exception to this inclusiveness. Within BP there was embedded a small section about which other sections were supposed to know nothing and did in fact know little. And within this small section was an even smaller unit which was fenced off in the same way. This is where I was. These sections were concerned with the machines used for ciphering communication between the higher commands in the German armed services. The machines were of two main kinds: Enigma machines (all basically alike but with minor differences between naval and other Enigma) and a variety of so-called *Geheimschreiber*, much more cumbrous and used only at the very top. The Intelligence which came from deciphering these machine ciphers was not just Secret or even Most Secret: more secret than Most Secret it was classified Top Secret Ultra. It was the least accessible of all German secret communications and it was the most valuable for two distinct reasons: in as much as it consisted of messages between German commanders themselves it was uniquely authentic, and if and so far as the ciphers might be broken promptly, which some were, the information from them was not merely useful background but operationally crucial to British and American commanders engaged in planning campaigns or fighting battles. When I was in Germany after the end of the war I had occasion to interview General Martini, who had been the head of the Luftwaffe's Information and Intelligence services. Without divulging to him how far BP had succeeded – I was not allowed to do this – I discussed problems of cipher security and got the strong impression that although he knew that many Enigma ciphers were vulnerable and even sporadically broken he had no idea that some were broken not only regularly but with amazing promptitude. The main cipher of his own Luftwaffe, for example, used throughout the Luftwaffe on all fronts, was read at BP daily from March 1940 to the day fighting stopped, and normally from the early hours of the day in question.

The widespread use of ciphers and, later, machine ciphers was the natural sequel to two modern inventions in the field of communications: the internal combustion engine and wireless telegraphy. The first enabled armed units to travel much further and faster than the foot soldier or the horse: the second kept these units in touch with each other and their superiors in spite of the distances which separated them and made semaphores and even telephones useless. As generals saw their forces disappearing over the horizon they could nevertheless issue orders and receive information by wireless. They kept their grip on what they were doing. But there was a price to pay. A wireless message thrown into the air can be heard by an enemy with adequate listening equipment. So the next step was to make these messages unintelligible without a special clue – to encipher them. And the next step, on the other side, was to crack the ciphers. In this duel two developments were paramount: the interception of the wireless traffic, and turning the ciphered messages back into their original language. If these processes were successful a third ensued: interpreting the information and using it. In this chain of interception-cryptography-intelligence I belonged to the third link.

This link had not at first loomed large. Between the wars GC & CS consisted of cryptographers only. Their successes were mainly in diplomatic ciphers. In peace time there was not much military traffic since telephones met the needs of the services except on special occasions such as annual exercises or in a crisis. When war came the bulk of the military traffic put into the air was in medium or low-grade ciphers which could be read with comparative ease but contained information of only transient interest. High-grade ciphers, it was anticipated, might be intercepted but not massively and they would not be speedily deciphered; and if this proved true no great Intelligence outfits would be needed. There would be little to interpret and that little would probably be gleaned too late to be of much practical use. The falsification of these pessimistic expectations created my job and others like it. Within a few months of the outbreak of the war the listening or 'Y' service was intercepting masses of traffic, including Enigma traffic, in spite of being uncomfortably far from the transmissions and out of line with them; and the cryptographers were beginning to break German Enigma far more regularly, copiously and promptly than anybody had foreseen.

The original version of the Enigma machine was invented and patented in 1919 in Holland and was developed and marketed in the early twenties by a German who incorporated the Dutch invention with his own and gave the machine its name. It was a commercial machine which anybody could buy. Patents were taken out in various countries including Britain and these were open to inspection by anybody who knew where to look for them and had the curiosity to do so.

Among the purchasers of this commercial machine were the German armed services. The German navy had been thinking of finding and adapting a machine for its ciphers as early as 1918, and in 1926 it began to use an improved version of Enigma. The army followed suit three years later; there was as yet no air force, but eventually the Luftwaffe used Enigma too and so did the German security services (police and SS) and other services like the railways. Over the years the Germans progressively altered and complicated the machine and kept everything about it more and more secret. The basic alterations from the commercial to the secret military model were completed by 1930/31, but further refinements both to the machine itself and to operating procedures continued to be introduced before and during the war. The Enigma machine was to be far and away the most important tool for the Germans' strategic battlefield communications during the Second World War.

Essentially Enigma was a transposition machine. That is to say, it turned every letter in a message into some other letter. The message stayed the same length but instead of being in German it became gobbledegook: it was garbled. That the Enigma machine did this was obvious. The problem was to find out how it performed its tricks. Only if its hidden workings were known could a cryptographer even begin to turn the gobbledegook back into German.

Even when he had got as far as to understand how Enigma worked the cryptographer was still no more than halfway to deciphering any particular message. This was because the machine had a number of manually adjustable parts and the cryptographer needed to know not only how the machine was constructed and how it worked but also how these various movable parts were set by the operator at the moment when he began transmitting each particular message. These parts were adjusted every so often – in peacetime once a quarter and then once a month, later once every 24 hours, and from September 1942 some of them every eight hours. In addition some parts moved automatically as the machine was operated. And, final complication, each separate message contained its own, individual key-within-a-key and this key was randomly selected.

At first glance the Enigma machine looked like a typewriter but a peculiarly complicated one. It fitted compactly into a wooden box measuring about 14 x 21 inches and 8 inches high. It had a keyboard like the standard three-row keyboard of an ordinary typewriter but without numerals, punctuation marks or other extras. On the German Enigma the letters were placed in the same order as an ordinary typewriter, beginning with Q on the left of the top line, but in the models made first by the Poles and then by the British the letters were in strict alphabetical order beginning with A where you would expect Q. This was simply an accidental peculiarity and of no significance. When the Poles constructed an Enigma machine they did not realise that in the electric wiring attached to each key the A wire and not the Q wire ran first into the keyboard. This detail is unimportant. Although its keyboard was simpler than a typewriter's, the Enigma machine was in all other respects much more complicated. Behind the keyboard the alphabet was repeated in three rows of small round glass holes which were set in a flat rectangular plate and could light up one at a time. When the operator struck a key one of these letters lit up. But it was never the same letter. By striking P the operator might, for example, cause L to appear; and next time he struck P he would get neither P nor L but something else.

The operator called out the letters as they appeared in lights, and a second operator sitting alongside him noted them down. This sequence was then transmitted by wireless in the usual Morse code and was picked up by whoever was supposed to be listening for it. It could also be picked up by an eavesdropper. The Germans experimented with a version of the machine which, by transmitting automatically as the message was enciphered, did away with the need for the second operator, but they never brought this version of Enigma into use.

The legitimate recipient took the gobbledegook which had been transmitted to him and tapped it out on his machine. Provided he got the drill right the message turned itself back into German. The drill consisted of putting the parts of his machine in the same order as those of the sender's machine. This should cause no problem since he had a handbook or manual which told him what he had to do each day. In addition, the message which he had just received contained within itself the special key to that message.

The eavesdropper on the other hand had to work all this out for himself. Even assuming he had an Enigma machine in full working order it was no good to him unless he could discover how to arrange its parts – the gadgets which it had in addition to its keyboard. These were the mechanisms which caused L to appear when the operator struck P.

These parts or gadgets consisted of a set of wheels or drums and a set of plugs. Their purpose was not simply to turn P into L but to do so in so complex a manner that it was virtually impossible for an eavesdropper to find out what had gone on inside the machine in each case. It is quite easy to construct a machine that will always turn P into L but it is then comparatively easy to find out that L always means P: a simple substitution of this kind is inadequate for specially secret traffic.

The eavesdropper's task was to set his machine in exactly the same way as the legitimate recipient of the message in spite of not possessing the relevant manual of instructions. He would then be able to read the message with no more difficulty than the legitimate recipient. The more complex the machine and its internal workings, the more difficult – and more time-consuming – was it for the eavesdropper to solve this problem.

As the operator sat at his machine he had in front of him, first, the rows of keys, then the spaces for the letters to appear illuminated, and beyond these again three slots to take three wheels or drums. Each wheel was about three inches in diameter and had 26 points of entry and of exit for the electric current which (as described below) passed through them. The wheels were much more than half embedded in the machine and end-on to the operator. They were covered by a lid and when this lid was closed the operator could see only the tops of them, but he could move them by hand because each wheel had on one side a serrated edge which stuck up through the lid.

In addition to this serrated edge each wheel had, on its other rim, a ring which could be moved independently of the wheel itself into any one of 26 positions round the wheel. Thus the wheel could be manipulated and so could the ring. Further, each wheel moved automatically when the machine was in use – the right-hand wheel at each touch on a key, the middle wheel after 26 touches, and the left-hand wheel after 26 x 26.

Although there were three slots for three wheels, there were by 1939 five wheels. The operator had to use three of his set of five. He had to select the correct three and then place them in a prescribed order. This was crucial because the wheels, although outwardly identical, were different inside.

The German navy introduced a four-slot machine at the beginning of March 1943. At this point the naval operator had six wheels for four slots but the new wheel had distinct limitations: it had to go to the left of the other three and it did not rotate, so that the number of permutations, though much increased by this innovation, was not nearly as large as it would have been if the four wheels had been as freely interchangeable as the three and if all four had rotated. In July of the same year a seventh wheel and fifth slot were added to the naval kit. The greater flexibility and inventiveness of the navy, which was still in evidence at the end of the war, may be ascribed to the fact that it used far fewer machines than either the army or the Luftwaffe. It was therefore easier to alter or replace them. Most naval Enigma machines were static either in naval HQs ashore or in fleet units. In this context a ship, even when at sea, provides a static home for its machinery in a way which is impossible for an army division or an air squadron, for which moving means considerably more upheaval. The total number of Enigma machines in use in 1939 – most of them with the army and air force – was perhaps 40,000, at the end of the war half as many again. So altering was laborious. It was simpler and quicker, but less radical, to alter the operational drill.

Besides the wheels were the plugs: in German, *Stecker*. These were in pairs. They looked like the plugs on a telephone switchboard. They were added to the machine in the thirties: by the army in 1930 and the Luftwaffe in 1935. At first they were at the back but in later models they were in front. There was one plughole for every letter of the alphabet. Each pair of plugs coupled a pair of letters. Putting them in and taking them out was the work of a moment. In theory there could be thirteen couplings of the

26 letters but there never were. At first six pairings were used, then a variable number between five and eight, and from the beginning of 1939 a variable number between seven and ten. During the Spanish Civil War the Germans in Spain used the old Enigma machine without plugs and so did the Italians and the Spanish rebels. The British read some of this non-Stecker traffic. (They also read Italian non-machine ciphers during the war in Ethiopia.)

The Enigma machine ran on an electric battery. When the operator of an ordinary typewriter strikes P on his keyboard he mechanically and immediately produces P on the paper in his machine. When an Enigma operator struck his P the effect, though all but instantaneous, was neither mechanical nor immediate. The operator's touch did not move a key and there was of course no paper in his machine. What he did by his touch was to release an electric pulse and this pulse went on a tortuous journey round the machine before returning to illuminate not P but L. The electric current passed through the plug system; then through a fixed wheel at the far right of the back of the machine; then through each of the three removable wheels from right to left, entering each in turn and leaving each of them by any one of the 26 different points of entry and exit; then – after bouncing off a second fixed wheel or reflector to the left of these removable three wheels – back from left to right by a different and equally multifarious route; and so to the light for L. The variety and unpredictability of each of these journeyings every time a key was struck were the inventor's pride and the cryptographer's headache.

Each journey from key to light – such was the complexity of Enigma's entrails – might take any one of an astronomical number of routes. The outcome, as shown in the row of lights, was not so multifarious. P could turn into only one of 25 different letters, i.e. 26 minus one. But that was not the point. The point was not what happened at the end of the journey but how it happened. What the cryptographer needed to know was the route, for without being able to establish and reduplicate the route he could not discover the journey's end.

Enigma, in the form in service when the war began, multiplied its permutations in various ways. First, there was the wheel-order. When there were just three different wheels to place in three slots the number of possible wheel-orders was six. Call the wheels A, B and C: the possible wheel-orders are ABC, ACB, BAC, BCA, CAB, CBA. But when the Germans added a fourth and a fifth wheel for the three slots, the number of possible three-wheel-orders rose from six to sixty. But that was only the beginning. Whatever wheels were chosen, they were neither identical nor stationary, so that the revolutions of their diverse intestinal passages posed the cryptographer's toughest conundrum in his struggle to catch and map the machine's entire anatomy.

Finally, the further changes introduced by the pairings of the Stecker raised the total of the permutations obtainable at each touch of a key to an astronomical figure which ran into billions.

All this sounds horribly complicated and so in one sense it was. But not in another. Although the Enigma machine was a highly complex piece of electric machinery it was easy (if rather slow) to operate, and a brief description of what the operator actually did may help to explain both the machine itself and the cryptographer's task – bearing in mind that the essential difference between the legitimate recipient of an Enigma message and an enemy cryptographer was that, even when both possessed and understood the machine, only the former had the instructions which told him how the machine's parts were to be arranged each day.

The German operator had two documents: a manual or handbook of general instructions about the machine, and a set of detailed instructions for the setting of the various movable parts at different dates over a period. The betrayal of some of these documents by a German official to the French secret service and their transmission to the Poles enabled the brilliant Polish cryptographer Marian Rejewski – who had already gone a long way to reconstructing the machine – also to break and read its enciphered traffic. This final achievement was made possible when he discovered how to set his machine as required by the detailed setting instructions, but without having those instructions all the time.

The German operator, consulting his detailed instructions at each point of change (quarterly, monthly or finally daily) had to do four things. Three of these things related to the wheels, the fourth to the plugs or *Stecker*. First came the selection of the wheels and the order in which they were to be placed side by side. Each wheel was numbered and the handbook simply gave the numbers of the three wheels to be used: eg. IV I II. These three numbers also indicated the order of the three selected wheels from left to right.

Secondly, the operator had to fix the rim of each wheel. His instructions were again in figures. They might, for example, read 7 21 12 – which meant that the rim of the left-hand wheel had to be fixed at the letter G, the seventh letter of the alphabet; the middle and right-hand rims to U and L. This operation fixed the rims of the wheels in relation to the wheels themselves. It was called in German the *Ringstellung*.

Thirdly – in an area which was to provide the Poles with their major critical insight into the working of the Enigma machine – the operator was required to adjust the wheels themselves as distinct from the rings on the wheels – in German, the *Grundstellung* as distinct from the *Ringstellung*. He did this by following instructions handed out to him in the same way as he received his instructions for setting the rest of the machine. Three figures, each corresponding to a letter of the alphabet, told him into which position to twiddle the wheels. But from September 1938 this general instruction was abolished and, mainly in an attempt to secure a greater degree of randomness, a new drill was introduced. Before this date the operator tapped out, twice, the prescribed three-letter sequence and embodied the resulting six-letter group in his signal; after this date there was no prescribed three-letter sequence and the operator himself had to pick one at random, which he transmitted *en clair* at the beginning of his signal. (To conform with the standard five-letter group the three letters were preceded by two throw-away letters which the recipient ignored.) He also chose another three-letter sequence which he tapped out twice and then proceeded to transmit his text as before. These keys-within-keys were called the discriminants.

This change, however, did not go to the root of the weakness which lurked in the *Grundstellung*, for although the change added to randomness it did not eliminate the double-encipherment of a three-letter group. This double encipherment was cancelled in May 1940 on the eve of the German invasion of the Low Countries and France, but by that time it was too late because the BP cryptographers had meanwhile learnt enough about Enigma to retain their hold on the traffic without the benefits given them by the double encipherment. The flaw in the double encipherment, as practised both before and after September 1938, was this: that as soon as an enemy cryptographer sensed that it was present in the enciphered text, he knew that the first and fourth letters of this group were the same, and likewise the second and fifth and the third and sixth. This transformed his task from the unmanageable to the manageable. It was a defect, not of the machine itself, but of the operating instructions.

Finally, to complete his setting of his machine for use, the German operator had to fix his *Stecker*. His instructions gave him pairs of letters: DO LH FM etc. These told him where to put his plugs. With one pair he coupled D with O, with another L with H, and so on.

Such was the Enigma machine. A machine of this kind may in theory be made ever more complex by adding to its parts, and this was to some extent what the Germans did when they added extra wheels. But there were practical limits. Most Enigma machines in use during the war belonged to relatively mobile units which had to carry them around in their baggage whenever they moved. An electrical pulse occupies no space but the gadgets in which it functions do – or did in those days. The practical problem therefore was not scientific but technological – making things smaller and lighter. The Germans did have and used more complicated machines than Enigma but they were too cumbrous for use outside a static office or HQ. These were the *Geheimschreiber*. Their transmissions were on-line (non-Morse) and high speed and they needed no second operator. Various models were developed from about 1930. From 1940 a network was created which eventually embraced some twenty higher HQs in Europe and at least one in North Africa. Some machines were captured by the British in Africa in 1942. Their existence was no surprise to the British and in that year a special intercept station was brought into operation in England and a special section at BP which, in cooperation with the Post

Office, designed and built machines culminating in the Colossus which came into service at the end of 1943. Ten were in use when the war ended. BP, whose coverage of the Luftwaffe's Enigma traffic was thorough, concentrated on the German Army's *Geheimschreiber* traffic and began to read it in 1942. It was read with delays of only a few days but was entirely lost four days before the landings in Normandy in July 1944 – to be recovered in September. (Unlike Enigma material, *Geheimschreiber* intercepts and decipherments have not been lodged in the Public Record Office.)

From the early thirties German Enigma traffic was read by the Polish secret service. The Poles were the only people to do so in these years. They realised that the Germans had started using a machine for their more secret ciphers. They discovered what sort of machine it was. They unravelled its workings – a problem in mathematics posed by the machine's engineering. And they broke a number of daily settings of the machine over a number of years. On the eve of war, when the increasing sophistication of the machine defeated their own resources, they passed on all they knew to the French and British, one of the more signal services ever rendered by one ally to another and all the more remarkable in the case of Britain since the Anglo-Polish alliance was only a few months old.

The brilliant work of the Poles was stimulated by their political and strategic stringencies and helped at a crucial point by the French secret service. The Treaty of Versailles had recreated the Polish state which had been partitioned and finally extinguished by its neighbours at the end of the eighteenth century. The new Poland was in the same vice as the old, between Germany and Russia; it was to last only twenty years before being partitioned once more as a consequence of the pact signed by Ribbentrop and Molotov during the night of 23-24 August 1939.

The new Poland went to war almost as soon as it was born. The Poles attacked the hardly less new Soviet Russian state which counter-attacked and was only prevented from taking Warsaw by French intervention. For this salvation the Poles were also indebted to their cryptographers who were able to intercept and read Russian military wireless traffic from Trotsky downwards. At about this time the Poles were also reading German military and naval ciphers. None of these was a machine cipher but the Poles realised at this early stage how vital to their existence it was to get this kind of intelligence.

When in 1926 the German navy began to use an adapted Enigma machine the Poles were for a time stumped. They divined that the Germans had gone over to some sort of Enigma. They bought the commercial model, and when a lucky chance enabled them to inspect a package which had been despatched from Germany to the German embassy in Warsaw, they were able to confirm that what the Germans were developing was the Enigma. They established a special course in cryptography at the University of Poznan and recruited for it a small and select group of young mathematics students. Three of these, working as a team, were then recruited into Polish Intelligence – one of them also did a course in advanced mathematics in a German university – and within a year this team broke some Enigma traffic. This was at the very end of 1933.

The Polish triumph had begun when Marian Rejewski spotted the double encipherment in the six-letter group at the beginning of each encipherment text. This flash gave him the theoretical basis of the adaptation of the machine from its commercial to its secret military version. Rejewski also worked out that, upon each touch of the keys, only one wheel moved – until, after 26 keyings, the middle wheel also moved by one notch. He continued his work with the assumption, which was true 25 times out of 26, that at each step the middle wheel stayed put. Given that *a fortiori* the left-hand wheel also stayed put, he was able to treat all three wheels as a single unit. But he was still some way from reading Enigma traffic when he had a stroke of luck which is one of the more astonishing episodes in the entire Enigma story. He received a batch of invaluable documents – from Germany, indirectly.

Towards the end of 1931 a certain Hans Thilo Schmidt, an official in the German cipher office, approached the French Secret Service in Berlin with an offer to sell secret papers. His motive was pecuniary. He was a womaniser and short of cash. The French Secret Service in Paris had a cryptographic section, headed at this time by Gustave Bertrand who was to become the head of the Service, a general and the first to publish a book about the Ultra secret (1973). Bertrand's section did not decipher anything. Its job was to collect material which might be useful to the separate *Service du Chiffre*. Bertrand took his precious haul to his colleagues who told him brusquely that they dealt with German ciphers and they were undecipherable. Bertrand seems to have tried to interest the British, who were equally dismissive, but he then travelled to Warsaw where he found the Poles despondent but receptive. This first journey by Bertrand to Warsaw was at the end of 1931, several months before Rejewski and his colleagues moved there from Poznan.

The documents sold by Schmidt, in 1931 and thereafter to August 1938, included drawings of the Enigma machine and instructions for settings. These settings were old and out-of-date, but the Poles had kept the relevant intercepted traffic and by great good chance the dates happened to fall in two different quarters (the changes to the settings were made at that time quarterly). With the help of these documents, which made them partially privy to the instructions given to German operators, the Polish cryptographers speeded up their reconstruction of the Enigma's internal wirings and workings and were also able to set their own machines so as to read intercepted Enigma traffic. Without the German documents they would, by their own later testimony, not have got as far as they did.

The Polish and French Secret Services also cooperated in exchanging intercepts. Both were intercepting German ciphered signals and, since cryptographers can never have enough raw material to work on, this swap agreement was mutually beneficial. It gave the Poles more to play with. There was, however, no exchange of deciphered texts, nor is there any evidence that the French deciphered any intercepts.

Although the Poles were able from 1933 to read German high-grade ciphers regularly the volume of intelligence which they reaped was not great, since in peace time the armed services used landlines for most of their chat. But they used wireless and ciphers during exercises and also in a crisis. Thus in June 1934, when Hitler turned on the SA (the brown-shirted *Sturmabteilung*, in effect a private army) and its leader Ernst Roehm, the Poles intercepted this message: 'To all airfield commanders: *Oberführer* Karl Ernst, adjutant to SA Chief of Staff Roehm, is to be arrested and sent to Berlin dead or alive.'

In these years the Polish government and general staff learned a certain amount about the German order of battle and mobilisation plans, the German armament industry and spies in Poland. They also gleaned a modicum of political information, e.g. which French ministers were expected by the Germans to collaborate with them. By the winter of 1937-38 the Poles reckoned that they could decipher 75 per cent of what they intercepted. On the other hand they got nothing from this source about the German invasion of Austria in March 1938 because that operation was conducted in wireless silence.

The main problem of the thirties was keeping up with the various changes introduced by the Germans for the purpose of keeping one step ahead of possible decipherers, if only for the fun of it: professional pride fuels progress. The Germans always had great faith in Enigma but they realised that the original commercial version had been freely available and that it was only prudent to go on making their service version more and more complex. The Poles coped with each fresh challenge until 1938. In that year the Germans first altered the rules for the *Grundstellung* and then introduced two new wheels. The Poles were able to cope with the first obstacle because they were reading SS traffic as well as military traffic and the changes did not at first apply to the SS. There was a precious overlap. But a few months later came the introduction of the fourth and fifth wheels, raising the permutations for the three slots from six to sixty. Although they managed to work out the wirings of the new wheels, their deciphering procedures were swamped: their resources were overloaded. To make matters worse the *Stecker* pairings were, almost simultaneously, increased from 5-8 to 7-10. Deciphering required brain power and machine power, and suddenly the Poles had too little of the latter.

Faced with the loss of the traffic, and convinced that war was round the corner, the Poles decided to find out whether either the French or the British knew anything that they did not know. They were looking for help. A tripartite meeting was arranged in Paris – whether on Polish or French initiative is disputed. The Polish representatives were instructed to judge for themselves whether the French or British had anything useful to impart. If they thought they did, they were to put all their own cards on the table and offer full collaboration. If not, not. They formed the opinion that neither French nor British had anything to teach them and so they went back to Warsaw to carry on single-handed. It has been generally assumed that the Poles were right, but it is not impossible that the British went to Paris with the same instructions as the Poles and came to the same negative conclusions about their opposite numbers. But with only one cryptographer working on Enigma in London it is certain that they were a long way behind the Poles and behind the developments progressively introduced by the Germans.

However that may be, the Poles soon decided to take a larger and more generous initiative. In July 1939, with the situation getting grimmer and grimmer, they convoked a second tripartite meeting which was held in secret near Warsaw. As in Paris the British were represented by Commander Alistair Deniston, head of what was soon to become Bletchley Park, and Dillwyn Knox, chief cryptographer (and brother of an editor of *Punch* and of an eminent Oxford *Monsignore*). They were accompanied by a third man who was then the deputy chief of the Special Intelligence Service, Colonel Stewart Menzies, shortly to become its Chief. He was introduced as Professor Sandwich, a mathematician from Oxford, although his evident unfamiliarity with that subject gravely impaired the disguise.

At this meeting the Poles told all. They described what they had achieved and how. They demonstrated the mechanical aids which they had invented to help their deciphering. One of these, which they called a *'bomba'* was a combination of Enigmas yoked together to simulate the workings of the German machine; but it was not an electronic computer. The other was a glass table, lit from below, on which were piled layers of lettered charts. The light, by shining through gaps in these charts, helped to identify the discriminants of the particular messages. Both machines became inadequate when the Germans provided the extra wheels for the three-wheel Enigma. As parting gifts the Poles presented the French and British with an Enigma machine apiece, the secret German version but manufactured in Poland. The Poles thus handed on a torch – just in time. A few weeks later Poland was wiped off the political map by the German army and air forces and partitioned by Hitler and Stalin.

There is a sequel to this story. After the Polish defeat the French asked a number of Poles who had escaped to Romania to go and work with them at their equivalent of BP which was in a country house at Vignolles 25 miles from Paris. A Polish proposal to invite British cryptographers too was rejected by the French and for the next eight months, until the French too were scattered by the Germans, work on Enigma went on separately at BP and Vignolles. There was some collaboration. Each outfit agreed to give the other any Enigma daily settings which might be unravelled. Vignolles was forced to shut up shop on 23 June 1940. By then the

Franco-Polish team had broken 110 Enigma settings, often with considerable delay: a key for 26 October, for example, was broken on 17 January. In all Vignolles read 8,440 German messages. Rather more than 1,000 of these related to the Norwegian campaign, some 5,000 to the campaigns in France. During these months 83 per cent of all Enigma breaks were made at BP. The first was made at Vignolles in January 1940 on the basis of work done at BP.

After the defeat of France in June 1940 the undaunted Poles set up a new centre in the unoccupied zone of southern France, but when this zone too was occupied by the Germans in 1942 they fled towards the Pyrenees and Spain. Five of them were captured and held by the Gestapo in horrible conditions. They possessed the most vital secret of the war – and kept it. This was an heroic final service to the allied cause.

From this point the cracking of Enigma ciphers and the exploitation of the traffic was a British and then an Anglo-American endeavour. At the same point Enigma traffic proliferated. The Enigma machine was a versatile tool which could be used to produce as many different ciphers as the machine itself had permutable settings. In the course of the war the Germans used some 200 different Enigma ciphers, some far more copiously than others. Some we read sporadically, some not at all, but the volume of decipherment together with its speed forced the authorities to create an Intelligence outfit to cope with it and also to operate a direct service from BP to commanders in the field. This service opened on 14 March 1941 with the British HQ in Cairo as its sole recipient. Between 28 April and 28 May some of the signals sent to Cairo were repeated to Crete. As the war went on more recipients were added and by the end over 100,000 signals with army and air Intelligence from Enigma ciphers had been despatched to British and American commanders (excluding naval Enigma which was handled separately at BP and by the Admiralty in London). At their peak signals of this kind were going out to commanders at the rate of one every ten minutes round the clock. This Ultra weapon, which started as a gleam in the eye, had become a major element in the fighting of the war.

When I sat in my room in Hut 3 at BP or roamed its crabbed corridors I was wholly dependent on two other groups of people besides my immediate colleagues. The first of these groups was the 'Y' service which consisted of people whom we never set eyes on and were scattered about the country and (a few of them) abroad. Their patience and skills were astonishing. Their job was to take down streams of meaningless letters which were often barely audible. In the course of doing this they developed the ability to recognise the touch or fingerprint of individual German operators. It has been said that Ultra's greatest victory was breaking the U-boat cipher and so defeating the German navy's attempts to starve Britain and keep the Americans away from the European theatre of war, but it is no less true that the 'Y' services performed an equal service at a crucial time in the Battle of the Atlantic when we lost the U-boat traffic for nearly a year. Until early in 1942 the U-boats used an Enigma cipher which they shared with other sections of the German navy and which we were reading fairly regularly and promptly. But at that point the Atlantic U-boats were provided with a new cipher of their own and although BP knew from current decodes that this change was about to happen cracking the new cipher took several months during which British losses at sea became extremely alarming. The breaking of the new cipher towards the end of 1942 was one of BP's greatest triumphs and was followed by a steep drop in the number of sinkings and then by the total withdrawal of all U-boats from the northern Atlantic. But during that blank period we did not entirely lose touch with the U-boats, thanks to the 'Y' service. Listeners were able to identify particular operators and since their transmissions could be located by D/F (direction finding) it was possible to track the course of an individual U-boat by tracking the operator sailing in it.

The work of interception was capped by the second group on which we depended for intelligence: the cryptographers. Them we did see because their workplace (Hut 6) was only a few yards away from ours. Their job was self-explanatory but how they set about it is not. It had been transformed by the application of machinery to decipherment. Before machines the cryptographer's task was to pore over a particular message. After mechanisation his task was to unravel the workings of a machine – and of a system of communications. If he mastered the workings of the machine and got its settings right, all relevant messages came out: if not, none did. So knowing the way the machine worked was the first, but only the first, requirement. The second was knowing how its parts were arranged at the moment of transmission; and thirdly, the cryptographer had to be knowledgeable about the context in which the machines and their operators worked. All Enigma machines together constituted a system of communications which could be used for the dissemination of orders and reports in a number of different but related ciphers or keys. Mechanisation created a family of ciphers. The cryptographer's target was this family.

He tackled the first part of his task by a combination of prying and mathematics: getting hold of a machine or, in so far as this was impossible or incomplete, working from what was known about it to deduce yet more. Intercepted messages were part of the means to reconstruct the machine even when these messages could not be deciphered. For the second part of the task the basic tool was the crib. In cryptographer's language a crib is a section of an enciphered message which may be presumed to correspond, in the original, to some stereotyped set of words which can be guessed more or less accurately: for example, the addressee of the message or its signature or some common salutation. (Arabic messages tended to begin with a stereotyped theological phrase.) The aim of the cryptographer is to reduce his problem to manageable proportions by concentrating on parts only of the enciphered text. And here machines made a second contribution. Having helped the transmitter to put his messages into inscrutable form, machines helped the decipherer to reverse the process. The decipherer may spot what appear to be weak points susceptible to cribs but these are no more than guesses, variable and numerous, and he needs to test his hunches by running selected ciphered passages against guessed versions of the original text. If he wants his answers quickly – not in weeks or months or years – he must find a way to discard false trails, in fact to design a machine to make with superhuman speed comparisons which he could himself make only with time not in the circumstances available. In response to this need cryptographers and engineers at BP evolved the first digital computers.

And there was another angle to the breaking of machine ciphers, for each operator and his unit (division, squadron, ship) was part not of one family but two families. They belonged to the family of those who could read each other's secret communications because they had the necessary key. They belonged also to the family of those who were in communication with each other because they were using the same wavelength. Both families were exclusive but they were not identical or co-terminous. The entirety of all these families was BP's field of study. Grasping this fact – the interlocking of Signals Intelligence (on wavelengths, call signs etc.) with cryptographic Intelligence – was a crucial insight at the core of BP's successes.

And so to Hut 3 which was the third link in the chain which began with interception and reached intelligence via cryptography. For all but a few weeks of my years in Hut 3 I was deputy head or head of Hut 3's Air Section (3A) which was matched across a corridor by a similar Military Section (3M). We worked on Luftwaffe Ultra, they on German army Ultra. 3A consisted of twenty officers called Air Advisers (only one was female) and about two dozen girls of our Air Index who most expertly catalogued the Ultra output on hundreds of thousands of cards. It was our business to read, digest, record, interpret and disseminate Luftwaffe Intelligence and with our Military equivalent we were part of what was called Hut 3. It really was a hut when I first knew it. Its roof was of wood and its outside walls were wooden planks on a brick base. The lighting was poor and the heating elementary. About half way through the war we moved into more commodious quarters but by this time Hut 3 had become the name for what we did rather than for where we did it and so Hut 3 we remained even after exchanging timbers for bricks and mortar. The total strength of Hut 3, including humble breeds like teleprinter operators, was somewhere between 100 and 150.

Hut 3's first task was translating the Ultra decodes from German into English. The decodes arrived from Hut 6 by being pushed through a short tunnel connecting the two huts. Translation was not as straightforward as it sounds since the texts were frequently corrupt, spotted with gaps or peppered with wrong letters owing to the difficulties which the 'Y' Service had in hearing them accurately. Much head-scratching might be needed to make them intelligible. This was the job of the Watch, a group of about ten people working an eight-hour shift round a semi-circular table with a chief presiding inside the half-moon. The volume of the Watch's work depended on the flow of decodes from Hut 6. After the huts were replaced by a brick building the decodes arrived in Hut 3 on a conveyor belt, at times in a flood, at others a trickle. Every time Hut 6 broke a particular day's setting of a particular key the accumulated traffic on that setting could be rapidly decoded and released into Hut 3. The first question asked by the oncoming Hut 3 Watch was: 'What's running?' – meaning which keys for which days were being currently decoded – and it was up to the head of the Watch to allot priorities for translation. The atmosphere varied from a frantic intensity to a more relaxed pace which permitted some chitchat and brewing coffee.

Each decode was on a separate piece of paper and all the decodes for a particular key were in a box of their own. Each member of the Watch fished out a decode from the Priority One box and, pencil in hand, divided the German text (which came in five-letter groups) into German words. He corrected obvious mistakes and filled in obvious gaps: for example, Gesodpader or Ges...d.r was quickly amended into Geschwader (squadron); for less obvious slips or gaps he suggested emendations, sometimes complex or even daring when the text was specially corrupt. He then made a literal translation into English and passed decode and translation to the head of the Watch for scrutiny. He in turn, if satisfied, passed the bits of paper to the Air Advisers and their army colleagues sitting, two of each, at a nearby table.

Everybody was new to the job not only in the sense that the jobs were themselves new but also in the sense that nearly everybody had been recruited from civilian occupations or straight from universities – to which some of them later returned to finish the courses which had been interrupted by war. The basic requirements were a knowledge of German, a meticulous attention to detail, a good memory, equanimity under stress and good health. In Hut 3 university dons and schoolmasters were the largest single group but I recall also a couple of museum curators – one of them had had to take the blame for his department's use of a deleterious detergent on the Elgin Marbles – a businessman or two, lawyers and writers, and the man or woman whom you cannot classify even after knowing them for two or three years. In Hut 6 the leading lights were mathematicians and chess players. (In a nearby naval hut a figure who looked every inch a sailor – beard, bearing and uniform – was a marine biologist or cryptogamist who had been recruited by somebody who thought a cryptogamist must be good cryptographic material.) Some of us wore uniforms as temporary members of one or other of the Services, some remained civilians. Most of us were between 25 and 30 when we went to BP; some were older, a few younger still. Of the Services Departments the Admiralty had been most alive before the war to the need to recruit civilians for wartime Intelligence but none had foreseen the extent of the need. Prewar recruiting had been on a modest scale. A few potential recruits had been marked down, quietly and privately. The Admiralty had a list of 'Gentlemen who had offered their services to the Admiralty in the event of Hostilities', and in the months immediately before the war began the Director of Naval Intelligence got an outsider – the novelist Charles Morgan – to go through the list and pick out 45 of the more promising volunteers. The City of London was another source of suggestions; the Governor of the Bank of England, Montague Norman, recommended among others Ian Fleming, creator after the war of 007 James Bond. All three Services and the Foreign Office also made discreet inquiries of relatives and friends, tapping universities, public schools, the business world and similar reserves of talent and discretion. This process continued after the war began, but the reservoirs dried up with general mobilisation. The somewhat discredited but undoubtedly efficacious old-boy network was brought into play as scouts asked those veiled questions which, over a glass of sherry, are understood without being made too explicit. Characteristically perhaps the old-girl network was overlooked until needs pressed and one senior BP cryptographer turned to his sister who had been a don at Newnham College, Cambridge, and diverted a posse of clever girls to Hut 6.

Similar girls were secured for Hut 3 and formed the corps of the Air Index whose importance cannot be exaggerated. The Index was the repository of what Ultra knew about the Luftwaffe. It received a translated copy of every decode which passed through the Watch and proceeded to index every word, name or phrase which anybody in the hut might conceivably want to look up in the months or years ahead. This monumental store of knowledge was constantly being consulted for quick answers to straight questions or for recondite answers to buried questions. At all hours of the day and night there was at least a handful of people looking for something. Has Major So-and-So been heard of before? What sort of a gadget goes by the name of PX7Q? How many serviceable aircraft were on Foggio airfield the day before yesterday? An Air Adviser teased by the thought that the decode in his hand had something to do with something he remembered from maybe eight or eighteen months earlier would rush into the Index for help in getting the penny to drop. The cards stacked in stands which stood in rows down the length of a long room contained facts beyond the capacity of even the most retentive memory. Today they would be sorted and arranged by computers but then girls did it all. There is unhappily no truth in the story that at intervals all the cards were photographed and the copies safely buried under the Bodleian Library in Oxford to guard against the awful possibility of their being destroyed by enemy action. Since the war they have been destroyed by officialdom, which is a pity since more than anything else they exemplified the scope and range of Ultra Intelligence. It required method and organisation. Sometimes somebody had a flash of brilliance but even then the flash came not out of the blue but out of a well-stocked mind backed by a well-stocked index. It was an alliance of individuals with a system and it was hard work.

The raw material of Ultra came in snippets, superficially unrelated and each in itself apparently trivial. These snippets had to be put together in rather the same manner as a classical scholar pieces together in his mind the bits of a broken Greek vase which he has seen in various scattered museums. A typical decode would be a terse order to X to proceed to Y – not very interesting unless you know from another snippet that X is an important man in a special field, so that his whereabouts are always of some interest; or that Y houses special activities which you very much want to monitor. The fact that X is being sent to Y is never an isolated fact. It is simply one fact in an enemy world where you cannot know too many facts. A large part of the business of Intelligence is to be in possession of associated facts, recent or remote, and to be skilled in making the correct associations. Another example: a message about the movements of '65 Corps I G' is transformed if you know that this officer (for that is what the initials denote) is Obersturmbannführer Dr Hoehne, the commandant of the SS Wehrgeologen battalion which is engaged in the seismographic plotting of rocket missiles.

Looking back our collaboration was astonishingly easy and smooth. There was of course the high seriousness of war which required us to assume responsibilities which we had not expected to have at our time of life. There was the fact that we were extremely busy and knew that what we were doing was valuable. There was the further factor, not entirely palatable to some, that nearly all of us had similar educational and social backgrounds and, unwittingly for the most part, the same assumptions about work and discipline and values, so that although we had never met before – among several thousands of people at BP there was only one, Henry Whitehead, whom I had known before the war (at Balliol ten years earlier) – we half knew one another and fell easily into comradeship and collaboration. And these facts go some way to explain the astonishing further fact that the Ultra secret was kept not only during the war but for thirty years afterwards, a phenomenon that may well be unparalleled in history.

Another factor was the way Hut 3 was run. Its first head was a controversial figure who was replaced by a triumvirate, a blindingly silly formula abandoned before my arrival in 1941. For much the greater part of the war the head of the Hut was Eric Jones, a civilian turned officer, at first sight an unlikely choice but an excellent one. Unlike the officers whom he was required to rule he was no intellectual but a Midlands businessman of medium rank. While respecting and indeed admiring his subordinates he intimated firmly that, however strange they might find the prospect of being governed by a man less clever than themselves, that was how it was. He left us alone to get on with our work, he knew how and how far to delegate, he had a clear and correct understanding of his own limitations and strengths, and his unexciting solidity admirably suited his position over a crew which included more than one male prima donna. The phraseology of his relatively rare written circulars tended to invite ridicule, but those who succumbed to this temptation soon found that their colleagues did not see the man as ridiculous and on the contrary esteemed him. Of his conscientiousness I had personal experience. Shortly after the end of the war, when I began to feel that I might not go back to the career which I had begun before the war, I wrote to ask him if he would give me a commendation which I might use in looking for new employment. I received in reply an eight-page letter in his own hand together with four typed copies. It is my war medal.

The security of our source was naturally a matter of the very first importance. We were all well aware of it without becoming obsessive about it. Secrets are, I am sure, in danger when people become obsessive. The ridiculous and demeaning behaviour of the Thatcher government over Peter Wright's *Spycatcher* proved that by drawing attention massively to what you wish to conceal you make a fool of yourself without hushing anything or anybody up: mediocrities in a lather, besides being a disagreeable sight, do a lot of needless harm. The security of Ultra beyond the confines of BP was in the hands of the users and of the communication channels between them and us. The channels were a distinct network under Secret Service control. The recipients were kept to a minimum: commanders-in-chief at the level of Army HQ and higher, their deputies and a few senior Intelligence officers. There was a general rule that no item of Ultra might be used operationally without confirmation from another source, so that the enemy could not draw the conclusion that Enigma was being read. This rule was not as constricting as it seems for although the C-in-C in the Mediterranean, for example, might not despatch an aircraft to sink an enemy tanker whose route had been reported by Ultra, he might send a reconnaissance aircraft to see and be seen by the tanker and then sink it. Churchill ruled that the protection of the source had priority over the winning of a particular battle. The attempt to hold Crete against the Germans in 1941 shows how this rule worked.

The decision to try to hold Crete, ill-prepared though it was, was made principally because of the fear that the Germans might use it as a stepping stone to the Middle East. General Freyberg was chosen to command its meagre forces and Field Marshal Wavell flew from Cairo for a day to discuss plans and prospects. After a general discussion Wavell draw Freyberg aside and told him about Ultra and that he would be receiving Ultra material, including a summary of recent Ultra traffic with a bearing on Crete. From this Intelligence Freyberg was able to conclude not only that his forces were dangerously inadequate but also that their disposition, which he had inherited, was wrong since it now appeared that the attack on them was to be airborne and not, as originally supposed, by sea. But

Freyberg had been instructed by Wavell (now back in Cairo) that a condition of the receipt of Ultra was that it might not be used unless confirmed by other Intelligence. Freyberg therefore sought Wavell's permission to override this restriction and re-deploy his forces. He got no such authority. Crete was pounded into submission in little more than a week and Freyberg's reputation was seriously damaged. But if this seems a sorry waste of valuable Intelligence it must be remembered that, if Ultra had been compromised over Crete, it probably would not have been available for the vital battle against U-boats in the Atlantic.

Criticism of the restraints has been most stridently – and ignorantly – voiced in connection with the blitz on Coventry on 14 November 1940. It has been alleged, and the story dies hard, that Churchill knew in advance from Ultra that Coventry was to be attacked that night and that in order to avoid compromising the source he refused to allow action to be taken to minimise the death and destruction. None of this is true. Ultra never mentioned Coventry. The question of safeguarding Ultra never arose. Three days before the raid a procedural message, revealed by Ultra, gave a list of frequencies and other items for an operation codenamed Moonlight Sonata. It was evident from the message that the operation involved an exceptional effort. No date was given. No target was specified, but certain target areas were referred to in code. From other available evidence these were believed to be areas in and near London. In a separate section of the message appeared the word *Korn*. In retrospect it has been suggested that Korn stood for Coventry – on the grounds that the initial letters were the same, a common German practice with cover names. A day or two later another routine message gave bearings from a series of beam emplacements in northern France used by the Luftwaffe to direct its bomber aircraft onto their targets. The bearings intersected at Birmingham, Coventry and Wolverhampton. These targetings indicated that, at some unspecified future date, these three cities were likely to be bombed if only because they were being added to a target list (which already contained several dozen names). At almost the same time a prisoner of war stated that Birmingham and Coventry were shortly to be bombed. His was the only direct reference to Coventry by name. These pieces of information were taken to portend a major raid at the full moon (15 November) with London as the main target but the industrial Midlands as a possible alternative. Certainty would have to await the activation of the beams which could be relied upon to point to the target a few hours before sunset. Between three and four in the afternoon on 14 November monitoring of the beam frequencies showed that Coventry was to be the night's main target. The usual counter-measures were taken, including special measures which had been prescribed some weeks earlier, although one of these measures – the jamming of the beams – was rendered largely ineffective by a mathematical error. In addition 'intruder' operations by the RAF were flown that night against targets all the way from Berlin to the west coast

Myself with my mother, her mother and her mother.

My grandparents' home at San Stefano.

In Greek costume.

My father, Pandia Calvocoressi.

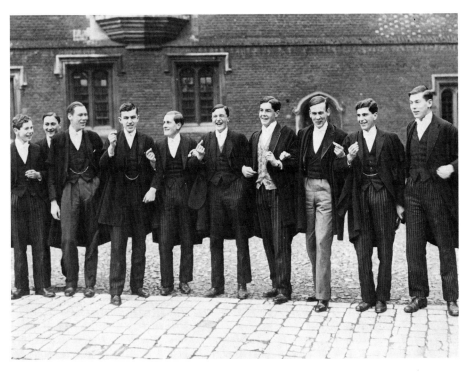

Eton: College Sixth Form.

Balliol: the Brackenbury Society.

Barbara Eden in 1937.

Wing-Commander, RAF VR.

10 September 1938.

10 September 1988.

Bletchley Park: the officers of the 3A Ultra group.

Nuremberg: Telford Taylor at the lectern with me and my colleague Oliver Berthoud.

Guise House, Aspley Guise, Bedfordshire.

With the Penguin Editors.

Honorary doctor of the Open University.

Four-score years.

of Brittany. Churchill, so far from pondering whether to save Coventry or safeguard Ultra, had been under the impression that the raid was to be on London.

Another contentious episode I have particular reason to remember. It concerned the role of Intelligence, including Ultra Intelligence, at the time of Hitler's last offensive in the west in December 1944 – his attempt to break westward through the Ardennes to the Channel coast with Antwerp as the main objective. I was by this time the head of the Air Section in Hut 3, and after the scare was over I was charged to help the late F.L. Lucas of King's College, Cambridge, with a special inquiry and report on the alleged failure of Intelligence in that affair. (I wish I had kept a copy of this report but it never occurred to me that all sorts of people, including the very highest, were in the habit of illicitly keeping copies of secret papers in their private archives for use after the war.) The issue over the Ardennes was not the restrictions on the use of Ultra but its availability and interpretation. Had it, or had it not, produced information which should have led us at BP or others at Eisenhower's HQ to foresee what Hitler was planning? By this date Ultra had become so regular and dependable that it ran the risk of being taken for granted. Such a source can lull its recipients into supposing that what it does not report does not exist. When therefore we were taken by surprise by the German attack in the Ardennes two accusations were levelled: that the Intelligence had not been provided or, alternatively, that it had been provided but had been overlooked.

What happened in fact illustrates the nature of Ultra, its relation to other sources of Intelligence and the complexities and subtleties of Intelligence work in general. The offensive was launched on 16 December and four days later it had failed. It was an attempt to seize the initiative even at this late hour in the war and was vastly overblown in terms of the resources available to Hitler, all of whose generals regarded the plan as hopeless and did their best to scale down what they could not prevent. But although the offensive was doomed to failure and was aborted within a few days it caused great perturbation on the Allied side. The Germans were not thought to be capable of anything of the kind and Allied Intelligence had so pronounced. Preoccupied with their own debate on how best to finish the war the Allies were not thinking about any disruption of their plans by Hitler. They were more worried by the slackening of the pace of their own advance than by a possible German advance. With their eyes on the Rhine they gave no thought to the possibility that Hitler might have his on the Meuse. The German attack involved 25 divisions and a great deal of preparation and movement of men, equipment and supplies. The complementary moves by the Luftwaffe – Goering promised Hitler 3,000 fighter sorties a day – were equally difficult to conceal. The plan had been foreshadowed as far back as September, since when more and more people had been drawn into discussions. Hitler personally briefed his senior generals with exceptional solemnity and threats in October. Orders were issued and units moved. D-day was postponed three or four times and all the time the circle of those in the know expanded. On the allied side Ultra revealed that the German army had created a new wireless network comprising an Army HQ and subordinate formations (all of which were named), that it was somewhere to the east of the Ardennes, that it included Panzer Divisions recently transferred from the Russian front, and that all units had been ordered to maintain wireless silence. This last item was itself a significant piece of information. It was in fact impossible in those days to keep perfect wireless silence without running the risk of losing contacts; wireless silence meant sending no messages, but it did not prohibit the exchange of brief but regular call signs which our signals Intelligence could observe, thereby gaining a picture of the size and general location of the forces involved. That picture showed a large force in a definable area and apparently holding its breath. In addition we knew from deciphered Enigma that the Germans had ordered special measures to prevent reconnaissance by us over the Eiffel (the hilly country which rises from the left bank of the Meuse). So presumably something was being carefully prepared and hidden there. We knew too from Ultra of transfers of Luftwaffe units from the Russian front and of similar transfers from the northern to the central sector of the western front. We continued to have a great deal of Ultra about the German army's order of battle, while breaks of railway Enigma enabled us to report the number and size of trains routed to the crucial area. We saw Luftwaffe units suddenly being brought up to strength. We could not give a precise date but we did show that a substantial and offensive operation was in the wind. Lucas and I expected heads to roll at Eisenhower's HQ but they did no more than wobble. The damage had been limited, the war climate was no longer so grim as a mere year or so earlier, and positions – if not reputations – remained intact. The war had changed, for we had come to the point where we could afford a slip-up.

Taking part in these events was exciting and exhilarating even though we were hundreds of miles away in the safe seclusion of the English countryside. It was also strenuous and, much of the time, routine. We knew that what we were doing was important, for we could see the results, often from our readings of the German traffic itself. Handling an item of Intelligence which was juicy, unexpected and urgent fired one and at the same time demanded a combination of judicious evaluation and prompt action. There were never fewer than two Air Advisers on duty at a time and they had the added support of Army colleagues beside them, a Duty Officer with experience and composure, the reserves of knowledge in the Air Index next door and specialists along the corridor: these special sections dealt with such matters as German military terminology, scientific developments, German cover words and so on. We operated among ourselves a system of rigorous but acceptable criticism. There is, if it has not been destroyed, a set of papers which would admirably demonstrate our peculiar amalgam of rigour and freedom. The main product of every eight-hour shift was a sheaf of about thirty Enigma decodes which had been selected for their special importance and sent by teleprinter to the Service Departments and the SIS in London together with the texts of any related signals sent to commands in the field (the bulk of Hut 3's output was sent to London not by teleprinter but by bag). One set of these teleprints lay in the office of the head of our section and his deputy. We went through it with a hyper-critical eye and wrote comments which all the Air Advisers were required to read and, if so minded, amplify or rebut. These exchanges could be quite sharp but they did not have the character of a dressing-down: nobody stood, even mentally, to attention. This was a debate between equals which generated remarkably little ill feeling. It did not occur to an Adviser under fire to remind his critic that it is human to falter at the end of a gruelling shift. Still less would the Adviser who disagreed with criticism of himself stifle his riposte because his critic held a higher rank. Our collaboration and mutual respect could not have been excelled.

Although 3A and 3M worked side by side in Hut 3 and seemed to be doing pretty much the same thing there was a sizeable difference between our work and theirs. Luftwaffe Ultra was more regular than the Ultra derived from German army keys and for most of the war fuller. Whereas the Luftwaffe had one main key which was used in every theatre of operations and was read by us every single day from early in the war until the very end, the German army had no similar key nor was any army cipher read with such regularity or promptitude. The campaigns in North Africa illustrate this difference. Initially there was no Ultra at all because there were no Germans in Africa, only Italians. After Rommel's arrival we read assorted German army keys patchily for two months towards the end of 1941. This intelligence was supplemented by what another section at BP was getting from decodes of Italian messages dealing with sea traffic in the Mediterranean and also by Luftwaffe Ultra which included much information about German military matters unwittingly relayed to us by Luftwaffe liaison officers at various German command headquarters. German army keys were read again, usually with delays, during the second quarter of 1942 and then became a plentiful stream. They contributed, for example, to the German failure to get to Cairo but could – so we at BP felt – have been more usefully exploited than they were against Rommel's retreating forces after Alamein. In the final phase of the war from the preliminaries to the landings in Normandy, including our assessment of what the Germans were making of our deception strategy, German army Ultra was copious and only rarely lost: one temporary loss was the cause of our failure to take Caen at the beginning of the campaign.

Although BP was miles away from any battle we did not feel remote. This was due to our direct service to commanders in the field and it was specially so in relation to North Africa which was very much a Hut 3 theatre as distinct from the Atlantic which was the concern of Naval Section (not part of Hut 3). North Africa was a fairly self-contained theatre of modest dimensions in terms of the men and equipment deployed over the deserts, and after the arrival of the Germans Hut 3's service grew gradually from modest support to comprehensive, steady and daily supply of valuable intelligence. It was comparatively easy to picture the situation on the ground and in the air both in periods of lull and during battles and in a sense to get to know the main personalities. Chief among these was Rommel who was sent to Africa early in 1941 partly to stem and retrieve the damage done by Wavell's defeat of the Italians but also in pursuance of the hugely ambitious German scheme to occupy Egypt, carry on into the Middle East and threaten the British in India. Rommel commanded joint German and Italian forces – there were always more Italians than Germans – for more than two years with only rare and brief absences. He was under 50 when he arrived and became a Field Marshal less than two years later. He had his failures as well as his victories, but he was a star and no other senior commander on either side served in Africa as long as he did. He left Africa in 1943 a defeated man. He was criticised by his professional peers – echoed by some military historians – for being less than outstanding in command of anything larger than a division and for trying to be everywhere and do everything himself, but the root cause of his ultimate defeat is beyond dispute. As he himself frequently complained his supplies from across the Mediterranean were always uncertain and often inadequate and, as he himself never knew, the prime source of this crippling undependability was Ultra, which sank the ships and revealed his plight and his dispositions. Rommel also figured in Ultra's most bizarre achievement. On one occasion instructions from Kesselring in Rome to Rommel in Africa were delivered to Montgomery before Rommel himself could read them. The explanation was that the text received by Rommel was so corrupt that he had to ask for a repeat. There is, however, another explanation: that he disliked the instructions and asked for a repeat in order to gain time while he hurriedly did something different.

Ultra's secrecy was kept for nearly thirty years after the war. It began to crack with the publication of Bertrand's book in Paris which led the British authorities to license Group Captain Winterbottom of the SIS to write his first book on the subject. There followed a spate of books by writers who were more excited than knowledgeable and wrote much nonsense. I myself refused to write unless and until relevant material was released to the Public Record Office and I would be able to verify my recollections. Other responsible authors did the same, so that there was an interval during which Ultra's role was weighed by overheated conjecture rather than rigorous appraisal. People asked silly questions and gave themselves silly answers, such as: Do we need generals any more? Why did we not win the war earlier? The correct answers are: In a sense we did win the war earlier – earlier than we otherwise would have – and after all we did not lose it, as we could have done if the battle of the Atlantic had gone the other way, cutting our supplies and preventing the Americans from coming to Europe. Generals are needed as much as ever, although it is more and more important that they should be attuned to Intelligence. At one point in the summer of 1944 my opposite number in 3M, Captain Alan Pryce-Jones, and I made a tour of all superior British and American HQs on western fronts to explain to commanding generals what Ultra was, where it came from and what it might be expected to do and not to do. Some of them had already received it in earlier campaigns. We caused some problems for those in charge of accommodation since our comparatively humble rank clashed with our direct access to Commanders-in-Chief. (On another occasion another of my BP colleagues on a similar mission perplexed his hosts even more since he was a civilian with no rank at all until it was decided that in war a Professor counted as a Brigadier.) As Alan Pryce-Jones and I flitted from one exalted caravan to another we reflected on the variety of the military mind but only rarely did we feel that the wrong officer had got to the top. Temperaments varied but quality was high. They were intrigued, receptive and not at all inclined to tell us to go back to Buckinghamshire and not interfere in matters we knew nothing about, like winning battles. I specially remember one US Air Force general. He sat in his caravan in a rocking chair and whenever one of us said anything that particularly caught his fancy he exclaimed, 'You don't say – you don't say', and rocked more vigorously. He was holding a small hair comb and from time to time he broke off some of its teeth and threw them over his shoulder.

Ultra did not go only to generals. It went also to those with supreme responsibility – to Churchill for example – and its contribution at this level was both incalculable and very big, although difficult to assess. At the political apex the steady flow of Ultra created a state of mind which transformed the taking of decisions. To feel that you know your enemy is a vastly comforting feeling. It grows imperceptibly over time if you regularly and intimately observe his thoughts and ways and habits and actions. Knowledge of this kind makes your own planning less tentative and more assured, less harrowing and more buoyant. Directing a great war is exceedingly tiring. Good Intelligence reduces the strains wonderfully. It conditions the two major elements in warmaking: the choice between strategies and the choice between ways of implementing the strategy you have chosen. When, for example, Churchill, Roosevelt and their Chiefs of Staff met at Casablanca in January 1943 to decide what they should do after they had cleared North Africa and recovered control of the Mediterranean, they had been receiving a steadily increasing stream of Ultra Intelligence about their enemies for three years, including reliable information on the overall size of the forces at Hitler's command. They knew they were dealing with an enemy who did not have a hat to pull rabbits out of: even Hitler's secret V weapons were nothing like as secret as Hitler imagined, although how to counter them was a sore worry. Without all this Intelligence their view of the war would have been very much less distinct. With it they still had to take fearfully difficult decisions but they could go about them without having to grope.

Below this level Ultra contributed Intelligence of varying importance in particular theatres at particular tiems, and it played also a valuable part in discerning and monitoring the progress of Germany's new weaponry and war science. This last part of the story has been expounded by Dr R.V. Jones in his *Most Secret War*. Much of the relevant cipher Intelligence came from Luftwaffe Enigma, so that my colleagues and I were closely involved and Hut 3 had also a special section – characteristically it consisted of just three persons – devoted to these topics. At BP we read the Enigma cipher used by a special Pathfinder unit of the Luftwaffe which used radio beams to locate the targets for the main bomber force. The Pathfinders followed a beam until it crossed another beam and from that point they steered a short course by dead reckoning or map reading. Thanks largely to BP's breaking of this special cipher a month or two before the big German blitz on English cities Dr Jones was able to reconstitute the beam system in about two weeks and devise counter-measures to jam or bend the beams. On another occasion a single Ultra decode transformed his work. The message did no more than pinpoint an object on the Channel coast. It gave no hint of what the object was, but on the principle that anything the Germans so precisely located had better be investigated Jones had it photographed and it turned out to be the kind of transmitting station (called Knickebein) in which he was most interested. Without the Ultra mention it could have gone unnoticed but the photographs removed all doubts about the nature of the German steering aids which Jones was trying to identify and counter.

In more strictly service matters Ultra provided a sure overall picture of the size of the German armed forces and copious, if not complete, details of their deployment and day-to-day serviceability. A standard product of Ultra was the returns which each unit in the army and Luftwaffe was required to submit daily to its superiors giving – for tanks, vehicles, aircraft, ammunition, fuel etc. as well as men – numbers on station, state of repair or health and so on. This information did not come on a plate. Intelligence seldom does. The signals consisted of strings of figures corresponding to a *pro forma* which was held by all relevant German units but had to be worked out by us by trial and error. These forms varied from one command to another. In addition to Intelligence on enemy capabilities we got clues to his intentions. These too were copious but, especially with the army, patchy. The most striking area of Intelligence of this order was neither army nor air but the naval Ultra which proved crucial to the defeat of the U-boats in the Atlantic: a story first told in Patrick Beesly's *Very Special Intelligence* and from the German side in Jurgen Rohwer's *Convoy Battles in 1943*. Our knowledge of the Luftwaffe was always more comprehensive than our knowledge of the German army, but army Ultra was plentiful in all the main campaigns from North Africa onwards. The main limitations lay in the fact that, however many clues it gave to German intentions, it rarely revealed timing.

During the war the Germans had occasional worries about the security of Enigma. Reading their traffic we read too about these worries – queries, for example, from dispirited generals unable to account for the frustration of their operations. One high-level conference concluded after much debate that it was 90 per cent certain that Enigma ciphers were 90 per cent secure – and that that was good enough. And the Germans, of course, had their successes too. They read British naval ciphers from early in the war and were massively successful in this area during the Norwegian campaign. In spite of setbacks in 1940 and 1941 when the Admiralty made changes in order to make its ciphers more secure the German naval cryptographers or B-Dienst read British signals about Atlantic traffic and North Sea convoys at the rate of about 2,000 a month during the battles of 1942. Tighter security gradually hampered the B-Dienst but never entirely forced it out of business. In the Mediterranean and North Africa, the Italians, and the Germans, succeeded in 1941 in breaking the cipher used by the American military attaché in Cairo who was favoured by the British with much precious information, but early in 1942 Ultra decodes of German traffic revealed that his signals to Washington were being read and the leak was plugged. The Germans also garnered a great deal of information from their listening services on the Russian fronts and by breaking numerous low or medium-grade Russian ciphers.

Finally a question often asked: What did we tell the Russians? We never told them that we could read Enigma ciphers, for the simple and sufficient reason that Russian cipher security was so bad that the Germans were to our knowledge reading Russian ciphers. So telling the Russians that we were reading Enigma would be tantamount to telling the Germans themselves. Even Churchill, who was temperamentally more in favour of sharing Intelligence than withholding it from his allies, accepted the overriding need to keep the source secret. But we did give the Russians a great deal of Ultra Intelligence, although without telling them where it came from. Whether they guessed we do not know, but they did not have to be very clever to make a good guess. They knew much about Enigma since they captured Enigma machines and code books and presumably they tried to decipher Enigma traffic. If they failed, the cause would not be any lack of clever people (or chess players) but rather, I suspect, a much inferior organisation to our superb combination of brainpower and efficiency.

When it was all over two feelings emerged. The first was quiet satisfaction. We knew that as a group we had done well. The second was a surprise. It was realising how extremely intense the work had been. So long as the work went on routines were in control, but when it stopped the routine stopped and I was left with a mind overstocked with information which was no longer relevant or useful. It was as though my mind had become part of history and needed to be emptied in order to make room for new functions. But pushing things out of mind is not as easy as all that. A year or so after the war ended I was having my hair cut in the Grand Hotel at Nuremberg. Chatting with the German barber I asked him about his war services. He told me that he had been with the Luftwaffe on the Russian front. I asked him which was his squadron and when he told me I muttered something about the discomforts of flying He.IIIs on the northern sector of that front. He was so surprised that he almost jabbed his scissors into my scalp and so I refrained from adding that I could also tell him his commanding officer's name and his squadron's call sign.

Spending most of the war at Bletchley Park had one unforeseen sequel. In 1944 we bought a house, Guise House, in the nearby village of Aspley Guise. It cost £6,000 and we intended to stay there until the war ended and then go back to London. We stayed until 1983, a very happy home.

There was too a second sequel. That wars change lives is a truism. While the war lasted it seemed to me more an interruption than a transformation, but this was a delusion. For most people war means first and foremost danger, a persistent and sometimes terrifying danger of death. A second main facet of war, it has often been said, is boredom. My war had been neither dangerous nor boring, but it was subcutaneously unsettling. It made prewar life seem too cosy, too circumscribed. Postwar life had to embrace an extra, broader purpose besides family life and a personal career. A role, however modest, in great events makes retreat into a private world unattractive and undutiful. The war greatly stimulated my interest in public affairs and left me with the sense, well-known to the ancient Greeks, that the secluded life of a private person (or *idiotes* as he was called) was unseemly. When the war ended I had given no thought to how to turn these vague inclinations into a practical direction but as it happened I did not need to take any hasty decision since I found myself transitionally engaged for about a year in a great undertaking – the trial at Nuremberg of major German war criminals.

6

Justice at Nuremberg

The city of Nuremberg, home of Hans Sachs and other Meistersinger, has become in modern times a symbol first of Nazi racist ideologies and then of the postwar attempt to apply the rules of war to Nazi criminals, but in 1945 it was simply weird. So too were many other German cities. Flying from Croydon to Nuremberg over Cologne, which I had known well before the war, I saw what looked like a theatrical set for a Gothic drama of disasters and ruin, and walking round Cologne a year or so later I was not sure which was the Hohestrasse. Nuremberg was specially weird because the inner city had been a medieval showpiece and was now wrecked, twice bombed by the RAF in the last months of war and then flattened by the US army. Outside the medieval limits were a large courthouse and gaol which, although badly damaged, could be put back into good working order and equipped with modern paraphernalia such as a multiple translation system. So, after an initial ceremonial session in Berlin, the International Military Tribunal for the Trial of Major War Criminals sat in Nuremberg. Most of the staffs of the Tribunal and the four prosecuting teams were accommodated in the Grand Hotel which was only partly destroyed. For the better sort houses were commandeered outside the old city and staffed with living-out servants who were only too glad to get jobs and wages, opportunities for extra food and cigarettes and the use of showers and baths when the masters were away at work. For most of my time at the main Nuremberg trial I was billeted in a small house on the outskirts of the twin cities of Nuremberg and Furth which had grown together to make one large urban area. The house, presumably built by a local worthy, was the epitome of bourgeois comfort and tastelessness. My companions were two Americans, Telford Taylor and Sidney Alderman. The latter was Justice Robert Jackson's senior assistant, a southerner and former Chief Counsel to the Southern Railroad, a quiet man whose chief relaxation was playing the violin with great affection and a little less skill.

The Nuremberg trial was solemn and dignified but often tedious and even drab. The sense of occasion which envelopes any major trial was tautened by what had gone before it and what was felt to be coming – by the peculiar horrors of the war which was only just ended and by the virtual certainty that at the end of the trial some of the accused would hang. There was too the eminence of the accused who had fallen from great power to the abjectness of captivity and ill-fitting suits, men who had not only 'witnessed huge affliction and dismay' but had caused them; and there was the further unusual sight of an international bench of judges and an international prosecuting team. On the other hand these dramatic elements were offset by the sombre setting. The courtroom had none of the trappings of high proceedings, the judges were unglamorously garbed, and the rhetoric and exchanges were reduced by the needs of translation to the effectiveness of a gramophone record played at the wrong speed.

There were occasional diversions. For me much the most memorable was a trip to Salzburg to see its first postwar *Figaro*. I had not been in Salzburg for ten years or more and this visit was memorable in more ways than one. Our party consisted of Telford Taylor, who was now a general, myself and our wives. We drove peacefully to the German border with Austria where we found a motorcycle escort lined up to receive us. This was a surprise but, until we set off, not alarming. From that point, however, the escort made all the running. Not only did we proceed at great speed to Salzburg but we did not slacken pace when we got there. We were to stay at Leopoldskrone on the far side of the city, and as we roared through it, cycle sirens now wailing, terrified natives dashed for the safety of doorways or leapt into the bosoms of trams. Taylor, shamed by this performance by the new master race, insisted – not without difficulty however – that in the evening we would go to the opera unescorted. The cast included Irmgard Seefried, Elisabeth Schwarzkopf and Willi Domgraf-Fassbaender.

Without the Americans there would have been no Nuremberg trial or, if there had been a trial, it would have been very different. The Americans insisted on it and shaped it. The British, notably Churchill and John Simon, the Lord Chancellor, did not want a trial of any sort. They wanted leading Nazis to be executed without trial, and even when outmanoeuvred by the Americans they tried to have the trial reduced to a mere formality consisting of little more than the reading of charges followed by summary execution. The Americans were shocked. The Russians said they were shocked too. De Gaulle tersely said there had to be a proper trial.

In the event there were one major trial in Europe (and a counterpart in Tokyo), twelve further trials of exalted Germans arraigned before special American courts in Germany, a handful of similar British and French proceedings and very numerous trials of lesser fry by German and non-German courts extending over many years (and their counterparts in the Pacific and South-east Asian theatres of war). In all some 10,000 persons were brought to trial for breaches of the laws of war – much the most extensive attempt ever made to enforce and extend the laws of war and to propel the rule of law into international as well as national affairs.

The impact of the proceedings at Nuremberg has been considerable. The very word Nuremberg summons up remembrance, however accurate or inaccurate, of the principal trial, and in the succeeding half-century it has been constantly referred to, not only by lawyers. It has been responsible for revisions of the laws of war in the shape of international Conventions signed by many states. These Conventions, amplifying earlier Conventions, are part of international law and bring the laws of war into line with modern warfare. Further, the Nuremberg trial was not confined to war crimes as these have been understood for centuries. It also broke new ground in three respects: first, by bringing before a competent tribunal the question whether planning and starting a war may be in itself a crime; secondly, whether atrocities unconnected with a war in progress may amount to crimes in international law, cognizable by an international court; and thirdly, by affirming the accountability of individuals for war crimes and other international crimes.

Any criminal trial involves preliminary decisions on who is to be indicted and what for. The accused at Nuremberg were picked in a strangely haphazard way. Normally a defendant on a criminal charge is put on trial only after the prosecutor has precisely determined what charges to bring and, additionally, has a pretty clear idea of the evidence available to support the charges. But although much thought was given to framing the indictment little was known or, until late in the day, done about assessing the evidence available against individuals. The identity of the accused was treated as a secondary matter. Some of the accused virtually picked themselves – Goering, for example – and the prosecutors had a broad idea of the sorts of things that he and his fellows had done over the years, but the discussions between the four chief prosecutors turned more on what they had been than on what they had done. They were picked to represent the Nazi German state in all its main aspects and activities. Lists were drawn up and exchanged. There was bargaining over which names to drop and whom to add. There were different views about the number to include in a single trial and one scandalous muddle – for which the British were chiefly to blame – when one member of the Krupp family was indicted although moribund and then an attempt was made to substitute another member of the family against whom evidence of criminality was unpersuasive.

What was done at Nuremberg owed a great deal to what was not done after the First World War. Then, plans for an international trial had been scuppered by the Americans and although the victors produced a list of 845 Germans who should stand trial before German courts only 45 were indicted, fewer were tried, sentences were light, and many of those convicted found it mysteriously easy to escape from their gaols. After the second war the Americans were in little doubt that this time there must be an international trial. They were, however, divided about what sort of trial.

Lawyers in Washington, where a high proportion of persons in and around government are lawyers, debated hotly whether to make the Nuremberg trial as simple as possible by limiting it to well-established war crimes (for example, killing prisoners of war) or to be more ambitious and take the opportunity to probe and extend the rule of law. The first course would have the advantages of simplifying and shortening the proceedings and making intelligible to the general public what would be essentially a murder trial. The latter course, which prevailed with President Roosevelt himself and other political leaders, turned the trial into a much more complex conspiracy trial embracing not only war crimes but also the two distinct categories of crimes against peace and crimes against humanity. This American decision, which was pressed on more or less hesitant allies, was adopted for an accumulation of reasons: the sense of outrage as the tally and toll of atrocities became known, many of them perpetrated from 1933 onwards, first in Germany and then over much of Europe, including crimes which were not war crimes since for most of the Nazi period there was no war; the strong, if imprecise, feeling that planning and initiating wars of aggression had become a crime in international law and that it was time to put the argument before a court of law; the more general lawyers' imperative to apply law, not to let it go by default, not to lose the opportunity to probe the efficiency and reach of law by the only appropriate means – a case before a court; a calculated desire to set the record straight and pre-empt the growth of myths, such as the belief that the Kaiser's armies had not been defeated but were forced to capitulate because they were stabbed in the back by weak-kneed civilians behind the lines; a fear of indiscriminate vengeance if no attempt were made to punish criminals by legal process. There were also obligations to Allied governments and to Jewry, the most obvious victims of the Nazi regime. A number of European governments had fled from the continent and established themselves temporarily in London. As early as 1940 the British and French governments denounced German criminal activity in Czechoslovakia and Poland, and the next year President Roosevelt denounced the taking of hostages by German authorities and the Russians protested against wholesale violations of international law. These steps gathered international momentum. In 1942 nine countries attended a conference on the Punishment of War Criminals which led to the creation by seventeen countries of a War Crimes Commission to collect evidence. After the entry of the United States into the war in 1941 the three major combatants declared that war criminals would be sent back to the scene of their crimes for trial with the exception of major criminals who would be tried by the principal Allied Powers. All these factors combined to tilt the balance in favour of a wide-ranging trial for which the term 'war crimes trial' was a misnomer. It embraced more crimes than that.

War crimes have an ancient pedigree. Broadly speaking they are acts of violence which even war does not justify. In the eyes of the law not all is fair in war, whatever may be the case in love. One of the characteristics of civilisations is making rules to regulate war: when war is permissible and what is permissible or impermissible in war. Moralists, legists and clerics have joined forces in making rules to restrict and tame wars. Over the centuries the rules have changed, as they still do. In modern times the principal expression of this trend has been a series of international treaties by which the signatories have proclaimed what they believe to be the state of the law. Thus the main aim of the Hague Conventions of 1899 and 1907 was to protect those entangled in war, notably prisoners and the wounded; they also proscribed some particularly noxious and obnoxious weapons, for example, expanding bullets. The Geneva Convention of 1925 added poison gas and germ warfare. Since the Second World War the four further Geneva Conventions of 1949 have brought the law up to date with more recent developments in weaponry. In 1945 there was no problem over the definition of war crimes in general and a considerable extent of positive law defining particular kinds of warmaking as criminal. There were, however, a number of related problems. There was the business of finding and presenting evidence against particular individuals. It quickly became clear that far from being hard to find the evidence was embarrassingly and overwhelmingly plentiful owing to the capture of a huge mass of German documents which showed that terrible crimes had been committed. But this mass of material had to be sorted and properly understood and at first sight it directly incriminated lesser fry rather than the senior officers and leading government figures whom the prosecutors were resolved to bring to book. Next, although the law clearly condemned the use of some weapons which had been developed in recent times, other means of making war had not been particularised in Conventions, if only because they had not yet been developed or foreseen. Thus the use of poison gases and germ warfare had been expressly declared to contravene the laws of war but the mass bombing of civilians had not, even though – no less than the use of gas – it was in some instances a breach of the rules which forbade the use of excessive and indiscriminate force.

This issue was never raised at Nuremberg because of yet another problem. German leaders could have been charged with criminality in relation to the bombing of London and other cities and, more plainly, the so-called Baedeker raids on cities such as Bath of artistic fame but no strategic significance. A standing international court with criminal juris-diction could have entertained such charges, but the Nuremberg tribunal was an *ad hoc* tribunal whose competence was limited by the Charter establishing it and by the circumstances of its creation – by the victors in a particular war. The Nuremberg tribunal was competent to hear charges against specified major German malefactors only, and it could not unblush-ingly have convicted them of war crimes arising from aerial bombardment since their antagonists had used mass bombing more heavily, no less indiscriminately and on occasions (on Dresden, for example) even less justifiably. The absence of a standing court with criminal jurisdiction – a counterpart to the International Court of Justice at The Hague which has civil jurisdiction only – was and still is one of the gravest weaknesses in the endeavour to extend the rule of law in international affairs. It makes the application of the law too selective for its own health.

The decision to go beyond war crimes and charge the accused with other criminal activities, together with the number and variety of the accused and the span of twelve years (1933-45) to be taken into consideration, imposed on the prosecution the need to devise a framework which would encompass all these things. The device chosen was to allege a common plan or conspiracy between the accused in the course of which each had been guilty of some or all of the crimes thereafter alleged. In addition, and in order to facilitate further proceedings against the hundreds or thousands of Germans beyond the mere 24 to appear in the dock at Nuremberg, six organisations were also indicted as such. The conviction of any one of these organisations would not automatically incriminate any individual member of that organisation but it would tar him with a black mark if he were subsequently to be put on trial in an international or national court.

The conspiracy scheme was an intellectually robust idea but it had its defects. Conspiracy as a crime in itself is a notion familiar to Anglo-Saxon lawyers but puzzling to others; historically it proved impossible to establish the conspiracy alleged; and for the lay public a conspiracy trial is much more difficult to follow than a murder trial. The centrepiece of the conspiracy was the so-called crime against peace: preparing and initiating and waging aggressive wars. There were two distinct charges – conspiracy to plan etc. aggressive war, and actually planning etc. such wars. There was no doubt that wars of this kind had been planned and fought by the Third Reich and there was no doubt that by 1939 63 states, including Germany, Italy and Japan, had condemned and renounced recourse to war by signing or adhering to the Kellogg-Briand Pact of 1928. But it was questionable whether the Pact made aggressive war (however that might be defined) criminal as well as illegal and, further, whether individuals might be held accountable as well as states. The Treaty of Versailles had included a clause requiring the Kaiser to stand trial personally before a special tribunal for breaches of the laws of war, but since attempts to extradite him from his asylum in the Netherlands failed the question of personal accountability at this level was not judicially tested. At Nuremberg defence lawyers argued that international public law dealt only with the acts of states but the tribunal rejected this plea. It also ruled that aggressive war was an internationally established crime at least since 1928. Eight of the defendants at Nuremberg were convicted on both the counts relating to aggressive war, while another four were acquitted of conspiracy but found guilty of planning and waging aggressive war. All those sentenced to death (twelve, including Bormann, tried *in absentia* but almost certainly already dead) were found guilty on other charges too.

These other charges included the crimes for which the term crimes against humanity had come into use earlier in the century, although it was not yet enshrined in legal usage. At Nuremberg these charges were designed to comprise atrocities committed at any time after 1933 and in any place inside or outside Germany. But the tribunal declared itself incompetent to entertain such charges in relation to anything that had occurred before 1939. This was the result of a muddle. In the course of the discussing and haggling among the chief prosecutors drafting the indictment the conspiracy charge which, in the American scheme, was central to the entire enterprise had got dropped in relation to everything except aggressive war, with the result that the tribunal found itself precluded by its Charter from taking the broader view and, on crimes against humanity, precluded from deciding how far such crimes were known to international as well as national law.

For the tribunal's brief was not to apply international law at large but the more limited one of implementing the Charter which had set up the tribunal and prescribed the scope of its proceedings. This Charter was contained in an agreement of 1945 made by the four major allies on behalf of all the then United Nations and subsequently adhered to by nineteen of them. The right of these states to set up the tribunal was challenged but the challenge was rebuffed on the grounds that since every state possesses the sovereign right to set up courts sovereign states may together set up a court for prescribed purposes, provided these purposes are lawful. There was a further challenge to the law to be applied on the grounds that there existed no international legislature competent to make law. To this argument the tribunal itself replied by accepting the contrary argument that international treaties and conventions are declaratory of existing law rather than enactments of new law. If that is so, then the law declared by such treaties or conventions binds all states and not merely the signatories – an important conclusion since many states, including the Soviet Union, were not parties to some of the relevant conventions which the prosecution was seeking to enforce.

The conduct of the trial as well as its planning was dominated by the Americans. The American prosecuting team was much the largest and the American chief prosecutor, Robert Jackson, was the outstanding figure. He was the kind of lawyer who is unusual anywhere but even more unusual in England than the United States. He had a passion for justice which most lawyers fight shy of as though it were professionally unbecoming, and he entered a court not merely to argue points of law but to win. He had stepped down from the Supreme Court of the United States not unmindful of the limelight about to be focussed on a singularly dramatic occasion but also profoundly committed to the business of enlarging the rule of law and prosecuting to conviction a group of unusually baleful miscreants. His opening speech and, if to a lesser degree, his closing speech were powerfully intelligent and very moving statements. But he had his failings. The American team was about 2,000 strong, including 200 lawyers of whom fifty had court-room roles at one point in the trial or another. In this large body were many excellent lawyers, many mediocrities and quite a number of feuds. Jackson's qualities did not include leadership or diplomacy and he showed little interest in organising his team. He concentrated on his personal appearances before the tribunal to the exclusion of much else. When not working on his speeches he spent much time back in Washington or sightseeing in Europe. At an early stage he quarrelled with one of his principal deputies, a personal friend, and sent him packing. He was disdainful of his fellow chief prosecutors. For a short time he had uncomfortably at his elbow General William Donovan, a hero of the First World War and the autocrat in the second of the OSS – a hybrid intelligence and operations outfit famous for treading on many toes. Donovan arrived in Nuremberg nobody quite knew how or why, but with the evident determination to be little if at all less prominent than Jackson. He upset Jackson by pointing out to him that although he had recruited many excellent lawyers they knew little about the facts of the cases which they had been hired to present and were floundering in the mass of German documents where their evidence must lie. Donovan was not only right about this state of affairs but maintained humiliatingly that he alone could rectify it. Jackson managed to see him off his territory and Donovan disappeared from Nuremberg as mysteriously as he had arrived.

The British team was by contrast small, relatively harmonious and when it came to the crunch of public performance notably efficient. The Russian and French teams were even smaller. The British numbered about 200 with half a dozen barristers. Nominally the chief prosecutor was the Attorney-General, Hartley Shawcross, who appeared and spoke effectively on the big occasions but left the day-to-day conduct of those parts of the trial assigned to the British to David Maxwell-Fyfe, his predecessor as Attorney-General until the change of government in London after the general election in July 1945. With Maxwell-Fyfe were one KC – G.D. Roberts, a jovial, burly and experienced criminal lawyer with an imposing presence but no intellectual bent – and three juniors who all went on to higher things: Harry Phillimore to be a High Court judge, Mervyn Griffith-Jones to be Crown Counsel at the Old Bailey (where he won fame of a sort with a famously ill-chosen remark to the jury in the trial of Penguin Books for publishing *Lady Chatterley's Lover* unexpurgated) and Elwyn Jones to be Lord Chancellor. Maxwell-Fyfe tried to my surprise to recruit me for the Conservative Party, a strange misjudgment, and he was less than fair to Elwyn Jones whom he seemed to dislike on purely political grounds, but he was a thoroughly professional, hard-working and courteous lawyer who won general esteem for his performance before the tribunal. His pertinacity, equanimity and command of detail were impressive and effective, a foil to Jackson's rhetoric and breadth of vision. Between them they did more than anybody else to save the proceedings from becoming humdrum or on the other hand narrowly vindictive.

Thanks largely to them the trial served a purpose beyond legal history. To Goering's contemporaries it was axiomatic that the crimes attributed to the Nazis had occurred: the charges had to be proved by proper legal procedures but the substance of the matter was not in doubt in that generation. To a later generation, however, of Germans and non-Germans this belief was no longer axiomatic. Half a century later younger people would ask whether these terrible things could really be true. The answer lay in the documents, unimpeachably authentic, produced at and for the Nuremberg trial. The volume of this material was all but overwhelming – the archives of the German navy, for example, had been captured virtually intact for a period stretching back eighty years – and putting these documents on the record was not the least of the trial's achievements and one which justified those who had advocated a wide-ranging, if dauntingly complex, indictment and then presented the case with scrupulous professionalism.

I myself was not a member of any of the four prosecuting teams. My role was peculiar. Although a practising member of the English Bar I had had no experience of criminal or international law and my posting to Nuremberg had more to do with my wartime Intelligence work than my prewar legal career. I was seconded to all four of the prosecuting teams by my employers, the Joint Intelligence Committee of the Joint Chiefs of Staff, and took with me a little team of three or four persons recruited from former colleagues at Bletchley Park. Three of the four prosecuting teams were not interested in us. I was on friendly personal terms with the British lawyers. With the Russians and French I had next to no contacts and I doubt whether they knew I was there. My work was with the Americans, specifically with Telford Taylor who had been a colleague and friend at Bletchley Park and to whom Jackson had delegated the prosecution of two of the six indicted organisations: the German General Staff and High Command, and the SS. The former was a notional group which had been indicted because it was held to embody the core of the German militarist beast and Taylor, more aware than most of the need to collect and present hard evidence against members of the group, wanted help in an arduous task for which not much time was available. That I was a lawyer was useful but not the main reason for my presence. Together with my principal assistant Oliver Berthoud (whose splendid sense of dry humour, as comforting as his intelligence was useful, later made him an outstanding headmaster until his sadly early death) I was at Nuremberg because I knew a lot about the organisation of the German forces and the SS and about their wartime behaviour. Oliver and I were also familiar with the variety and the jargon of daily reports, war diaries and other documents which German units at all levels had to compile and copies of which were pouring into Nuremberg for the use of prosecuting and defence counsel. And when it came to interrogating Germans from Field Marshals downwards we started with the advantage of being fluent in their language and well-informed about their affairs. Senior officers in particular, men who had been used to giving orders and studying situations but had been shut away for months since the War's end with nothing to do and nobody to talk to, were delighted with the chance to talk shop, to explain and generally engage in conversation with people who knew what they were talking about. From our wartime work Oliver and I knew whom it would be most fruitful to interrogate and on what lines to interrogate them. Since most of them were in Russian custody we relied on the Russian delegation at Nuremberg to discover whether they were still alive and where they were and then to arrange for them to be despatched to Nuremberg where they were held so long as we wanted them to be there. We could not interrogate anybody who was under indictment in any trial – that would have been improper – but this was not a serious limitation since there were more than enough interesting characters for us to see. Some of them became so interested in our talks that they volunteered to write notes, even long essays, using the horrible blunt purple pencils which were all they seemed to be allowed by the keeper of the prison in which they were lodged until they were returned to wherever they had come from.

We had to establish two main points: that our indicted military group was a group or organisation within the terms of the tribunal's Charter, and that it had participated in the crimes alleged in the indictment. Telford Taylor and I were always doubtful on the first point and the tribunal decided against us. My advice, accepted by Taylor and then by Jackson, was to interpret the group narrowly – a small group of senior planners and field commanders, a group defined by function rather than rank and which would number about forty individuals in all over the entire period from 1933 to 1945. We could then present this group as a coherent power centre which had criminally abused its powers. We did not attack the military profession but we alleged a persistent disregard of the laws of war amounting at times to criminal atrocities. With oral testimony from senior serving officers to supplement the evidence from captured German documents we established our second point to the extent that the tribunal, while ruling that the indicted group was too fluid a group to satisfy the requirements of the Charter, judged nevertheless that members of it had been guilty of serious crimes: for example, implementing Hitler's order to execute without trial captured commandos even if wearing military uniforms; and participating in the enormities perpetrated by the special SS units which murdered tens of thousands of Jews and other civilians in areas under the army's control on the eastern fronts.

Since most of the culpable individuals in this group were not before the tribunal it was left to the several prosecuting Powers to bring cases against them. The British staged two or three half-hearted trials, the French fewer and the Russians none, but after the main Nuremberg trial the Americans conducted in the same city in 1947-49 twelve further trials, including two against senior military chiefs. The defendants in these twelve trials ranged from one to 23: 177 defendants in all, of whom 24 were sentenced to death, almost all of these being either members of SS death squads on the eastern front or doctors who had used living human bodies for medical experiments. Thirty-five were acquitted and the remaining 118 got prison sentences. Of the two cases involving military figures the one was concerned with the taking and killing of hostages and with unjustifiably reckless spoliation, mainly in Greece and Yugoslavia; in the other thirteen generals and field marshals were charged with planning and waging wars of aggression (of which all were acquitted) and with other crimes, notably executing captured commandos and Russian commissars even when captured in uniform. Of these thirteen, all but two army officers received prison sentences between life and three years while a single admiral and a single Luftwaffe general were acquitted. To help with these two trials I worked for three months in Washington on more piles of captured documents and then returned to Nuremberg as an employee of the US War Department which was responsible for all twelve trials with Telford Taylor as Chief of Counsel.

Putting generals on trial upset a lot of people. In the popular view military men might be stupid but they were honourable and clean. The military in other countries were outraged by allegations of brutality against their German brother officers, but while this professional loyalty across the lines of battle had its appealing side it was based on ignorance of the facts and often on a determination to remain ignorant. German generals were not all bad, but some were and the attempts of apologists to close ranks to defend the criminals among them and shield what they regarded as their professional honour were misguided and unsustainable. These apologists were particularly concerned to insist that the German army had had nothing to do with the excesses of the SS in occupied territories and abhorred all that sort of thing, but the evidence of military complicity in SS operations was convincing and the passage of time has steadily reinforced it as more and more has become known about the wartime cooperation between the army and the SS, on the eastern fronts in particular. By the time war came in 1939 the Nazis had corrupted even the self-assured and standoffish military caste where, even though outright villains were few and far between, a cowardly hypocrisy in the face of SS villains and a pharisaical disposition to look the other way attested the persuasive power of propaganda. This insidious power has no more grisly illustration than the well-attested accounts of officers in once reputable regiments who hunted down and killed mental patients turned loose for their sport in the grounds of institutions.

To anybody sitting in the court at Nuremberg one of the hardest facts to digest was the brevity of the Nazis' rule: only twelve years and yet so much damage and so many horrors before they were put down. The trial had promised to be a great occasion with the word historic dripping from every writer's pen. Unforgettable it has proved to be, but not in the mode anticipated. It was not showy or dressy, as court scenes – in England at any rate – are expected to be. The judges wore sober suits and black gowns, except the two Russian judges who wore unexciting uniforms. Nor was there anything of the savage tenseness of the television court drama. The most dramatic element was the mere presence in the dock of once high and mighty men, led into it at the beginning of each session by one of the most famous men in the world, Hermann Goering. Yet for all their fame the accused were more rumpled than glamorous and what made the scene awesome was not what was going on but what had gone before. Among the accused Goering was pre-eminent. While his fellows retreated into aloofness or collapsed into pathos he displayed an alert intelligence. He did not disavow Hitler or his crimes and had come to terms with the certainty that when the trial ended he would die.

The pace of the trial was leaden, not merely because of the complex scope of the indictment and the number of the accused but also and most drainingly because of the requirements of translation. The judges and prosecutors spoke three different languages and the accused and their counsel a fourth. Few in the court understood all four and even those who could still could not follow the proceedings in more than two tongues since nobody has more than two ears. Simultaneous translations and the earphones with which we were all provided did no more than give each person a choice of what to listen to. It fell to me to cross-examine Field Marshal von Rundstedt. I put my questions to him in English and he answered in German, questions and answers being translated three ways simultaneously. But I needed to know, first, how my question had been put to him in German, since he replied not to my words but to the German translation of them. His reply came to me across the court in German but also, through one of my earphones, in the English translation which some, but not all, of the judges were hearing. Ideally I wished also to know how both sides of this exchange had been rendered to the Russian and French judges, for if one of the judges interposed a question he would be reacting to the words of the translator to whom he was listening. It was, in short, impossible to keep track of everything that was being said and the business of conducting examinations in a mere two languages made the sessions slow and tedious, quite apart from the possibilities of error posed by the other two sets of translations. In the circumstances the ten months which the trial took were a commendable achievement but at the time much of that period was grindingly dull. The eight judges had to listen all the time but nobody else did.

Yet never did the proceedings seem unimportant. The trial was part of something that mattered very much. The ghastly war and its grisly concomitants hung about the place like a pall which had not had time to blow away. There was a strong conviction that the failure to make the world a safer place after the First World War must not be repeated and that one essential item was to attach responsibility to the individuals most responsible for starting the second war, deploying the SS death squads put together to cull Slavs, and devising the holocaust of Jews and gypsies from all over Europe; and to punish them. The trial was not without its defects, not in the sense that it was unfair or unjust to those in the dock but in its appearance of one-sidedness, more a consequence of victory than of law-breaking. It was also disappointing to the extent that the court – and the courts which heard the subsequent American trials – ducked the issue of crimes perpetrated before the war began. The question whether rulers may with impunity commit atrocities in peacetime within their own borders remained unanswered, although it had at least been raised and a few years later in 1949 a Genocide Convention explicitly condemned as criminal wholesale attacks, in peace or war, intended to destroy wholly or partially a national, ethnic, racial or religious group, and declared that such attacks were justiciable by national or international courts. The trial also produced useful statements on the law relating to the taking of hostages, forced labour, deportation and official looting and the principles applied by the tribunal were codified by the UN as an accepted part of international law.

But no permanent court has been established to entertain these matters and so long as this is so governments and individuals may continue to break the law with the fairly confident expectation that nothing unpleasant will be done to them. The thorniest obstacle to the creation of such a court is the reluctance of powerful states to establish an institution which may then criticise them. After the Gulf War of 1991 many people wanted Saddam Hussein to be arraigned before an international court but there were others who did not. Arabs, however much they deplored Saddam Hussein's misdeeds, did not relish the prospect of an Arab leader being tried by non-Arabs; Americans recoiled from a trial in which Saddam Hussein's criminality might be affirmed but charges might also be voiced about their own conduct of the war and against Israel's many infractions of international law in their occupied territories and in Lebanon. There is furthermore a distinction between a criminal and a civil court which, politics apart, bedevils plans for creating a permanent international tribunal with criminal jurisdiction. A civil court adjudicates between the claims of parties before it. A criminal court imposes sentences – but how effectively? Before an individual can be punished he must first be caught and, preferably, be induced to plead. Alternatively, if he is not caught he may be tried and condemned in his absence but in that event the implementation of the court's sentence presents peculiar difficulties. The culprit is presumably in a country where his supporters are unlikely to yield him up to justice. The court which condemns him has neither the jurisdiction nor the beadles to go and get him. The UN will be loath to invade and in effect start a war in the role of tipstaff, while measures short of war such as economic sanctions must fall largely on a blameless populace.

These weaknesses in the international order have encouraged national governments into unlawful courses. Criminals or suspected criminals living in one country have been kidnapped by another. Adolf Eichmann was abducted from Bolivia by agents of the Israeli state to stand trial by prosecutors who flagrantly flouted the law in order to stage the trial. Eichmann's guilt was clear enough and superabundantly odious, but Israel too was guilty of criminal action. So too was the government of the USA when it sent the American Army to kidnap Manuel Noriega in Panama for a trial in the USA which was an extension not of the rule of law but of the domain of anarchy in international affairs.

On the question of war crimes trials decades after the events I endorse unreservedly the general rule of law that time does not efface a crime. (An amnesty may do so but an amnesty is a political, not a judicial, act.) Nevertheless it does not follow that it is always proper to indict a suspected war criminal. For such an indictment to be proper there must be good evidence to support the allegations and a sound prospect of a fair trial. Time erodes these requirements, particularly where condemnation will largely depend on reliable identification. The extreme instance of an improper trial was that of John Demjanchuk, extradited from the USA for trial in Israel where he was convicted. Not only was he almost certainly the wrong man, but even had he been guilty as charged the reliability of the testimony to prove his identity was deplorably low (and the conduct of the trial seriously degraded by the introduction of inadmissable hearsay). But this particular trial, in which the pursuit of justice was vitiated by zeal for vengeance, was only one departure from the rules of law in similar circumstances. In Britain Parliament passed a belated Act to permit otherwise impermissible trials of persons who – guilty or not – had taken refuge in Britain after the Second World War, and this Act was doubly distasteful since it both altered the law in retrospect and facilitated trials which would depend on evidence of identity to be presented after the passage of nearly half a century. The upshot of these arguments is that some criminals may stay free and unpunished. So be it. Not all criminals get caught, and the nature of the crime alleged makes no difference in law to the force of the argument.

7

The World as Oyster

When the war ended I had the Bar to go back to and I did so, but only briefly. Although I found the law truly interesting I was uneasy at the Bar and I had acquired wider interests and above all a surer footing in the world. I was disposed to change course.

But leaving the Bar was more than a change of course. It turned out to be a change of pattern. I did not simply swap one fixed career for another but began a medley of careers – a riskier way of life but one more to my taste. So far as people may be classified as specialists or generalists I was a generalist, even a pluralist. My bent was for variety, for doing several things at once and not just one. In the event two topics dominated the years to come: foreign affairs and publishing. Sometimes the one dominated and sometimes the other but at no time after the war were foreign affairs out of my mind.

I first got a sense of a wide world from *The Times* when I was still a child. I did not then read *The Times* but it arrived every weekday and had its special place in the drawing room and represented something which was a way off since it came from outside, permanent since it came regularly and changeable since it was different every day: in other words, a living world. I had a second intimation of this world which, like *The Times*, was daily but for Sundays. About an hour or two after getting home from his office my father had a telephone conversation in which most of the talking was done at the other end of the line while my father listened, frowned and pondered and at intervals pronounced a name and a figure. My father was 'in cotton' and it was somehow clear to listening children that the figures were prices which were being set for the next twenty-four hours for various kinds of cotton and that the names were distant places where these cottons grew. The names – I have forgotten them all except one, Comilla, which sounded like a girl's name out of place – were romantic and Indian and brought a whiff of farflung activity directed by my father.

They were also echos from the wide horizons with which I had been born. At the age of three months I travelled from Karachi to Liverpool. Maybe I gave no thought to India or Asia for many years after that transplantation but there was a tentacle which lived on. My parents' origins in Greece, of which I have written at the beginning of this book, planted in me an interest which, although slow to awaken, became deep and broad. In my teens I began to experience a lifelong delight in many parts of Europe and to feel the impact of European politics on private lives. History at Eton and Balliol gave me a taste for current affairs, for although history academically stopped around 1870 this arbitrary cut-off could not prevent one's mind from running on, linking the past with the present, dead people with myself. This was particularly so in my case because my 'special subject' at Oxford had been the Congress of Vienna and the post-Napoleonic settlement of Europe and I was naturally led to compare that period with the First World War and the Paris Peace Conference. Wars, regrettably or not, have their enticement and when I was still at school I had begun to delve into the literature of the Great War, as it was then called. The College at Eton had a reasonably well stocked library which was open to half the members of the College for borrowing books, reading newspapers or simply sitting around: this was one of the College's greatest advantages. Each House had a 'library' too, but a House library was usually a pokey little place reserved to a tiny elite and innocent of books. At Eton I ploughed through all Churchill's volumes about the Kaiser's War ('I see,' said one wit, 'that Winston has written a book about himself and calls it *The World Crisis*'). Memoirs and novels followed, randomly. I read Robert Graves' *Goodbye to All That* but did not at this time come across Philip Sassoon. The first war novel I read was Erich Maria Remarque's *All Quiet on the Western Front* and the next was R.H. Mottram's *The Spanish Farm*. The four Tietjens novels of Ford Madox Ford, perhaps greater and certainly more perplexing books, I did not discover for many years.

Then too, part of growing up was reading grown-up newspapers which meant once more *The Times*, then the most famous and prestigious paper in the world and specially renowned for its coverage of world affairs alongside its other principal function as the Mayfair Parish Magazine. We were as a family *Times* folk and I had myself appeared in its pages not only when I won my scholarship to Eton but also when I was born. On that earlier occasion, 17 November 1912, *The Times* did not appear, not for any sinister reason but because it was a Sunday. On the following Wednesday my birth was tersely announced on the front page along with thirteen others, two of them besides myself born in India. That day's *Times* had sixteen pages, six columns to a page. Advertisements occupied less than nine columns out of 96. Much the most prominent of them concerned 'Eczema: Its Torment and the Significance of the New Treatment Endorsed by Doctors'. On another page unnamed doctors recommended gas fires and a drawing showed a somnolent gentleman reading a book in front of one. A smaller advertisement listed 'Mr Heinemann's New Books' in a half-column. Other enticements were for a piano with a brain (available in exchange for your existing piano) and an auction of 1911 German 'natural' wines. Among the small ads the most numerous were for domestic jobs in town or country; gardeners, for example, looking for places and stating that they intended to get married 'when suited' – suited meant finding the right job, not the right girl.

On the one hand *The Times* catered for top people, telling you all you wanted to know about people you knew or wished you knew and serving as a directory announcing dates of impending departures for Baden Baden or Cannes or Scotland and intended dates of return. On the other hand *The Times* took the world for its oyster and boasted foreign correspondents of special learning and social consequence in their respective bailiwicks. This day's *Times* gave eight columns to its 'Imperial and Foreign Intelligence'. Half of this Intelligence was about the wars in the Balkans, notably the race between Greeks and Bulgarians to be the first to evict the Turks from Salonica. Relations between these two Christian allies were so bad that the Greeks, having got into the city first, refused to admit the Bulgarians with the result that the Bulgarian crown prince and his brother had to sleep the night under a bridge. The rest of this page – one third of it – was given to theatre reviews and announcements. A preceding page carried a miscellany of foreign reports, including a disquisition on Turkish place names, torrential rain in Jamaica, the failure of electric light in the French Senate, and the shooting by New York police of an international crook and his female companion. The paper had next to no financial or business news.

We 'took' *The Times* as a matter of course but so long as the distinction between adults and children lasted (longer in those days than now) I was provided with the weekly *Children's Newspaper* which I found dreadfully boring. I read enough of it each week to satisfy a feeling that I ought to do so since my parents were kind enough to get it for me. I remember being fired by it only once, when for several weeks on end it ran an intriguing competition consisting of dozens of silhouettes of famous historical characters. My mother and I hunted for likenesses in illustrated history books and when we went to London on my way back to school we rushed round the National Portrait Gallery, the Wallace Collection and other likely places trying to identify profiles of the famous by the kind of wig they wore or the aquilinity of their noses. At some point I graduated from childish newspapers to *The Times* and when I went to Balliol I began sixty years of regular subscription. It cost me at first a farthing a day. The price was 2d. – all other papers except a racing paper were 1d. – but undergraduates got it half price and four of us clubbed together to share the penny. This was not a sign of poverty or meanness but a sensible calculation that it was wrong to give a presumably flourishing newspaper more than the inescapable minimum.

I first put a toe seriously into the business of foreign affairs with an organisation called the Liberal International which was created after the war as an association of (mainly) European Liberal Parties with a superstructure of eminent liberal personalities – Benedetto Croce, Gilbert Murray, Salvador da Madariage, Theodor Heuss and others. I was asked to be its secretary, head of a staff of two in a minuscule office in London which, with luck and good management, might become the nub of an influential international organisation. I went to Naples to see Croce, a pre-fascist ancient monument who received me in the vast house where he was attended upon by middle-aged daughters. He showed me round room after room, almost bare except for books all over the place, until we arrived in one room where books in many languages were tidily arranged in a glass-fronted bookcase to which he pointed saying: 'Un autel dédié a Vico' – of whom I knew at that time hardly anything. On this visit to Naples I made my first and last public appearance in a great opera house. The San Carlo has been hired for a political rally and I was given a seat of honour on the stage. Italy's first post-fascist elections were intensely exciting, joyous and kaleidoscopic, ranging from efflorescent democratic rhetoric to – from one candidate – the distribution of free spaghetti.

The Liberal International was designed as a counterpart to the famous Socialist Internationals but was even more fissiparous than they. It was held together by tolerance and good manners rather than shared doctrines. It was not easy to identify which party in a given country was the right party to enrol. There were free traders in one part of Europe, Victorian libertarians in another, anti-state entrepreneurs and landowners in yet another, and everywhere parties which were being squeezed between Right and Left without being sure which they regarded as the less congenial. There was also a strain, particularly evident in France, Italy and the Roman Catholic parts of Germany, which harked back to medieval notions of a supranational Christian polity and at the same time forward to a brave new united Europe: Robert Schuman, Alcide de Gasperi, Francois de Menthon. Men of this kind were totally incomprehensible to the British and Scandinavians who distrusted their Catholicism as something entirely alien to liberalism and failed to cotton on to the quasi-federal nationalism which, when it was adopted also by German conservatives such as Adenauer, created the base for the European Community.

I was chosen to orchestrate this disparate band probably because I had stood as a Liberal candidate in the first postwar general election in Britain and, unlike other available candidates for the post, could speak a number of the relevant languages. Our finances came from a few rich men and a few political parties and we held conferences in various cities where much sense was talked but not much unity was achieved. After a bit I came to see that I was out of place since I could not convince myself that the organisation was doing much except survive and I no longer called myself a liberal in politics. (From 1950 I voted Labour regularly and unhesitatingly.) So I resigned to seek a more substantial job.

As luck would have it two presented themselves. The one I sought after it was advertised and the other came out of the blue just after I had accepted the first. It happened like this. One day Willi Bretscher appeared in my office. He was the editor of the *Neue Zürcher Zeitung*. He had become

editor at almost exactly the same moment as Hitler had become Chancellor
of Germany and he had played a critical part in making the paper and
German-speaking Switzerland much more anti-Nazi than they might
otherwise have been. I had met him once or twice and he now told me of
plans to create in Zurich an International Press Institute, an association
of newspaper editors for the promotion of international understanding, the
training of journalists in new states, and so forth. He asked me if I would
become its Director. Since I was settling in to a new job and since I did not
want at that stage of my life to go and live in Switzerland I said no, but I
also told him that I knew the man for the job and sent him to see my friend
from Bletchley Park days, Jim Rose, who took it.

The job which I had taken I imagined to be a job for life. I remained in
it for five years. It was at the Royal Institute of International Affairs,
commonly called Chatham House after Lord Chatham who was one of
three British Prime Ministers to live in the house in St James's Square
which was presented to the Institute on its foundation at the end of the
First World War. I joined the staff in November 1949 with a salary of £875
a year (after a probationary year at £600) and I worked there until October
1954 – five years which saw the production of five fat volumes in the series
of Annual Surveys of International Affairs – volumes of about a quarter of
a million words each covering the years 1947-53 (we began with two double
volumes). I had one assistant with whose help I wrote about four-fifths of
each volume, the remainder being commissioned from a couple of eminent
outside specialists.

The presiding genius of Chatham House was Arnold Toynbee, an
extraordinary man. At this date Toynbee was famous but not yet the world
star which he improbably became by publishing his *Study of History* in ten
volumes. He was not strictly speaking an historian except in the limited
sense that Greco-Roman history was one ingredient in the make-up of a
classical scholar. He came of a middle-class family of intellectuals and
philanthropists which was having difficulty in making middle-class ends
meet – his father spent about half of a long life in a lunatic asylum – and
as an only son with two much younger sisters he had had to make his way
by brains and hard work to Winchester and Balliol. He was prodigiously
intelligent and prodigiously industrious and even before he took his degree
at Oxford he seemed set for a career as a classics don. His degree was in
Lit. Hum., commonly known as Greats, which required a knowledge of
languages, literature, philosophy and archaeology as well as history. All
his life he read philosophers of all ages, including his own, wrote poetry in
Greek and Latin as well as English and even wrote a letter to *The Times*
in Greek verse. In so far as the university system permitted he was a
generalist rather than a specialist although within this general education
his specialism was Greek and Roman history. His career, however, was
quickly deflected from the university by the Great War and in spite of some
postwar flirtation with university appointments he became one of those

figures whom it is difficult to locate in conventional categories, particularly when he acquired two distinct roles which were at first sight poles apart. The first of these was his work at Chatham House where, as it turned out, he spent his entire working life.

Ill health debarred Toynbee from active war service so that instead of going into the trenches he became an early example of the backroom boy recognised as more useful behind a desk than as cannon fodder. When the war ended he proceeded to the Peace Conference and so to the foothills of public affairs, for which he discovered in himself a taste. And not just a taste. Like many people in that war and the next he felt an obligation to contribute in peacetime too to public affairs and so to veer away from the more serene and cloistered paths of a university career. Like Keynes, his near contemporary and intellectual equal, Toynbee returned from the Peace Conference feeling that things could have been a great deal better managed. His task there had been to provide politicians with some knowledge of the past to help them give the future a sensible start. The conference boosted the notion that international affairs would be better conducted in the context of an enlightened public opinion and these two strands – the tutoring of the mandarins and the education of the public – led to the creation of Chatham House where, a few years later, Toynbee settled for life with the job of producing an Annual Survey of International Affairs and with the title of Director of Studies. Over fourteen years he produced 21 volumes in the Survey series and wrote the bulk of them himself. Although he simultaneously held a Chair in the University of London the Institute, not the University, was his base and the Surveys were the first call on his time and his mind.

Their aim in his time – and again for a few years after the resumption of the series by me after the Second World War – was to produce each year an account of world affairs in the previous year. Toynbee's Surveys did much to make 'contemporary history' respectable against the view of historians who maintained that the very idea of contemporary history was a contradiction in terms: in my days at Oxford in the thirties history stopped before the eclipse of Bismarck. Toynbee may have been encouraged to flout this limit by his familiarity with Thucydides who wrote about the stirring crises of his own time or, even more, Polybius who in the days before newspaper clippings missed no opportunity of buttonholing a living witness or tramping over a scene of action. But given the academic disdain of contemporary history the inception of the Surveys as an attempt by historians to educate politicians and other public servants was a bold venture. It is hard to tell whether it succeeded. Although many such persons were happy to take an hour off to listen to lunchtime talks at Chatham House there is little in their memoirs to suggest that they read the Surveys – except in self-defence as when the Foreign Office seethed over Toynbee's passionate denunciation of Britain's failure to stop the Italians from gassing the Ethiopians. Toynbee was an emotional man with an admirable capacity for indignation and an ingrained sympathy for underdogs: for the Turks, for example, after the First World War and in his unfulfilled wish to see a history of the Punic Wars written from the Carthaginian point of view.

One of the attractions of Chatham House for Toynbee was the freedom it gave him to pursue simultaneously with the Surveys his cherished and vastly ambitious plan for a *Study of History*. At first sight the Surveys and the *Study* seemed wholly unrelated enterprises but that appearance derives largely from a single feature – their utterly different timescale. They share, however, a common field which Toynbee brought to the Surveys from his early reflections for the *Study*. That field is the world as the habitat of mankind: the whole world but the world in relation to man and increasingly under the dominion of man. The Surveys contributed to the conversion of the British intelligentsia from parochialism and Eurocentrism to globalism, a shift of vision in politics and economics not unlike the Copernican revolution in the natural sciences. Secondly, both Toynbee's Surveys and his *Study* are infused with the powerful element of faith alongside and sometimes in conflict with the innate rationality which moulded his erudition and his judgment. In current world affairs, from the Peace Conference to the Abyssinian crisis, Toynbee placed his faith in the liberal and rational humanism which underpinned the League of Nations, but when the League failed adequately to confront that crisis he was thrown into violent dispair. He devoted an entire volume of the Survey for that year to the crisis and put the whole of the rest of the world into a separate volume; he thought the world lost; he threw up his hands, lost his faith in the League and transferred it blindly to God. Likewise, the first six volumes of the *Study* are constructed round the concept of human civilisations but the sequels transfer the focus, much less optimistically, to religions.

There was in Toynbee an element of instability, something more than uncertainty, which was evident in his private and his professional life. Traumatic events such as the suicide of his eldest son and the collapse of his first marriage tormented him to the verge of madness. He had mystical experiences on a number of occasions, moments when he apprehended a cosmic current passing through him and glimpsed a great truth, incidents not easily reconciled with the quest for historical truth by modern scholarly procedures. They created an acute conflict which is most manifest in the *Study*. The *Study* uses rational language and rational modes of argument to chart the rise and fall of human civilisations, the entities which Toynbee first defined and identified as the basic material for his *Study*, but he also mystically leaves open a small window of escape for our own civilisation. He presents a grimly deterministic world with ourselves helplessly perched on the verge of disaster but perhaps redeemable by a sporting flash of mutant will. Not, however, free will. Toynbee's history presents a recurrent pattern modifiable not by chance (as some might grant) but by choice, yet not by free human choice since the choice has been put into the system from the outside by God. Toynbee applied in human history methods used by natural science to explore and explain the cosmos, the planet and everything in the planet bar human destiny. He then invoked the supernatural in an escape clause – a familiar dramatic device from the days of Aeschylus – in order to conclude that in human affairs the patterns revealed in the past may after all not rule the future.

Toynbee's *Study of History* is a goldmine of footnotes and appendices wrapped round a spate of discourse on a stupendous theme. The trouble of course is the theme. Toynbee sketched his master plan on a scrap of paper in his youth and held to it thereafter with extraordinary inflexibility. At one point he drew up provisions for the execution of his plan by others if he should die young. He gave them considerable latitude but insisted that his outline remain sacrosanct. On the other hand this certainty was offset by doubts. In private he would refer to his *magnum opus* as his 'nonsense book' and in a grand international colloquy towards the end of his life he failed plausibly to defend his grand theme.

The *Study* starts with definitions which Toynbee tries to establish as nearly as circumstances permit to Euclidean axioms or unimpeachable starting points. He defines his unit of study, enumerates extinct and surviving examples, posits laws of their organic rise and fall and their interactions or, as he tellingly calls them, affiliations. All this has been sharply attacked and derided: civilisations – his chosen units – are not organic and their history cannot be explained morphologically. That term comes in the subtitle of Spengler's no less celebrated contribution to controversy and Spengler was thinking of Goethe's work on plants. But humans are not plants and there is no sufficient ground for equating human societies with natural species. Furthermore, critics continue, history has no laws or patterns apart from generalisations which are so broad as to be neither specific to historians nor useful to them as such. Yet Toynbee's impulse, if not his chosen path, was more human than vegetable, for he was looking for explanations and that is an uniquely human endeavour. On this analysis the flaw in the *Study* is not the quest but the analogy by which it is pursued. And this flaw, if it be admitted, means that the *Study* is not history. But if not history, what? Is it a rhapsody – an appropriately vast and Homerically repetitive elaboration of achievements and calamities pointing a moral, and above all a prophetic, tale? Or is it apologetic theology by the back door? Or an illusion, like perhaps the Beatific Vision upon which Toynbee set his gaze on the day when he concluded his great work? These are valid questions but not the basic ones. The value of the *Study* lies in the very grandeur of its conception, in the richness of its stuffing and in the implied assertion that such summations ought to be essayed. Toynbee has been compared with Herodotus and Thucydides but I prefer to liken him to Plato, or Jung – mind-stretching myth-makers. Or to those Victorian polymath-pedagogues who pursued knowledge for its own sake but also with the obligation to present its lessons to the public with unashamed superiority. Like, for example, Ruskin lecturing the working classes on morality, taste, industrialism and suchlike grand themes, so Toynbee told historians to take a deep breath and have a go; and since he himself did so with immense learning and seriousness and more than a dash of imagination he enriched the store of knowledge and ideas of the rest of us.

As a colleague Toynbee was accessible, friendly, without side, ready to advise and help but readier still to let you get on with your work on your own. In my five years in Chatham House he was still Director of Studies, was actively involved in organising the team of writers who were filling the gap in the Surveys between 1938 and 1947 (where I took up), and was writing more volumes of his own *Study*. Over and above all these commitments he was becoming a univeral sage, particularly in the United States and later in Japan where at one point he assumed the mixed role of the Pythian oracle and an intellectual agony aunt, answering questions about the fate of the world and mankind daily over several months in a leading Tokyo newspaper. He remained as zestful as ever over current affairs. I remember his elation at the news that the United States had resolved to counter with force North Korea's invasion of South Korea. During the morning coffee break in Chatham House he was sitting with a few of us at one of the small formica-clad tables peculiar to canteens and proclaiming with rapid sentences and bright eyes his belief that here was a saviour with a sword, a correct response to a crisis, a moment of hope.

Writing the Surveys was arduous, absorbing, enjoyable and immensely instructive, both for its worldwide scope and in the techniques of handling the very raw material and shaping it into accurate and intelligible and readable nuggets. It expanded my horizons from European affairs, with which I was relatively familiar from my university days, into larger and remoter areas about which I knew to begin with precious little. It was exciting to learn more, not merely from the newspaper cuttings of yesteryear but also from history books where I sought the necessary background to the current affairs of, for example, Latin America or Africa. Writing the Surveys required discrimination, conciseness and a good intellectual digestion. The indispensable bedrock of the work was the famous Chatham House press cutting library (later sadly attentuated) which was run by a small army of girls who cut, sorted, tabulated, filed and cross-referenced a mountain of material from all over the world. My practice was to use half a dozen papers comprehensively and up to fifty more in varying degrees for special areas. My assistant and I were always awash with papers and notes, and the key to getting a whole year's events chronicled in eleven months (the twelfth, one hoped, was holiday) was ordering one's material and one's thoughts with rigorous, even ruthless, method. My last volume, covering 1953, was followed by one more produced on these lines but thereafter the size of the Survey team was expanded and so, ironically, was the interval between the year surveyed and the appearance of the relevant volume until eventually the whole series was abandoned.

I expected to stay in Chatham House for all my working life but I fell out with the Director-General (as he had pompously come to be entitled) and in spite of offers of eventual promotion to either his or Toynbee's position I insisted on resigning. My resignation unexpectedly produced one of the most disagreeable experiences of my life. I had expected to go quietly but when the Institute's Council heard of my departure it asked to learn from my own mouth why I was doing this. The Council consisted of about twenty elders drawn from Academia, the City and the Services and I was duly ushered into the presence of this puissant body sitting round the traditional oblong table, in this case polished wood rather than green baize. I delivered my critique of the running of the Institute which, as I saw it, was crassly insensitive and self-glorifying and in a Parthian shot I averred that, so far from being eccentric or isolated in my views, I differed from my colleagues only in having a private income (about £1,200) which enabled me to risk expressing them. I hated the whole proceeding which gave me nightmares before and afterwards. My embarrassment and discomfort must have been apparent to some at least of the Council, since the next day I received kind notes from two of its members (Elizabeth Monroe and Alan Bullock) – gestures which count. I also learned what two other Councillors had had to say. The one, a professor, said: 'This Council has not been doing its job.' The other, an Air Chief Marshal, said: 'In the Services we do not allow people to talk like that.' The upshot shortly afterwards was that I was myself elected to the Council on which I served until 1972 when my appointment to Penguin caused me to resign all part-time positions, and the Director-General was given a knighthood and invited to resign. On his resignation I was offered his job but it seemed to me unfair to abandon so abruptly the friends who had taken me into partnership in the publishing house of Chatto & Windus when I left the Institute. The offer from Chatham House was repeated some years later but by that time my career was set in a different direction and I again said, regretfully, no.

After leaving Chatham House I maintained my interest and my active involvement in international affairs through two regular commitments: a monthly symposium which I ran for about sixteen years and a commission to write a weekly column which I fulfilled for about the same length of time. The symposium or dining club was nicknamed – by Andrew Boyd of the *Economist*, if I remember right – the Speakeasy. It was a very pleasant affair. It was started by myself and a few friends for the profitable discussion of some international topic and, in equal measure, in order to have an enjoyable evening. At first we met in a private room in some Soho restaurant or West End club but later and for most of its life in our flat above the offices of Chatto & Windus near Trafalgar Square. Its members were all professionally involved in foreign affairs as teachers, scholars, journalists, civil servants, cultural bureaucrats or indefinables. We regaled ourselves for an hour and then discussed a preset topic for an hour and a half, with or without a guest who might have been caught by one of us on the wing through London. At first we had no diplomats because we feared that they would listen and say nothing, but when we broke this rule we found in them some of our best members: Duncan Wilson, Denis Wright, Paul Gore-Booth, Adam Watson, Peter Ramsbotham and more – but a fluctuating category since they tended to slip away to foreign postings. Members of Parliament on the other hand were a dead loss because they too often found something more urgent or more appealing to do at the last moment: we gave them up as a bad job. The discussions were well informed, constructive, relaxed, witty. I cannot remember anybody ever getting cross. Absurdly we never had women in spite of a succession of attempts by me and others to breach this silly and anachronistic barrier. The only woman ever to attend the Speakeasy did so when Guy Wint got Owen Lattimore to come and talk about Mongolia and he refused to do so unless he might bring his wife with him.

The task I set myself in the Speakeasy was to nudge the discussion of current problems a little way into the future. It is easy enough for a group of well informed and intelligent persons to debate and dissect the present with the necessary reference to the relevant past, and it is easy enough to allow an hour or so to go by doing nothing else, but the special value of our evenings was the attempt to look forward, not impossibly far but far enough to give present problems a pragmatic as well as an academic context. This was not too difficult given our membership but it required a certain diligence in spotting and spurring a likely line of thought thrown up in the course of our exchanges. Scholars of the quality of Geoffrey Hudson and Martin Wight, rooted in the past by their professions, proved notably valuable in probing the future. We could too, in the twilight of empire, draw on the unusual experience of people such as Philip Mason or Maurice Zinkin whose years of service in India imported into our circle not only close knowledge of distant parts but also the character and attitudes of men who had been entrusted from an early age with responsibility in governing and passing judgment: a whiff of wisdom on top of cleverness. Among the most valuable of our members were the unpredictables. They were not without their convictions, even prejudices, but they were men who used their convictions as a springboard to enlarge, not to foreclose, argument, while the uncertainty about where in argument they would come down gave spice and weight to their contributions: Alastair Buchan, for example, or Paul Bareau or Christopher Dilke. The tone of these gatherings was optimistic. Our group assumed that it knew a lot and could learn a lot more and put this learning to good use. But our main purpose was to inform one another and we did not suppose that we had any more public role. I think it fair to say that no members of the Speakeasy displayed self-importance. I received many protests when I decided to decree the Speakeasy's demise, but after sixteen years I felt that we were getting a little stale and predictable and that we should bring a singularly successful venture to a close instead of allowing it to run down.

Alongside the Speakeasy but four times as often I would sit down to write a short piece on foreign affairs for syndication in the provincial papers owned by the Westminster Press. I nearly came unstuck at the start by writing an article condemning the Suez War, not so much on the grounds that it was immoral or illegal (which it was) but because it was idiotic. The editor-in-chief of the group rang me up to say that their head office took the opposite view. They thought that it was a good war. After some argument he agreed to run my piece so long as I did not object to a leader on the same page saying the opposite. Writing this column was excellent discipline. I had to compress what I had to say into 800-1,000 words and I had to be perfectly clear about what I wanted to say. I was writing for readers who were presumed to be interested in what was going on in the world but were not expert or even at all well informed. So I needed to make two or at the most three points precisely and without any of the sophisticated circumlocutions with which well educated writers contrive to hide the fact that they cannot quite make up their minds. Initially I was invited to contribute for four weeks, the idea being that a succession of different writers would take over the job from month to month (I was the second), but the proprietors forgot to look around for my successor and I carried on for sixteen years. During most of that time the proprietors forgot also to raise my pay. Foreign, incidentally, meant anything anywhere so long as it was not in Ireland.

These two regular occupations, the one monthly and the other weekly, were my main but not my only peripheral commitments in these years. I served also on the governing bodies of Chatham House and the Institute for Strategic Studies; I was for nine years a member of the UN Sub-Commission for the Prevention of Discrimination and the Protection of Minorities; I was chairman of the Africa Bureau, and a strange encounter with Amnesty led to a stint on its International Executive. All these were positions from which I could look and learn more about world affairs.

When the war ended few people in Britain had noticed how much it had affected Africa. The eviction of the Italians from their empires in Ethiopia, Somaliland and Libya, followed by the departure of the British from India immediately after the war, gave decolonisation in Africa an actuality which it altogether lacked a few years earlier. Before the war decolonisation was talked about but only in the vaguest way and without any attempt at a timetable. Even after the war the end of colonialism, although envisageable, was barely visible: African leaders themselves toyed with dates round about the last quarter of the century. Yet in 1956 the Gold Coast was promised independence the next year and by 1960 most of the French and British colonies in west and central Africa and the Belgian Congo became independent. If the pace in east Africa seemed more leisurely it was nevertheless expedited by the Mau Mau insurrection in Kenya which, besides temporarily holding up the process, at the same time instilled into the British the need to move ahead in order to escape from the perils of having again to commit an alarming proportion of their armed forces – some 50,000 troops – to master a few bands of a few hundred guerillas in one colony, a task which took six years and £60 million.

The Africa Bureau came into existence in response to this general situation. In Britain African independence was on few people's agenda and high up on fewer. The only safe generalisation about the British and Africa was that they knew where it was. Of Africans and African history they knew virtually nothing. African history was not taught in schools or even in universities where it was a non-subject except as an adjunct of the history of British colonial endeavours and conflict between European states. Africa had none of the glamour of India. There were in Britain a number of people who felt more familiar with India than the European continent – the wogs in India, unlike those in Europe, were at least our wogs – but nobody felt that way about Africa. Yet it by no means followed that the British would not care about the loss of colonial possessions. Decolonisation might be seen as feeble, humiliating, a dangerous blow to prestige and whatever of power and profit goes with prestige. Appearing unexpectedly on the international agenda decolonisation could cause spasms which would be all the more harmful owing to the prevailing ignorance about African affairs and African leaders and their intentions. One of the Bureau's functions therefore was to spread correct information about what was going on in Africa – a task better assumed by an unofficial body than by government or by political parties, even supposing these were willing and competent to tackle the job.

There was a no less important counterpart. Leading figures in Africa knew what they wanted for their countries but did not know a great deal about the workings of the government in Britain from which they had to get what they wanted, i.e. independence and post-independence links political and economic. They needed also to know about and, if possible, influence the state of public opinion in Britain. The Bureau helped to get them interviews with politicians and newspaper editors, instructing them in advance that this one was genial but a fool, another was interested and well informed, a third a boor on his way to a knighthood. On both sides – the African and the British – there was a need to dispel ignorance, facilitate communication and lessen the resentments and hostility which decolonisation might otherwise be expected to arouse. Two episodes showed the dangers lurking in the situation.

The first was the banishment from Bechuanaland of Seretse Khama by the British government. Seretse was heir to the Chieftaincy of the Bamangwato and was duly elected to this position in 1949, but the previous year he had married a white girl and the South African government, which outlawed mixed marriages in 1949, demanded that Britain should refuse

to recognise Seretse's position on the specious grounds that the marriage
had so sorely divided the people of Bechuanaland that Seretse should not
be allowed to succeed to his hereditary position as Paramount Chief.
Britain caved in, refused to recognise Seretse and banned him from his
own country. (He was allowed back in 1956 and was successively Prime
Minister and President before he died in 1980.) The second episode
concerned the Kabaka of Buganda, heir to a monarchical title bestowed on
his family by the British in 1900 on condition that its bearer should do
what he was told by the colonial power in Uganda, of which Buganda was
a part. The Kabaka was caught in two traps. On the one hand he was under
obligations to the British but he had also come to distrust their intentions:
he interpreted some silly remarks by a British minister in London as
evidence that Britain was planning to create in East Africa a federation
on the Rhodesian model which would be dominated indefinitely by the
white settlers of Kenya. On the other hand the Kabaka, as monarch in
Buganda, distrusted the wider Ugandan freedom movement whose aim
was an independent Uganda in which Buganda and its ruler would lose
their separate identity and status. The Kabaka, who was not in all respects
an admirable young man, quarrelled with the exceptionally liberal British
governor of Uganda who in 1953 exercised his power to send the Kabaka
packing. He went into exile for two years. After his return he made an
adventitious alliance with Milton Obote's freedom movement and was
eventually rewarded with the presidency (1963-66) of independent Uganda
until it suited Obote to make himself president.

The merits of these two episodes were different but both had a disagreeable smell. The treatment of Seretse Khama was scandalous and the
Kabaka was a victim of anachronistic highhandedness: he, too, although
not blameless, had a case and the right to have it heard in Britain which
was still the ultimate ruler over Uganda. There was a need for accurate
and dispassionate accounts of what was being done and the Bureau filled
this need. But at the same time the Bureau was also something different
and rather odd. It existed to support the efforts, the principles and the life's
work of one man: Michael Scott.

Michael Scott was a single-minded man. He was also a good man. He
knew right from wrong, good from evil, and he devoted his life to righting
wrongs – principally but not exclusively in Africa where he was born and
took Holy Orders as a Christian priest. He hated injustice, particularly
when it stemmed from racial contempt. He was horribly pained by the
racial brutality in South Africa which for him was not only an affront to
his principles but an almost physical hurt. He was bitterly disappointed
by the strong-arm methods adopted by some leaders in new African states,
whom he rebuked privately. He was not an easy man to work with or for,
partly because he saw the world and its problems in extraordinarily simple
terms and brushed aside complexities as merely subordinate impediments.
Incapable of conspiracy himself, he was nevertheless inclined to spot

malevolent combinations, particularly capitalist machinations, as explanations for the persistence of manifest evils and he spent in consequence some time barking up trees which were no more than shrubs. But these were the minor faults of a man who commanded trust and an often awed admiration.

The Bureau, although it revolved round Michael Scott, was not created by him. It was created by David Astor, one of numerous enterprises which he animated in his curiously covert way. David Astor did a great deal of largely unnoticed good. Being very rich was a help but the main force was his determination to make good use of his talents and his money. He was not the only very rich newspaper proprietor but he was unique among them in the thoughtfulness of the ways he chose to apply his wealth. He spanned conventional divides. He was a good judge of persons but was over-diffident about his own considerable abilities. He was a thinking man who did no good in the conventional academic sense at Oxford. He was kind as well as generous but could also be tough and, I suspect, did not lose too much sleep when he felt compelled to act hardly. He did not like the limelight and so he would start things and then find others to take the lead and, very often, the credit. He was a man with courage and a great deal of common sense and quiet mischievous humour. He once rang me up rather late at night and after some beating about the bush asked me if I might find the time to write a book which he had in mind. When I asked what book he replied: a life of Lord Beaverbrook. I expressed surprise and reluctance since I did not see myself as a biographer and was not attracted by the subject. He then added that the book would probably not be published – not an added inducement. I asked him what he was up to. He explained that he had heard that Beaverbrook was commissioning a book about Lady Astor, his mother, the purpose of which was to be disobliging about her. Whatever his views about his mother's public and political activities (and I did not know what they were) he was going to do what he could to stop attacks on her by Beaverbrook. So he had hit upon the idea of getting a disobliging book written about Beaverbrook as a deterrent to a Beaverbrook book about his mother. The aim was that neither would see the light of day. I was not captivated by this plan, although I was tickled by the motives and the bizarre ingenuity. Nothing came of it.

The Africa Bureau was not one of those organisations which have members. It had a guiding committee and it had a secretary. The committee was one of the best I have known. It was recruited mainly by David Astor and contained at one time or another men and women of the calibre of Jock Campbell, Rita Hinden, Colin Legum, Mary Benson, Andrew Cohen, Elizabeth Longford, Peter Parker. The Bureau could not have existed without David Astor or Michael Scott – or without its secretary Jane Simmonds. She acquired an amazing knowledge of African personalities and problems, understood Michael Scott's aims and peculiarities, extemporised solutions to impossible situations and ran an organisation centred on an individual who was the antithesis of organisation man. Historians will find that the Bureau played an honourable and considerable part in providing Africa's new men with advice on how to present their case to British officials, politicians and journalists – in the absence of the Bureau most of the advice would have come from the Communist Party – and in persuading the British public that decolonisation was not the end of the world. The Bureau was not purely political. It established an Education Trust to help young Africans to get training in Britain, particularly in nursing.

My connection with the Africa Bureau brought me some strange experiences. One day I got a telephone call from an unknown man who wanted to see and consult me and came to my London flat. He was a young white South African and he was very frightened. He had fled South Africa with a quantity of documents which he intended to use in writing a book which the authorities were determined to nip in the bud. He had entrusted the documents to a friend and was living in rooms, flitting from one place to another. He told me his story calmly and coherently but from time to time he trembled. He told me of sinister men who trailed and jostled him on the platform of underground stations and had followed him into Hyde Park and made as if to throw him into the Serpentine. Whether these men meant to kill or terrify him I could not tell. He was less uncertain; he feared the worst. I told him to get his papers copied, lodge them in a bank and let his persecutors know that duplicates existed out of their possible grasp. I related his story to a friend who had worked for a time in MI5 and had also been a junior minister: he knew what are called the right people. I never learned precisely what happened but I was given to understand that the thugs had been warned off and many years later I noticed in a newspaper that their intended victim was back in South Africa. At the time when he came to see me the practices which he intended to reveal were not commonly known or believed beyond South Africa. On another occasion an African from another part of the continent, a man who had fallen from high estate to manual work, came with a white friend to tell me his political enemies were after him and that he was afraid for his life. He was right. Not long afterwards he was killed.

People love to say how much they hate committees and committees can be a dreadful waste of time, but a good committee with a purposeful exchange of views is as enjoyable as it is useful. I have been lucky with the various committees or boards which I have known. I recall particularly the committee of the London Library of which I was for a time chairman. There are three ground rules for a chairman. First, do not talk too much. Second, do not allow anybody else to talk too much. It is useful to remember that if you have to deflate one member he may be miffed but all the others will be delighted and will tell each other after the meeting what a good chairman they have. Third, establish the rule that every meeting ends sixty minutes after it begins and see that this rule is kept much more often than not.

David Astor was again the man through whom I became associated with Amnesty. I was introduced to it in a most bizarre way. David Astor asked me to meet three or four people in his home. When I got there they asked me to undertake an inquiry into ructions which, they said, were destroying Amnesty. I had to say that I had never heard of it. It had been brought into existence in 1961 by an advertisement in the *Observer* and by the vision and enthusiasm of two men in particular: first and foremost Peter Benenson but also Neville Vincent. It invented the phrase 'prisoner of conscience' to denote persons imprisoned for their beliefs and for no other reason and campaigned to get them out of prisons all over the world. Besides inspiring Amnesty's activities Peter Benenson directed them personally for the first few years. In 1965 he appointed Robert Swann to be director of the organisation which was still quite small and operating on the proverbial shoestrings provided by a few wealthy well-wishers. It was, however, spreading from Britain to other countries by the establishment of other national groups with the same aims and affiliated through an International Executive Committee. By 1967, when I made its acquaintance, Amnesty had become an unhappy place. Benenson and Swann did not get on and Benenson suspected Swann of using Amnesty for ulterior purposes and so putting its repute and very existence at risk. The purpose of my inquiry was to give the Executive Committee an independent appraisal of these internal commotions and one of the people whom I met at David Astor's house was the International Executive's chairman, Sean MacBride – Irish lawyer and former Foreign Minister of Ireland. I had never met MacBride or Benenson or Swann. I agreed to do what they asked of me on condition that Peter Benenson agreed, which he did when the proposal was put to him. I then conducted in my flat in London what amounted to a private one-man commission and came to the conclusion that Peter Benenson had been mistaken in his suspicions and accusations. He was, I think, surprised and he was certainly angry with me, although many years later, when we happened to run into one another at a party, he came up to me and generously conceded that I had done well by Amnesty and incidentally for him. My report was considered by the Executive at a special meeting convened with elaborate secrecy at Elsinore in Denmark, each copy being carefully collected each evening and locked away from prying eyes. Amnesty was understandably anxious to safeguard its reputation from the likely effects of gossip in the press. Soon afterwards Robert Swann resigned. Although I had told the Executive that charges against him were insubstantial there had been circumstances surrounding his original appointment which could damage Amnesty and both he himself and the Executive Committee considered that he had better go. His departure was a loss to Amnesty and so was Benenson's, but circumstances necessitated both. Intermittently for years afterwards some journalist or other would get in touch with me and probe me about my report and ask if I had kept a copy. I always replied that I had no copy, which was a lie.

In the course of my inquiries I came greatly to admire what Amnesty was trying to do and so I was delighted to be invited to join its Executive. I was also asked to become Director and I was much tempted, particularly when urged to do so by Robert Birley for whom I had special respect. But I would have had to give up most, if not all, of what I was doing including the University teaching which I had begun only two years earlier. I remained on the Executive and was asked a few years later to be a candidate for the chairmanship of its International Executive. The circumstances were these. MacBride was in many ways an excellent chairman for Amnesty. He was very intelligent; he was genuinely concerned for its aims; his international connections were invaluable; and he was skilful in managing an international committee, by hook or crook. But when trouble in Northern Ireland made its way into Amnesty's ambit his partisanship raised some eyebrows. I advised him and so did others that he should cede the chairmanship whenever Anglo-Irish matters came up, but although he assented he could not bring himself to do so. It was the obvious thing to do, as must have been clear to a man of his intelligence, but partly out of vanity – he wanted to insist on his ability to rise above prejudice – and partly too out of the very partisanship which his critics imputed to him he carried on as though Anglo-Irish affairs were no different from any others. Nor did his acknowledged qualities dispel the disturbing feeling that he loved to be devious, so that even if he were broadly right in his anti-English stance on particular issues he ceased to command the confidence of colleagues for whom rectitude and the appearance of rectitude were everything. I was approached by members of the Executive who wanted to displace him when his time for re-election came, but although I thought that MacBride was behaving badly I did not like the conspiratorial manner in which his removal was being compassed and so I refused to stand against him and he was re-elected. I remained on the Executive and gave special attention to developing Amnesty's research departments which were essential to sustaining the credibility of its reports, and I resigned only when the press of other business made it difficult for me to give enough of my attention to its affairs. As it happened these affairs were about to be transformed. Its influence and good standing – even with governments – were steadily increasing and in the seventies its starveling fortunes turned into affluence when the award of the Nobel Prize for Peace brought cash as well as acclaim. With a combination of wise guidance and growing resources Amnesty won worldwide credibility, a remarkable achievement. Fewer and fewer governments were able to scout its strictures or refuse to permit its investigations, since to do so was tantamount to self-condemnation.

Amnesty became as important as any organisation in the world. This is a big claim but it can be justified. Amnesty's task is to combat the gravest scourge and disgrace of the twentieth century – the recrudescence of injustice and inhumanity in their most appalling form, torture. I have said in an earlier chapter that the anti-semitism which culminated in the piteously nauseating slaughter of millions of Jews in the Nazis' new-model slaughterhouse may be counted the biggest blot on Europe's civilisation with the possible exception of the slave trade, but torture, practised or condoned by governments all over the world, afflicts many more millions than the victims of the holocaust. There was a time when torture, in Europe at least, seemed to be receding in the comparatively enlightened climate of the eighteenth century. The Milanese marquis, mathematician, econo-mist and criminologist C.B. Beccaria wrote a pamphlet on crimes and their punishment which denounced the death penalty and torture, was trans-lated into virtually every European language (the French version had a preface by Voltaire) and won influential attention as far afield as the Russia of Catherine the Great and Revolutionary France. The optimism of the next century contributed to the belief that torture was permanently and progressively in decline but the twentieth century has belied this belief, so that Amnesty's concern with prisoners of conscience broadened naturally into a campaign against the barbarous treatment of all prison-ers. The thoroughness and carefulness of its investigations and reports have given its strictures a credibility and force which less well grounded pressure groups cannot command and its work has had undoubted, if unmeasurable, success in relation both to individual victims and to the sluggish awareness of public opinion. I believe that I was of some service to Amnesty at an early and critical stage in its existence and I am proud of that.

In 1965 the University of Sussex created a part-time Readership in International Relations and offered it to me. This was done at the instiga-tion of Martin Wight who was one of the university's founding fathers and one of the most accomplished scholars and inspiring teachers of his generation. When accepting the offer I wrote that I did so on the condition that I would sit on no committee – a condition which elicited no reply because it was taken mistakenly to be a joke. I taught at Sussex for seven years. These were years when people outside the universities, and some inside, were wringing their hands over the awfulness of the young, par-ticularly the university young. There were fusses at Sussex from time to time and on one occasion a student threw a pot of paint at a visiting ambassador, but the students whom I knew and taught were admirable and likeable and hard-working and, so far as I could tell, counted them-selves fortunate to be at the university. Their handwriting was far worse than their manners.

The expression 'international affairs' covers a number of overlapping subjects. For some it is synonymous with current affairs, meaning com-mentary on what is going on in the world. Commenting on current affairs is an aspect of journalism with as a by-product the occasional ephemeral book. Its purpose is to explain although many of the people who tune in to it want prophecy as well as explanation. The prudent writer sticks to explanation, leaving his readers to deduce prophecies if they want to. There is, secondly, recent or contemporary history. There is no hard and fast line between recent history and current affairs. It is just as futile to try to explain current affairs without a sound historical background, as it is to sever one chunk of history from an earlier chunk. The writer on current affairs limits his excursion into the past in order not to overburden his explanation of the present; for equally practical reasons the historian limits his advance into the present in order to avoid entanglement in matters which are still so far submerged and inchoate as to be unsuitable for his professional discipline. Thirdly, international relations is more than either current affairs or contemporary history. It is a complex academic subject for which an historical background is essential and, in my view, primal. It is also a branch of politics in the academic sense – invented by Macchiavelli – of the study of the relations between independent states, what they are and how they may best be conducted. And it requires some knowledge of international law and international organisations. This complexity makes international relations a difficult subject to teach to undergraduates, since some of them come to it with little history, most of them with less politics and virtually all of them with no law. Starting from scratch is no bad thing but starting from different points creates awkward problems, most noticeable in relation to history: some of my pupils at Sussex knew a good deal of nineteenth and early twentieth century history while others seemed uncertain of the differences between Metternich and Bismarck. Against these problems, however, was the considerable advantage that students who chose international relations did so because they really wanted to do it. It was not a subject that they drifted into because they could not think what to do or because they thought it a soft option.

The forty years after the Second World War constituted in international terms a strangely odd period. It was a period dominated by the Cold War between the Superpowers, by the conversion first of Europe and then the whole world into fields of battle between these two enemies and their allies, and by the development of nuclear weapons as their principal weapons of war with unprecedented but untestable catastrophic possibilities. The Cold War was a state of affairs which overshadowed everything else, and yet it was also in my view phoney – in this sense, that I did not believe that the Cold War was a prelude to a shooting war or that nuclear weapons were at all likely to be used by the protagonists. There is no way of being certain about the future but it is always a mistake to allow the horrors of what is possible to turn possibility into probability, and when the two main crises of the Cold War – the Berlin crisis of 1948-49 and the Cuban crisis of 1962 – both passed without a shot being fired I held ever more strongly that a war between the Superpowers was extremely improbable. The arms race was not so much a race to the abyss as an appalling piece of economic lunacy and the debates between learned strategists about the numbers of nuclear warheads, launchers etc. on either side reminded me of the equally learned arguments between medieval theologians about the number of angels who could without jostling dance on the point of a small needle.

The Cold War was a reality which ballooned out of myths. It owed much to old antagonisms and distrust but more to misconceptions, miscalculations and plain mutual ignorance. Stalin feared in 1945, as he had feared in the thirties, a western alliance to attack him and destroy the Soviet Union, but although the West hated communism it had not the slightest intention of starting a war against it. The West feared that Stalin would use his victory over Germany to advance his armies further into Europe, even to the Atlantic, and subvert western Europe through communist parties, but his exhausted armies and shattered economy had not the slightest capacity for any such ventures and western communist parties were never more than a moderate nuisance in the few countries where they counted at all. In its course the Cold War created a new myth – the myth that the Superpowers were roughly equals, a proposition that was never true or even nearly true. It promoted and accelerated the revival of Germany and Japan which, undertaken by the United States in the mistaken belief that the Korean War was the first act in a Russian bid for worldwide dominion, made Germany the greatest power in Europe within little more than a generation after the defeat of Hitler and made Japan within a similar timespan the greatest rival to American economic power in the world. It wrecked the economy of the Soviet Union and, aided by the profligacy and inanities of the Reagan years, demoted the United States from its extraordinary pre-eminence in world affairs. And it distracted attention from an enormously important and entirely new problem.

This was the problem of how major Powers may secure for themselves essential resources which lie outside their own territories. The answer to this problem had been relatively simple: use the power you have to get the resources you need either by seizing the territory which contains them or by making it clear that you will seize it if the resources are not made available to you in quantities and at prices which satisfy you: use force or at least look as though you are ready and willing to do so. But this solution had become anachronistic. Even the veiled imperialism called the mandate system which, between the World Wars, ensured to the major European Powers – Great Britain and France – the Middle Eastern oil which they needed had been abandoned, not least because the new Great Power – the United States – had denounced and then undermined it. Yet major Powers avid for essential foreign resources must get them; it is a function and even a duty of their governments to do so. Most essential was oil. The optimistic view that oil as the world's main source of energy was about to be replaced by nuclear power, home manufactured, quickly faded, leaving a number of lucky states in the Middle East sitting on a precious commodity which was both a source of wealth and a weighty political bargaining counter – called blackmail by those at the other end of the bargaining. Since the Middle East was, and in spite of new discoveries elsewhere remained, the main source of exportable oil I became more and more interested in that part of the world. When the war ended I knew comparatively little about it and I knew no Arabic, but I have always had a liking for learning about a subject on which I am ignorant rather than learning more about a subject on which I am not.

In one sense this deviation could be called flying off at a tangent, but it was not if I was right in judging that the Middle East was not a region among others but a region of more than regional importance. It raised therefore the question of the limits to the use of power in a world which was trying to extend the rule of law at the expense of the rule of the sword. In 1945 the founding members of the United Nations had gone so far as to abandon voluntarily and for ever the use of force except in self-defence, a revolutionary step, and yet it was to say the least doubtful whether the stronger among them would keep their word if threatened by the loss of whatever they might choose to call essential materials. The founders of the UN did not imagine that they could eliminate the use of force from international affairs. The UN Charter expressly provided for its use – but by the UN as a body and not by states on their own volition. The Charter made provision for UN forces and their uses but these provisions never came into effect, mainly because the Cold War turned the UN from an organ for collaboration into a forum for confrontations.

The Middle East most strikingly exemplified the dangers of this conjunction between the Cold War on the one hand and, on the other, the open question of how to secure the flow of oil from independent minor states to oil-hungry major ones. Whereas Europe, where a line was drawn dividing the spheres of the Superpowers, became the most stable area in the world, the Middle East was basically unstable. So long as the Cold War lasted neither Superpower dared, for fear of the other, to adopt policies in the Middle East which were not at the same time policies directed at one another. This situation was further complicated by the creation in one corner of the Middle East of the Jewish state of Israel and its virtual adoption by the United States as a strategic bastion of the Cold War. The United States' partiality for Israel was prompted by intense sympathy for Jews in the wake of revelations about the full horrors of the Nazi holocaust but also by the fear that Israel would incline to the Soviet Union rather than the United States: the Soviet Union was the first state to recognise the state of Israel and Israel's first rulers and leading spirits were aiming to create some sort of socialist paradise. But Israel's need for arms and money in quantities which only the United States could supply quickly converted it into alliance with and dependence on the United States. In addition, Israel, starting from a strategically weak position, committed itself to a policy which doomed it to perpetual warfare. It gained recognition as a state by accepting the UN plan for a Palestinian and an Israeli state but at the same time secretly conspired with the emir Abdullah of Transjordan for the seizure by him of what, under the UN plan, should have been the Palestinian state. Israel adopted as fundamental a refusal to accept any Palestinian state or acknowledge any distinct Palestinian identity. Since it had also irredentist (or biblical) claims against Jordan and Lebanon, and since the more distant Arabs – besides their anti-Israeli animus – felt uneasy about letting the Palestinians down, the prospects for peace in this part of the Middle East were extremely slim. One consequence was to drive the United States into an anti-Arab stance and construct a Middle East policy based on Iran, where its ally the Shah was eventually displaced by a passionately anti-American regime, and on Israel, whose military and budgetary requisitions, political intransigence and contempt for law increasingly embarrassed the United States. Obsessed by its humiliation at the hands of the new Iranian government the United States backed Iran's enemy Iraq which, besides other crimes, was preparing to attack Israel and to raise its stake in Middle East oil by wrecking Iran's and seizing Kuwait's. From this morass the United States was rescued by the Gorbachev revolution which both put an end to the Cold War in the Middle East as everywhere else and initiated the disintegration of the Soviet empire and the Soviet Union. A radically new set of problems emerged between 1985 and 1990. A dozen or more new or renovated states appeared in Europe alone, many of them with suppressed antagonisms endangering Europe's stability; conflicts in other areas were stripped of their Cold War context and constraints, whether with happy consequence or the reverse remained to be revealed; alliances and armouries which had formed the framework of international affairs lost their *raison d'être* – or perhaps did not; the UN appeared set to emerge from an ice age but whether under American leadership or American dictation was another question whose answer was buried in the future.

I greatly enjoyed teaching once I got into it. I was surprised by how much I enjoyed it, for after all many pupils are less than exciting and it can be a grind. But for me learning has always seemed incomplete without explaining and imparting. There is here an element of showing off, more pronounced in some teachers than others, but it does no harm to the pupil whatever it may tell about the teacher. I left Sussex because I got an entirely unexpected invitation to an exalted position in Penguin Books and in those days an offer from Penguin was something that few refused. Penguin left me no time for anything else, I resigned all my part-time commitments and virtually stopped writing, but when – as related in the next chapter – I was abruptly ousted from Penguin I reverted once more to foreign affairs and to writing books. My first book, first of nearly twenty, I wrote on my return from the Nuremberg trials; it was about those trials. At Chatham House my job was writing a book a year. The Suez War, two years after I left Chatham House, brought an offer to Guy Wint and myself to write a quick Penguin Special which we did in five weekends. Later, Guy and I worked together again on a much fatter book on the causes and courses of the Second World War, *Total War*, and at about the same time I undertook to write a book covering events throughout the world from 1945 onwards. This book, *World Politics since 1945*, I revised and rewrote every five years from its first appearance in 1968. From the end of the war I was rarely not writing a book. Collecting the material for a book, thinking about how best to organise and present it, setting it out in good flowing prose over blank sheets of paper – all these stages delight me. All my books except one have been about contemporary or nearly contemporary history, ending with an optimistic analysis of Europe's place in the world from Bismarck to the end of the twentieth century: *Resilient Europe*. The exception is a *Who's Who in the Bible*. How did I learn to write? By doing it *con amore*. I love sitting down before a clean sheet of paper, arranging facts and ideas, setting them out clearly and succinctly, choosing the right words and the fewer the better, with intelligence and perhaps a dash of enlivening wit.

8

Publishing

Publishing, so the saying used to go, is an occupation for gentlemen. This is an ambiguous characterisation. Gentlemen vary. This particular publishing gentleman was thought of as honourable, agreeable, well educated up to a point and somewhat relaxed, particularly around lunch time. When it came to salesmanship or reading a balance sheet he was, if not quite out of his depth, yet not in his natural milieu. He was, of course, male, but there were also plenty of females in publishing. Young girls flocked to it on their way to marriage, concubinage or nowhere in particular. Later, they were on their way to the top jobs.

But few publishers were like that. Most of them, like most of anything else, were competent people who were good at what they were doing, not brilliant but not fools, nice to meet and honest in their trade. Publishing also attracted an utterly different type who were few but prominent. These were the peacocks – self-indulgent poseurs, literary mountebanks or social climbers – who found in the book world a place to show off. They were a misery to work with and they were not good publishers since they were guilty of the cardinal sin of believing publishers to be more important than authors. But although they were not estimable and were certainly not gentlemen they could sometime be fun. Their besetting sin was vanity which, however unattractive, does less damage than the greediness which disfigured many of their successors.

Another category, a growing one, were the interlopers, the tycoons who bought up publishing businesses and peopled them with their satellites and sidekicks. These interlopers described themselves as publishers, which they were not since they knew little or nothing about publishing. Too often they had – in the words once used by one of my colleagues at Penguin to describe another – both feet well off the ground. A man does not become a publisher by walking into a publishing office and sitting down in a publisher's chair. The publisher needs skills, some of which are common throughout the business world: how to treat staff, how to read accounts, how to sell his wares, how to talk to his bankers. But however good he is at these things they do not make him a publisher and he is not entitled to call himself a publisher until he has mastered the skills peculiar to publishing. These are, first, the editorial function which entails deciding what kind of books you want to publish, finding good books, assessing manuscripts and making suggestions for shaping them for the better and with due regard to the author's susceptibilities; it entails also thinking ahead to the kind of list which your firm should have a few years on. The second qualification of the publisher is a combination of taste and know-how: choosing the typeface and the size of type, settling the page margins, ensuring that the text occupies an acceptable number of pages, designing the title page and other preliminary pages, choosing paper of the right quality and price, choosing illustrations or an illustrator, commissioning a jacket. I believe I got to know enough about the second function and more than enough about the first to qualify for the title of publisher, and I have commonly so described myself on documents ever since except where the title of barrister-in-law may make a more persuasive impression.

I was very lucky with my first incursion into publishing. Soon after the end of the war Ian Parsons, whom I had met transitorily during it, asked me to join Chatto & Windus as a partner. I was frying other fish at the time and so I declined, conscious, however, that I had been offered something exceptionally attractive. Books and the making of books fascinated me; I liked what I knew of the persons involved; I was looking for a new start and a new career; I liked the scale of things in the book trade and of a firm such as Chatto & Windus; I would have to learn a new trade but I supposed that I could. But the opportunity, besides taking me by surprise, came at the wrong moment. Some years later, when I resigned from Chatham House in circumstances which I have already explained, the invitation was repeated and I accepted it. I was a partner, later a director, in Chatto & Windus and The Hogarth Press for eleven years, the longest stint that I have ever devoted to anything except my own writing which has been going on in the background to whatever else has been occupying me.

Chatto & Windus was a firm which was customarily and correctly described as distinguished. It was distinguished by the quality of its authors and the quality of its book design and production. It was not one of the veterans of the trade like Longmans or John Murray, both born in the eighteenth century, nor was it what passed in those days for a giant: Macmillan or Heinemann, Collins or Hutchinson. It counted as medium-sized. It was most often bracketed with Faber or Jonathan Cape or Secker and Warburg, highbrow to middlebrow, literary, with a flavour of cosmopolitanism, but it was appreciably older than all these friendly rivals. Its beginnings had a certain ambiguity. Its founder, John Camden Hotten, son of a carpenter, was one of the buccaneers of the mid-Victorian book trade. After working as an apprentice to a bookseller he became his own master in 1855 and set up shop in Piccadilly on a site now overlaid by the Ritz Hotel. He was a man of mixed tastes who, before his death at the age of 43, had tacked publishing on to his bookselling and put his money into fine editions and into risky ones. He took on Swinburne when the poet's own publisher dropped him because of attacks on him for immorality, and he was prosecuted, unsuccessfully, for publishing Zola. He specialised in new American writers, pursuing this interest with piracy as well as flair. He published Mark Twain without permission or payment and after doctoring his texts – Twain called him John Camden Hottentot. The American strain was early and strong. Other Americans whom Hotten published were Poe, Whitman, Oliver Wendell-Holmes, Artemus Ward and Ambrose Bierce. When Hotten died the business was bought by Andrew Chatto who had begun work in it at the age of fifteen and was joined in partnership by W.E. Windus, an untalented poet already published by Hotten. The firm migrated gradually eastward, along Piccadilly and then to two sites in St Martin's Lane and thence to William IV Street where it was established a few years before the Second World War and remained until 1986. Along this road and about 1880 it dropped bookselling, although one of Andrew Chatto's sons kept the Chatto name in bookselling by creating the firm of Chatto & Pickering, antiquarian booksellers as well as publishers of fine collected editions of classical sages of the eighteenth and nineteenth centuries. Also along the way it moved into and out of paperback editions of saucy books with titillating covers, some of which were still reposing in the warehouse in William IV Street in the 1950s, a surprising discovery, apparently an overstock.

Andrew Chatto, with Percy Spalding, gave the firm stability and lustre with authors such as Ouida, Wilkie Collins and R.L. Stevenson, and in spite of some bumpy years early in the new century it climbed to the forefront of British publishing between the wars when it became preeminent for its array of famous novelists, poets and essayists. After the Second World War the stars in its fiction list were Aldous Huxley and William Faulkner, almost exact contemporaries in birth and death but both past their zenith by this time. Huxley's later novels lacked the sparkle of *Crome Yellow, Antic Hay* and *Those Barren Leaves* which had delighted the twenties, while the best of Faulkner – *The Sound and the Fury, Light in August, The Hamlet* – and his Nobel Prize lay in the past. They died within a year of one another in 1962-63. At this upper level Scott Moncrieff's celebrated translation of Proust added refulgence. In the Hogarth list Virginia Woolf was an equal star, followed by Henry Green, one of John Lehmann's contributions during his brief partnership with Leonard Woolf. But fiction lists cannot live by stars alone and there was a good array of writers of the next rank, good sellers in their day but without the power long to outlive themselves: Margaret Irwin, Compton Mackenzie, Sylvia Townsend Warner, Richard Hughes, Ann Bridge. Of a younger generation the biggest catch was Iris Murdoch whose first novel *Under the Net* was published by Chatto & Windus just before I joined and who went on being published by it for many years after all the partners whom she first knew there had gone. My own contribution to the fiction half of the list was almost nil. Novels were Norah Smallwood's domain – although Ian Parsons had a good nose for novels among much else and was an excellent editor, as witness *The Golden Warrior* by Hope Muntz which he cherished and coaxed through a parturition of many years. There was a tacit, if unstated, assumption that I did not have the fiction flair, a judgment with which I was inclined to concur although on one of my trips to New York I fell for a first novel which Alfred Knopf was about to publish and, greatly daring, I bought the British rights. If my partners were worried by this eccentricity they had no cause to regret it, for the author was Anne Tyler who was still ornamenting the Chatto list thirty years later. I subsequently revised this assessment of my critical ability, upwards, on the grounds that one could not read and enjoy as many novels as I did without picking up some appreciation of the *genre*.

The main strength of Chatto & Windus in those years was less its fiction than its literary criticism. This was the creation of Ian Parsons. It outshone any University Press in the English-speaking world and was so full, famous and various that it became necessary to ensure that the authors, not all of whom loved or esteemed one another, should not cross our threshold at the same time. They included William Empsson, Frank Leavis and his wife Queenie, E.M.W. Tillyard, Basil Willey, L.C. Knights, Muriel Bradbrook, V.S. Pritchett. Likewise in Hogarth, the works of Sigmund Freud and the associated Psychoanalytic Library provided a substantial part of the firm's renown and profits. Ian's range, and Leonard's too, was one of the marks of the firm. Ian would apply himself with equal energy and discernment to travel books as to poetry. Both Chatto and Hogarth had a niche in poetry publishing which went back to the poets of the First World War – Wilfred Owen, Isaac Rosenberg.

Ideally a publisher should start young, if only to be in a position to attract his contemporaries into his list. When I went to Chatto & Windus I was past forty and so most of my literary – or, as the saying now is, creative – friends and acquaintances already had publishers to whom they wished to remain loyal. About the first thing a publisher, young or old, needs to imbibe is the infinite variety of authors. These, the persons whom he exists to serve and without whom he would have no new books to publish, come in many temperaments. Some resent criticism; others welcome it, at any rate until it is offered. Some are stoutly independent while others like to be cosseted. I have known one or two not above tricking the publisher in order to get their own way. When, for example, I was handling Ernest Jones's *Life of Freud* I had to look sharp to stop passages which I had insisted on changing to guard against legal action – they were digs at Jung – from being changed back in revises of the proofs. Most of our authors were friendly to the point of dropping in for a chat or asking us to store some paraphernalia for them for a month or so. The stereotype of the bumbling writer is wide of the mark, for most are efficient and business-like. I specially recall Nirad Chaudhuri's laudable concern to make sure that I understood his views of the publisher's proper place. He had written a number of books before he came my way, including two classics of our

times, *The Autobiography of an Unknown Indian* and *Passage to England*.
Prompted by a mutual friend he wrote to me to ask whether I would be
interested in publishing his next book since he had fallen out with his
previous publisher. I replied that I would. He then wrote to say that he
had decided views on the author/publisher relationship and before going
any further he wished me to see his correspondence with his previous
publisher. He sent me a thick file which, since his own letters were untidy
copies of what he had written, took me some time to get through. Having
done so I replied that nothing in the file made me want to change my mind
and I stated, rather more concisely, my own view of the matter: that the
publisher was entitled to comment, suggest and criticise but (questions of
libel apart) not to insist. The book which then reached me was *The
Continent of Circe*, a marvellous compendium of erudition – Chaudhuri
was as amazingly well read in French as in English literature – forceful
argument and bizarre speculation. It is one of the best books I ever
published, although many Indians hated it. My relations with its idiosyn-
cratic author remained unruffled, largely because both of us knew in
advance where we stood in relation to one another.

Through one of my authors I had an unusual experience. Rosalind
Heywood was a woman with an independent and adventurous intelligence
combined with much common sense and humour. She wrote two books –
The Sixth Sense and *The Infinitive Hive* – in which she probed, using
personal experiences, such abstruse capacities of the mind as telepathy,
telekinesis and so on, but without ever losing sight of the distinction
between wanting to know and wanting to swallow tall stories: she had none
of the woolliness or credulity characteristic of these quicksands. Through
friends such as Aldous Huxley and the polymathic psychologist Humphrey
Osmond she was enrolled in a programme of experiments to explore the
mind through LSD and she asked me to be a guinea pig. Prompted by
curiosity and a flattering chance to be useful I agreed and so one day I
reported to a flat in London where Rosalind and a friend administered to
me a small dose of a discoloured powder. They were equipped with
notebooks and pencils and with an antidote in case I proved to be one of
those people who are plunged by the drug into nightmare and horror. I sat
in an armchair waiting for sensations such as Huxley had described in *The
Doors of Perception* but nothing much happened. Soon I became extremely
cold and was covered in blankets by the two ladies. I also felt weak, unlike
a previous guinea pig who had jumped from his chair, rushed into the street
and, accosting an astonished beggar woman, exclaimed: 'Ah, a Gainsbor-
ough' and rushed on pursued by the ladies with their notebooks. After a
bit I was asked what the objects on the mantelpiece looked like and was
obliged to reply that they looked just the same as they had an hour earlier.
I was beginning to feel a failure. I became agreeably drowsy and saw
flashes of shapes and colours, but found it hard to describe them because
they moved fast, my reactions were slowed and my speech hampered.

Although something was happening I was not doing my bit in reporting it. Several hours passed in much this way, punctuated by my surfacing from semi-consciousness into fitful consciousness, vaguely distressed by my disappointing performance and apologising for wasting the precious powder – I had been told that it was expensive – and contributing nothing to the advancement of the frontier of knowledge. When all effects had subsided I left disconsolate. Later, however, I was told that this encounter had caused some interest since no other guinea pig had evinced such concern with the experimenters and the experiment itself. Many years later still, when Rosalind Heywood died leaving instructions in her will to send me a gramophone record, her sons with inherited percipience chose a recording of Bach played by Andras Schiff.

The senior partner in Chatto & Windus when I joined the firm in 1955 was Harold Raymond who had been a partner for more than twenty years, had seen the business through the war, was renowned in the trade as the inventor of the book token, and was on the point of retiring. He was a courteous, peaceable and not very incisive man, one of those leading figures whom everybody knows because he takes the trouble to know them. His departure left Ian Parsons in charge together with Norah Smallwood who had been Harold Raymond's mainstay in the war years (in which her husband was killed) and was to become the most eminent of publishing's few women chieftains of that generation. Harold's son, Piers, a man of undentable good temper even when treated as no more than a fairly promising youngster, was made a partner at about the same time as myself. Cecil Day Lewis enjoyed the ancient and honourable title of Reader but was transformed into the more modish Literary Adviser and became a director after the partnership was turned into a limited company. Leonard Woolf was also a director.

London publishing was commonly described, half enviously, half irritatedly, as cosy. Chatto & Windus was not cosy. It was agitated, not to say noisy, and most evidently on the first or partners' floor. Three interconnecting rooms along the front of the building were occupied by Ian, Norah and Piers with Piers in the middle. Ian and Norah, who constituted a dominant tandem by right of long service and professional expertise, frequently found it necessary to rush into one another's rooms and they did so by using Piers's office as a corridor. A short time after my arrival Piers left to go to Methuen and I inherited his room. This change made the place yet noisier because I contrived to divert this through traffic from my room to the more public passage outside. Ian and Norah were both sensitive people and after I had raised the occasional eyebrow they stopped treating the front three offices as though they should have been designed as an open-plan area or race-course.

The staff at Chatto consisted of old retainers, who did not mind being shouted at (or had got used to it) and younger things, some of whom did. Ian and Norah were publishers to their fingertips, masters of the essentials of their trade, meticulous, imaginative and enthusiastic. Norah had the artist's eye as well as the craftsman's skills. I have seen her pick up a proof of a title page, cast an eye over it, shift one line by one em and send it back to the printer – who accepted this treatment without demur. They were devoted to the activity of publishing, to the firm itself and to its authors. They wanted to make money too and knew that they had to, since without profits there could be no future, but they were not in it primarily for money or at all for social uplift. Their insistence on standards and their love of the business of publishing permeated the firm.

If Ian Parsons and Norah Smallwood were eminent in the world of publishing Leonard Woolf was eminent in a wider world. The Hogarth Press, which he had founded with his wife Virginia in 1917 (as described in one of his splendid volumes of autobiography), moved in 1946 into the Chatto offices and became gradually fused with Chatto. By the time I came along the staffs of the two firms were identical with the solitary exception of Leonard Woolf's personal secretary. Leonard was by this time well into his seventies, a small greying figure radiating intelligence, muted humour and benignity. His movements were almost inaudible owing to the shoes with thick rubber soles which he favoured. He had a relatively large head and nose, blue eyes and a most engaging smile. His voice was low and he spoke slowly, almost hesitantly, but his thought was sharp as sharp and he dithered less than anybody I have ever known. He was exceptionally efficient and, in manner and style, economical: he never used two words or two minutes when one would do. He had the unusual trait of yoking strong commitment with balanced judgment and, as his novel *The Village in the Jungle* and, still more, his autobiography show, the patience to understand and sympathise with different kinds of people. His wit was precise, inclined to the ironical, fierce only against humbug. He was the only man I ever met who seemed to me to be right about everything that matters. He used to come to London from his home in Rodmell in Sussex only once a week and mainly to deal with specifically Hogarth correspondence and manuscripts from a poky little office which was all that his one-day attendance was thought to warrant.

The Hogarth Press maintained a distinct list. No book was published with the Hogarth imprint unless Leonard wanted it and no book that Leonard did not like was so published. As a publisher he was at the very opposite end of the spectrum from those American (and increasingly British) editors who treat a MS as a first draft to be rewritten by them or along their guidelines. Leonard believed that the author's business was to write his book how he wanted it and to the best of his ability and to submit an essentially complete work which the publisher would accept or reject with the minimum of comment. If the publisher had serious reservations about the book or simply did not like it he should reject it. Leonard's rigour led him to reject one or two good authors who would have graced and enriched any list, but he had no compunction about leaving an author to go elsewhere, since the multiplicity of publishers ensured his finding a place for his book so long as it was at least half good. Leonard Woolf was neither a jealous nor a greedy man and he did not in the least mind other publishers getting good books; it did not nettle him to see good books in other lists. When he died the Hogarth Press, so much his personal creation, should have stopped publishing new books. Turning it into a reprint list in the eighties was a sad indignity.

The directors of Chatto and Hogarth had few formal meetings. Business was conducted on the trot rather than round a board. There was a regular monthly meeting to look at the figures but the focus of publishing life was new books rather than old figures. Once a week we met not in the board room but in the senior partner's office. Both Harold Raymond and Ian Parsons were men of natural courtesy and forbearance but these are not the qualities which make for brisk chairmanship and the meetings were a mixture of publishing acuteness and a ragged indifference to the way time was running away towards the lunch hour. As each partner talked in turn about his clutch of hopeful manuscripts I began to wonder whether my turn was going to come or not. When publishers get talking about the books which they espouse they get carried away and their colleagues fall into the role of devil's advocate in order to redress the balance – all of which takes time. But these were stimulating hours and, more than anything else, they shaped the future of the business. They were also a schoolroom for me.

Some manuscripts needed no discussion because they were an established author's latest book – although that did not prevent them from being discussed and extolled, not in order to arrive at a publishing decision but for the exuberant fun of it. Aside from these sure starters we received about one thousand unsolicited manuscripts a year. These were first read by a reader. We had two – Cecil Day Lewis and his less senior and less permanent assistant. Between them they wrote reports on every MS submitted and these reports piled up on a table in the senior partner's room until one of us found time to go through them, despatch the bulk of them back to where they came from, or pull out the odd one for discussion and possible acceptance at the weekly meeting. We published very few of these offerings, getting most of our books either by recommendation from existing authors or other friends or by our own efforts in pursuing likely writers and topics: doing the publisher's job in fact. We took very little from agents, one of the big differences between publishing then and now. The pile of rejects, which included a great deal of pathetically bad verse, was a melancholy commentary on authors' aspirations, the more so when one reflects that it is just as hard for a bad writer to write a bad book as it is for a good writer to write a good one.

The centrality of new books was emphasised by a single piece of apparatus which was deposited every day in the senior partner's room round about midday. This was the 'board' – a sheet pinned to a piece of wood and recording the daily sales of books about to be published or recently published. The board told at a glance how sales were going and its daily appearance could occasion much genial commotion, satisfaction or alarm.

The Chatto offices were so inconvenient, draughty and bedevilled by passages and odd stairways that they would have convulsed any time-and-motion expert, but they were no worse than other such offices in London's publishing world and better than most of those which I visited in Paris. The top people put up with them because they had the best rooms and everybody else put up with them because they expected no better. I myself became particularly attached to the top floor which was a flat which my wife and I occupied from 1959 and for a number of years after I left the firm. It had marvellous views over chimneys, including those of the old Charing Cross Hospital; of the sculptures round the dome on the Colisseum, hardly visible from the street below; and, until the new Post Office was built on the site of an eighteenth-century mews, of St Martin-in-the-Fields and Trafalgar Square. The building had been a fish restaurant before Ian Parsons found it between the wars and it consisted of an incoherent jumble round an open space, with packing room and warehouse occupying the central area at street level. It had the slowest lift in London.

When I joined Chatto and Hogarth in 1955 their combined turnover was just over £200,000, one third of it from export business. Normally rather less than half of turnover came from new books, that is to say, books first published within the accounting period. When I left in 1966 turnover was approaching £500,000. Net profit before tax was rather over 10% of turnover. By 1955, its centenary year, Chatto had re-established itself after the wartime years of bare survival. In that year we published nearly 100 new titles; we printed some 800,000 books and sold 700,000 of them within the current financial year. Of the books printed in that year two-thirds were new and one-third reprints; of the books sold almost the reverse was true. After that year we reined back our new books to around sixty a year with an additional ten or so from Hogarth. Besides new books we had a back list of 600-700 titles in stock, a number which more than doubled over the next decade – a sign of good publishing. Our remainder rate in those years was about 3% of stock. Nearly all these books were tended from cradle to back list by three partners.

The fifties and sixties were the period between postwar recovery and the inflation and recessions of the seventies and eighties – and the destruction of much of publishing by predatory invaders, of whom more below. The firm was owned by the directors who were obliged by its articles of association to offer their shares for sale to their fellow directors on retiring from active participation in the business. The share capital was small – 16,000 £1 ordinary shares, increased to 20,000 around 1961, and a smaller number of preference shares. Borrowing was prudent and so was accounting. We had in 1955 a borrowing facility of merely £20,000, expandable to £25,000 for a brief period twice a year when royalty cheques went out; but the £20,000 grew to £50,000 before I left and presumably grew faster in the testing years thereafter. Stock valuation – a tedious business conducted by the directors in a series of lunchtime conclaves once a year – proceeded on the general rule that books should be written down to remainder value or nil within three years of publication; most novels were written down drastically after one year and altogether after two.

The principal outgoings of a publishing business are production costs, overheads and royalties. Our production costs equalled 40% of turnover; overheads and royalties, which were roughly equal with one another, nearly 50%. In order to achieve a net profit of 10% we had to pay special attention to two things: the pricing of each book and printing the right number – the right number being what could be sold within a reasonable period, basically three years but much the greater part in the first year.

On pricing we had a rule of thumb. This was a touchstone or check; it was not a straitjacket or pre-set regulator. I once asked a friend whom I reckoned to be the most successful publisher in New York how he priced his books. He said he picked up the book, handled it and then knew what to charge for it. I do not suppose that he was always right but judging by results he cannot often have been wrong. He had started in publishing as a traveller or bagman and by the time I knew him he was a master publisher who knew all aspects of his trade. In Chatto & Windus our rule of thumb was this: take the production costs, add the royalty, add 60% and that is the cover price. (It was, of course, not the price received by the publisher since he sold to the bookseller at a discount, normally one third off the cover price.) Anything below 40% on cost-plus-royalty meant a loss; going to 70% made our books noticeably more expensive than our rivals'. Reprints were more lucrative since their production costs did not include any cost of composition and the principal recurrent cost – paper – was still a relatively low component. This saving in the production costs of a reprint could be offset against rises in general overheads in order to keep the cover price steady.

No less crucial than the price was the print run. Printing too many meant capital locked up in stock which had eventually to be remaindered or pulped. Printing too few entailed an obligation, felt by most publishers but not all, to reprint and so incur some extra expense which could have been avoided by getting the figure right first time. Getting it right came from experience aided by such preliminary orders from the book trade as were available before setting the print run; getting it wrong came from an excess of enthusiasm over experience or from the vagaries of reviewers one way or the other. We aimed to sell half the impression before publication; half the remainder in the ensuing twelve months; and the rest in the next two years. That was the ideal but there were many books to which it did not apply, notably fast sellers.

We had in 1955 a staff of 60-70, all except our five travellers or reps (as the salesmen were called in those days) in our premises at 42 William IV

Street. This in-house total was unusually high for a firm of our size because it included the warehouse on the ground floor where some fifteen men were engaged in storing, packing and distributing the books delivered to us from the binders. A packing department in the middle of London was a luxury made possible by our wonderfully low rent of £1,000 a year for 10,000 square feet. The rates were not much more at 10s in the pound on, if my recollection is correct, a rateable value of £2,500. The pay of the staff was much the biggest element in overheads, although the figures look absurdly mingy forty years on. By the mid-fifties the annual bill for wages and salaries had passed £20,000 excluding the directors. Heads of department were edging up to £1,000 a year. Typists got £4 a week, invoice and royalty clerks £7. Directors' secretaries and girls with degrees in the editorial and production departments began with not much more but had better prospects. The packers, whose pay was negotiated with the appropriate union, got £8 a week or a little more. Wages rose only slowly over these years. As a director I believe I began with a salary of £1,500 and an expense allowance of £200. In 1962 an incoming new director began at £2,500.

Standard royalties, so far as such existed, were 10% on the first 3,000 copies sold in the home market, $12\frac{1}{2}$% on the next 3,000 copies and 15% after 6,000 with variations for export sales and an advance on royalties of £100-500. Higher advances betokened either exceptional expectations or exceptional love for the author. Some specially successful authors who had become established Chatto authors got a royalty of $17\frac{1}{2}$% after a certain point or even from the start: Compton Mackenzie, Ann Bridge and perhaps three or four more were in this last most-favoured-author class. From the end of the war Aldous Huxley got a flat 20% and in his final years 20% rising to 25%. A new Mackenzie would have an initial print run of 15,000-17,000 which we would hope to sell entirely within a year of publication. Ann Bridge much the same. With the rising star of Iris Murdoch we were feeling our way, buying paper optimistically and then giving orders to print in gulps as we watched pre-publication orders on the 'board'. For *The Bell*, her fourth book and a springboard in her literary career, published at the end of 1958, we ordered initially paper for 25,500 copies which we printed in three impressions before publication, followed immediately after publication by another 3,000 which also sold quickly but left a tail which lasted into the book's third year, whereafter a regular sequence of reprints began and continued indefinitely. The cost of these 28,500 books was £2,200 for paper, composition, machining and jackets but excluding binding; with the binding the prime costs over the four impressions came out at 3s a copy and we published at 15s – in this instance beating our rule of thumb quite comfortably.

The costs of a steady seller of this kind were held down by a number of refinements: the printed sheets were bound only in packets as and when needed; the unbound sheets were stored by the printer at little or no cost to the publisher; and the type was kept standing by the printer for the modest rent of 15s a month rising to £1 by the end of my time with the firm in 1966. A more considerable, sometimes indispensable financial benefit came with the English language. An English publisher of our kind frequently sold publishing rights or, if not publishing rights, at least printed sheets or bound books to an American publisher who had acquired American publishing rights directly from the author or the author's agent. Such arrangements were particularly common with serious non-fiction such as our lit. crit. and similar books. For example, *Culture and Society* by Raymond Williams: we printed initially 6,000 copies of which we sold 1,500 bound and jacketed to an American university press: that is to say, we recovered before publication the costs of a quarter of the first impression with a small profit. In 1960 when we published an abridged Gibbon in one volume we printed not only 13,000 for ourselves but a further 13,000 for the USA and 6,000 for the Reprint Society in London – a very handy increment which enabled us to produce a book of nearly a thousand pages at a cost, with jacket, of just over 8s a copy. We published it at 36s.

Then there was poetry. Poetry is notoriously difficult to sell but on the other hand a slim volume of largely blank pages does not cost a great deal to produce and we liked to keep up the Chatto and Hogarth traditions in publishing poetry. Together the firms produced in the Phoenix Living Poets five or six volumes a year, 48 to 72 pages long, elegantly clad in jackets designed by Enid Marx, printing 750 or so for an outlay of perhaps £150-180 per volume priced at 10/6 or 12/6. If the editions did not sell out the loss was not catastrophic. The one thing about them which bulked large was the time spent on them, mostly by Ian Parsons. Poets normally and naturally want to see in print more poems than the publisher thinks appropriate. Making a selection requires much quiet thought and tactful discussion to persuade the poet that the publisher's selection is the best one.

Like nearly all British publishers we were slow to cotton on to the paperback revolution pioneered by Allen Lane and Penguin. Three leading London publishers combined to establish Pan Books to publish their own and other titles as paperbacks and to compete with Penguin, but most publishers persisted in regarding paperbacks as a subsidiary branch of the trade, even scruffy (which it was before Penguin). They remained too long content to lease reprint rights to Penguin or other paperback specialists instead of equipping themselves to do the job themselves and reap the whole profit. Expansion, therefore, tended to be into new fields rather than diverse forms. Chatto added children's books, educational books and technical books to its existing lists and, in the first category at least, profited considerably by doing so. But we would have done better to put money into expanding our accustomed publishing into paperback rather than acquiring new lines. The reluctance of established publishers to go wholeheartedly into paperback publishing had a number of roots: a certain snobbishness about the inferiority of the paperback article, wariness of the unfamiliar marketing skills needed in the paperback business, and above all wariness of the complexity and cost of anything like the Penguin operation. These were small firms which liked being small. Their authors too liked them to be small. So long as they could make good profits without getting bigger – and most of them did – they felt neither the temptation nor compulsion to expand or revolutionise their traditional vocations.

With their virtues, which were many and pronounced, Ian Parsons and Norah Smallwood had a blind spot which increasingly bothered me. I can best describe it as an insensitivity to the need to share responsibility with younger people. Superficially this may seem a false judgment and ungenerous, since intellectually they realised the need and were on the lookout for successors to ourselves and they enjoyed the company of young people. Yet in the firm things did not feel like that, and the fact that they did not was largely their fault. Looking back I suspect they took too much on themselves and were too busy to spare time or attention for the climate in William IV Street. I felt that there was between us a gap – a gap perhaps in management or temperament – which would get wider but which was so much a matter of 'feel' as to be almost impossible to define or argue about. I also felt that my partners had a strong right to run the firm their way and would continue to do so in any case. I was therefore not completely averse to a move when after eleven years I was courted (for the second time) to go and teach at Sussex University. I explained my predicament to Leonard Woolf who, although he was much older than the rest of us, had none of the sort of possessiveness that made it difficult for Ian or (perhaps more so) Norah to modify their dominance of the firm. Characteristically he addressed himself to advising me in the position which I described to him and did not try to argue me out of it: he treated my statement of the position as data and said that if that was how I felt it was right for me to move.

I left Chatto and Hogarth with regrets and look back on my share in them with pride. We did well by our authors; we cherished our books as well as our authors; we made decent profits without striving after indecent ones; and I do not see what more a publisher should do if he is not personally greedy or a socio-literary climber. One thing conspicuously lacking in Chatto and similar firms was anything that might be described as planning. We did not think of a season's list as a planned or coherent whole, although it had a certain character owing to the firm's history and the present partner's tastes. Our books constituted a list only because one partner wanted to publish it and the others did not want not to. Each of us could handle so many books a year and there was no shortage of books coming our way. Many books published in this way are less than great literature and many are forgotten a generation later but they were not for these reasons unworthy of publication and looking at old catalogues I am gratified by the number of books in them of sound and abiding worth.

Not long afterwards – to complete my involvement with Chatto &

Windus – Ian Parsons told me of plans for a partial merger or association between Chatto & Windus, The Bodley Head and Jonathan Cape. The motives were partly economic (the advantages of shared distribution, accountancy and other services) and partly political – in order to fend off the attentions of American publishers intent on buying British firms which they needed to do in order to break the conventional division of the English-speaking world into two exclusive publishing areas – the British, which included all existing and former parts of the British empire, and the American, to which the Americans had succeeded in attaching only the Philippines (with some messy arguments over Canada whose proximity to the USA and leaky frontier made the British case hardly tenable in practice). I poured a lot of cold water on these plans. I did not believe in semi-mergers unless they were intended to lead to full merger, which this one definitely was not; I did not believe that the three firms would retain their vaunted and treasured editorial independence of one another; and I forecast that an American predator, far from being put off by the cost of having to buy three firms, would on the contrary leap at the opportunity of buying three of the most prestigious firms in London in one bite. What eventually happened was that the three were squeezed by circumstances, largely of their own making, into a tighter and tighter nugget, which was bought by another British firm, which was bought by an American firm, which was part of an American conglomerate. The surviving directors, having failed to avoid these surrenders, sold out and became millionaires. I was incidentally not at all hostile to Anglo-American mergers in certain circumstances and was keen in later years to make such a marriage through Penguin – but not the one which was actually effected and which I advised against.

When in 1966 I left Chatto & Windus and The Hogarth Press to go to teach at Sussex University I never expected to be an active publisher again but I was wrong. Some years later I got a short handwritten letter from Patrick Gibson whom I slightly knew. He was deputy chairman of S. Pearson which had recently bought Penguin Books and he asked me whether I ever thought of going back into publishing. He asked me to go and see him and offered me the post of Editorial Director of Penguin, which would be created for me. I was happy teaching at Sussex and since my job there was part time it allowed me the time to do other things that I wanted to do, but an offer from Penguin was not in those days one that anybody turned away and after some discussion at home I accepted it. I did so on two conditions: that I should work for Penguin only four days a week and that the appointment should be approved by Chris Dolley, chairman of Penguin, whom I had never met and who had not been consulted. I said also that I would retire on my sixty-fifth birthday and that I meant it: there would be no last minute decision that special circumstances made me an exception to what I believed to be a good general rule. I was approaching sixty, the age at which G.H. Lewes says in his biography of Goethe that biography ends and necrology begins.

Penguin was the most famous firm in British publishing, perhaps in world publishing. It had begun life in 1935 thanks to the flair and energies of Allen Lane and it was not only phenomenally successful but different. The first Penguins were followed within two years by the first Pelicans which revived the Victorian tradition of men and women of stature addressing a general audience on serious, even difficult, subjects. (Pelicans were also the most consistently profitable section of the list although the more money-minded found it hard to believe this.) After Pelicans the line ran through Penguin Specials, Puffins, Penguin Classics, King Penguins, Arts and Poets to Penguin Education (1964). This diversity was one of Penguin's main strengths and also characteristic of Allen Lane who was always looking for something new: although in temperament he was inclined to caution, in business he was also and sometimes confusingly an innovator. He had gusto which, with his firm's exacting standards in editing and production, put a stamp on Penguins which lasted all his life and a little longer. Shoppers knew a Penguin when they saw one and, seeing it, said to themselves that if it was a Penguin it must be good. Most paperbacks were scruffy but Penguins were not. Extra care was lavished on their content and their appearance. The Penguin English Library, for example, and the Penguin Classics departed from the usual practice of appending sparse and often cretinous notes to standard texts and provided instead long introductions of superior value. Talented typographers and designers gave Penguins style. Not all Penguins were outstandingly good or outstandingly successful but a high proportion of them were. Penguin never in those years deliberately published rubbish and there was never any need for the rueful apology made to me many years later by a Penguin director: 'We do publish good books too.'

Every publisher publishes books of which he is not proud. Some do so simply to make money, others through misjudgment or cowardice: it is difficult to turn down a book by one of your regular authors who may be also a friend. But it is quite another thing to publish trash knowing it to be trash. Soon after I arrived at Penguin I was pressed to make a bid for the British paperback rights in a truly awful book called *Jonathan Livingstone Seagull*. I refused. I was taken to task for perverse refusal to jump at a bag of gold but I insisted on my right to refuse to publish what I regarded, rightly or wrongly, as a rotten book. My critics were only partially mollified when I told them that I found the book blasphemous as well as bad. Publishers must make money in order to go on publishing but there is all the difference in the world between making money in order to publish books and publishing books in order to make money. Feeding a vending machine, whatever else it may be, is not publishing.

Allen Lane was more than a discerning publisher. He was also a man of courage. He had succeeded a distant relative John Lane (he himself was born Allen Williams in 1902) as managing director of The Bodley Head where he conceived the Penguin idea – cheap reprints of famous books, cheap in price but not in appearance. But he clashed with his colleagues over his determination to keep the price of these new editions down to six pence. They preferred nine pence. He was in effect saying that they should be able to print and sell enough of them to make six pence cover costs, overheads and profits; they on the other hand judged him too optimistic but, as everybody soon found out, they were wrong. The clash was resolved by an agreement to publish at The Bodley Head with the proviso that Allen Lane would take the whole risk of what they, and most of the publishing trade, took to be a ridiculously suicidal scheme. So the first Penguins carried The Bodley Head imprint.

One of them carried also a curious misprint – Penguin Book (in the singular), happily a fallacious omen. In spite of this sly jab from a wicked fairy Penguins survived and flourished and they were Allen Lane's property and he quickly set up on his own. His success bred imitators but – and here he had a bit of luck – the advent of war and paper shortages made it impossible for them to challenge Penguin until some years later, and when competition did appear they failed to match Penguin's standards so that although Penguin's monopoly was broken its pre-eminence was not.

I had only a slight acquaintance with Allen Lane. He was a good companion but not gregarious and he did not run with the main pack of publishers, many of whom disliked him for a variety of, mostly bad, reasons. They looked down on his paperback product; they envied his prodigious success; they particularly resented his success with reprints of books which they had themselves published in the first place. To me Penguin was an immensely admirable venture and, with the BBC of those times, evidence of Britain's vital creativity between the wars.

Allen Lane was not an easy man to know outside his own close circle of friends. Although he liked talking and was a careful listener, there was also a sense of reserve, an unforthcoming watchfulness which came close to suspiciousness. Even in a *tête-à-tête* he left you wondering what he was thinking. It was difficult to know whether this was because he had already made up his mind or because he could not make it up; and it could be either, since he was both impulsive and at other times indecisive. One of my first encounters with him occurred when he asked me what I thought about a senior appointment at Penguin which, it seemed from what he was saying, he was thinking of making. When I praised warmly the individual in question but said he was the wrong man for the job Allen said he was sorry to hear what I had to say because he had made the appointment the day before. (Within a year he conceded that I had been right and he had been precipitate.) He liked airing questions, but it was the airing rather than other people's injections that appealed to him. An even earlier encounter had given me some inkling of a puzzling character. He was casting around for a new sales manager and also for an excuse for removing the one he had. He was bad at hatchet work unless he could put the hatchet into somebody else's hands. In this particular case the person in question was still at Penguin a decade later. The man who had taken the bold decision to start Penguin on his own because he was determined to publish at six pence and not nine pence could be extraordinarily cowardly when it came to dealing with staff. On one occasion, having fallen out with one of his principal colleagues, he got rid of him by sending the victim's own subordinate to meet him at the airport and tell him not to come back to his office. Less chilling is a legendary story about Penguin in Australia. Allen Lane had gone there to sort out some managerial problem. During several days he said nothing about the question in everybody's mind until, within minutes of his embarking on his return flight to England, one of his acolytes asked bluntly what was to happen. 'Oh,' said Allen, pointing in turn at his two chief acolytes, 'you're in, you're out and I'm off.'

Allen Lane knew more about books than either he himself or his detractors made out, but where he got his knowledge was a bit of a mystery since I never had the impression that he spent much time reading them. His insistence on quality, however, was genuine and profound; and by quality he did not mean highbrow, but excellence at whatever elevation of the brow. His concern for quality in the design, production and appearance of the books was uncompromising. The idea that he was a prototype of the modern supersalesman is entirely wrong. His closest associates in Penguin were editors. He was the last man to throw money at anything, least of all at a marketing manager or a promotional binge. He would have regarded today's methods as a sickening waste of money and not a little vulgar: he was in many ways a fastidious man. His philosophy was of the counting house and like those other publishing knights of his generation – Stanley Unwin and Billie Collins – he was more shrewd than showy and made his fortune out of artisanal thoroughness. Sales and marketing were, of course, crucial. Penguins were cheap not because they had no hard covers (that was a popular delusion) but because they were printed and sold in large quantities. So Penguin was a market-oriented firm from the start, but never in Allen Lane's time or mine was the choosing of the books subordinated to the marketing. Penguins sold because they were good, not because they were puffed.

Allen Lane had no son and could not make up his mind what to do with his creation. He knew that besides being a huge commercial success Penguin was a cultural phenomenon and he treasured the service element in what he had created. He toyed with schemes for vesting it in a trust but he never discovered any plan which satisfied him and the progress of the cancer which killed him in 1970 eroded his capacity to tackle his problem. There was no lack of firms eager to buy Penguin – some of them believing that they had been promised an inside track – but in the end only two contestants remained: the American publishers McGraw Hill and the financial conglomerate S. Pearson. By sheer chance I played a small, probably insignificant, role in the final round. I happened to know what McGraw Hill were prepared to pay and I happened to be lunching with a banker friend who, unknown to me, happened to be advising Pearsons. When the conversation came round to Penguin and I casually mentioned what I knew, my friend asked if I had any objection to his making use of this information. When I said no, he left the table to go to the telephone. I have no idea whether this episode was in any way decisive. The fact, which is all that matters, is that Pearsons got Penguin for £14 million and so far as I had any interest in the matter I felt pleased. This was not because of any anti-Americanism – far from it, for I was sure from experience that the English language publisher should be Anglo-American, the language being the defining factor and providing the constituency – but I did not think that McGraw Hill was the right sort of owner or partner for Penguin. I hoped that Pearsons might be – perhaps the biggest misjudgment of my life. Pearsons already owned publishing businesses, notably Longmans, among a variety of other things and they were proud to add Penguin to their clutch. They had no intention of destroying what Allen Lane had created, but they were not book publishers, were profoundly ignorant of publishing and demonstrated how much easier it is to destroy than to create.

Round about the time of Allen Lane's decline and death Penguin had two central problems. The first was size: how to organise an expanding business in which individual initiative and individual responsibility are, because of the nature of publishing, of paramount importance. The second was Penguin's dependence on other publishers for the right to reprint their books as paperbacks under fixed-term licences.

Penguin was not a big business in general terms but it was big among publishers. A publishing business can be as big as you want to make it or nearly as small, size being measured by the number of new books published in a year. There is no virtue in bigness or in expansion for the sake of expansion: you expand only if and when you have a good new idea and the money to support it. My first question when I became Editorial Director of Penguin Books – put indeed at a meeting which I held before I took up the job – was how many new books were planned for the next year. The answer was somewhere between 800 and 900. That was more than I thought wise either in financial terms or in terms of the editorial skills available. Nor did I want to emit so many new books. I proposed gradually to retrench. An editorial director in a large firm has two main concerns and they conflict. He must retain and exercise personal responsibility for all the books published and he has to find and keep the best editors in the business, bearing in mind that they are not to be had unless they are allowed considerable freedom. My solution was this. I assembled all the senior editors and made them a proposal. Each of them would, within a defined area of publishing, publish a number of new books to be set by me and would operate independently subject to two conditions: first, that the advance on any book and the total of advances contracted in any year would not exceed set limits without reference to me; and secondly, that if an editor and I fell out because I did not like what he or she was doing the editor would go and I would stay. These guidelines were supplemented in practice by constant informal contacts among us which were at least as important, and by set practices on the costing of books. I retained control of the lists at the price of exercising it through a mixture of informality, financial rigour and long-stop review. Each month – we published once a month – I arrived home with a load of new books which I handled, inspected and, in most but not all cases, read with a beady eye for shortcomings in editing, proof-reading or production as well as for their quality. I am sure that this method or something like it is the only efficient way to run a large publishing business and that a firm which abandons it or smothers it with committees becomes a topsy-turvy firm in which the best people do not care to work for long. I suspect that it hardly survives in publishing today and certainly not in the conglomerates dominated by accountants, salesmen and wheeler-dealers, most of whom are not publishers in the proper sense of the word. When I went to Penguin it contained a high proportion of the best editors in London and was the best training ground for the next generation. These editors were Penguin's front line and first strength. They made it their business to cover their respective fields thoroughly and excellently. This does not mean that they did not have their prejudices, their likes and dislikes, but they published nonetheless fiction by authors whom they esteemed less highly than others and non-fiction by authors whose views they reprobated, provided the books were good of their kind and right for Penguin. Most of these editors were at Penguin when I arrived. Most were gone within a year of my leaving. Penguin was no longer the place for them. The essence of publishing is getting new books, which is what editors do. Without good editors, and without the conditions which appeal to good editors, a publishing business is reduced to acquiring old firms rather than new books, which is what Penguin under Pearsons increasingly turned out to do. Pearsons, like other conglomerates, were better at buying other people's businesses than at running them when they got them.

The second big problem looming in the sixties and seventies was Penguin's dependence on other publishers for getting its books. Penguin began as a reprint business, publishing as paperbacks books already published by other publishers and under licence from them. Most of these licences were for a fixed term, renewable but not bound to be renewed and increasingly unlikely to be renewed on the original terms or even on any terms as other publishers learned the value of paperback publishing and resolved to do it themselves. Like landlords they wanted to use breaks in the licence to raise the rent, extract a price for renewing the licence or repossess their property. Broadly speaking orange and green Penguins – fiction, crime and entertainment generally – were published under licence, while the blue Pelicans were partly reprints but increasingly new books commissioned by Penguin for publication as Pelican Originals. Allen Lane had foreseen the pitfalls of reprint publishing and had begun to offset them not only by commissioning books for first publication as paperbacks but also by starting a hardback list whose books could be, and mostly were, later re-issued as Penguin paperbacks. The first expedient was hardly controversial, but the second, which was crucial to Penguin's future and which I was determined to foster, ran into opposition from old Penguin hands who were wedded to Penguin as a paperback firm and nothing else, and from Pearsons who did not understand the importance of the hardback list and wanted to scrap it altogether on their accountants' advice. I had a hard tussle but saved a sufficient rump to enable it to rise again later on. Without it Penguin would have been in a grave mess.

The related problem of licences from other publishers was in the long run insoluble, since these publishers were bound to do more and more paperback publishing under their own imprints. The best that Penguins could do was to ensure that withdrawals of valued licences did not become a stampede. The threat of withdrawals was complicated by the fact that it was a threat to Penguin's pride as well as its revenues, while at the same time such a stampede was likely to be accelerated by Penguin's measures to expand its own hardback publishing. There was a true dilemma. We had to try to get the best of two worlds for as long as possible but without, in my view, going slow on the essential business of developing the hardbacks, for which a good basis had been laid (for example, Penguin could have become second only to Thames and Hudson in art books). The immediate task was to hold on to our paperback licences, paying generously but not idiotically for renewals and pointing out to the licensors that Penguin could do a better job for them and for the authors (i.e. sell more paperback copies) than they could themselves – an argument which I was able to use energetically since it happened still to be true and they knew it.

I was partially successful. A number of publishers resolved to terminate their Penguin licences, beginning with their more famous authors: they were less keen to reclaim authors with lower sales. The most important of these publishers was Secker & Warburg, if only because they were the publishers of the quintessential Penguin author George Orwell. So I went with one of my senior colleagues, Jim Cochrane, to beard Tom Rosenthal of Secker in his well-appointed den. We talked publishing for two hours, not without a certain amount of mutual flattery about services to literature and even a little wine brought in by an equally well-appointed girl. I indicated with the nuances appropriate between gentlemen publishers that Penguin was not interested in publishing only Secker's second eleven and would dump them if we lost the cream. Cochrane and I came away with every one of our licences renewed for a substantial period. I prepared to do likewise with other firms, but the Penguin board suddenly hit upon the notion that a better course was to tackle our problem by throwing money at it. This was a lunatic idea, not just because the sums proposed were absurdly large but because it was not primarily money that these publishers were after. In the ensuing muddle Penguin lost a string of famous authors; some of their publishers formed a new paperback list (which predictably failed to make a mark); and a number of authors found themselves transferred like footballers from Penguin to an imprint which they had never heard of. In time all these publishers would have set up their own paperback lists anyway, but the losses to Penguin could have been strung out and some famous writers who told me that they did not want to leave Penguin would not have had to do so. Further, the bungling and ineptitude dispirited Penguin editors and revealed the extent of the confusion and amateurishness which had crept into the conduct of Penguin with the Pearson connection. The temper of the times intensified a trend, which became headlong in the eighties, to preach the existence of a science of management independent of what was to be managed: hospitals to be run by persons ignorant of doctoring or nursing, museums by persons ignorant of art display or scholarship, businesses by persons ignorant of the business in question – and publishing companies by persons who did not know what or how to publish. At difficult moments such persons either dither or plunge, two equally disastrous ways of proceeding.

These were the main problems peculiar to Penguin at that stage of its life. There were, of course, others. One was its radicalism and the hostility provoked by it. This radicalism was a good deal more to the taste of its founder and many of its staff than to the new owners who were nervous about it. They were mildly conservative and did not relish being twitted by friends in their clubs or lobbied by pressure groups which accused them of owning a subversive left-wing enterprise. Penguin did not set out to serve left-wing propaganda, but some of its books had a decidedly radical cutting edge and, given the issues of the times, this was bound to be so. It was, for example, virtually impossible to publish a book on Conservative housing policy which any large number of people would buy and efforts (which were made) to find readable and exciting right-wing books on various current issues were on the whole unrewarding. A favourite target for disgruntled or suspicious right-wingers was the Penguin Latin American Library whose editor was openly and sometimes provocatively left-wing but also an exceptionally experienced professional publisher. Neither he nor anybody else at Penguin was going to publish a book in praise of General Pinochet of Chile, but when we did publish – among many excellent books in this section – one by a Brazilian communist it was seized upon by critics who attacked it for teaching people how to kill. It contained nothing that had not already been published in many languages and was most unlikely to be used by apprentice guerrillas in Brazil or anywhere else, but it served as a stick to beat Penguin with. Since the new owners of Penguin read little, if any, of its output they were easy prey for tendentious campaigners who took the opportunity to discredit Penguin

by selective and distorted attacks on books which stung – less because they
were radical than because they were well-written and authoritative and,
in a word, good. Another and peculiarly ill-chosen target was the Economics list. This admirably comprehensive section included books by authors
from right, left and centre; the most eminent British economist not in the
list had an open invitation to write a Penguin with a promise to publish
whatever he chose to submit and he was not on the left. It was an admirable
list. But that did not stop partisan critics from using particular books
which they did not like to snipe at the list as a whole and at Penguin as a
whole and so try to make the new owners uncomfortable.

A particularly outrageous example of partisan misrepresentation occurred shortly after my arrival and left a specially sour taste in the mouth.
The episode arose in this way. There had been a much publicised row at
one of the London Polytechnics in the course of which some left-wing
teachers adopted implacably intolerant attitudes which were all but certainly ideologically motivated. Three of their colleagues compiled an
account of what had been going on and hoped to get it published as a
Penguin Special. They sent it to Robert Allen, a former Conservative chief
whip who worked for Pearsons and was on the boards of both Penguin and
Longmans. Allen gave it to a Longman reader who turned it down on the
grounds that it was not good enough. He then sent it to me. I read it and,
without knowing that it had been turned down by Longmans, came to the
same conclusion. But since the subject – public education and how to run
it – was a natural one for Penguin I decided to ask a colleague for a second
opinion. I sent her the book with a note drawing attention to the suitability
of the subject but saying nothing about my estimate of the book's quality.
She thought the book not good enough but since she interpreted my note
as a wish on my part to publish it she too sought another opinion before
advising me against it. This third opinion was identical with hers and
mine. I told Robert Allen what we thought and why. By this point he had
four reports from four well-qualified editors, all of them saying much the
same and on the same grounds. He made no demur and that seemed to be
the end of that. The situation was a familiar one – a promising subject but
poorly executed. The publisher has in this situation two choices. He can
either reject the book or he may give the author his reasons for not
accepting it with suggestions for improving it and an offer to reconsider it
in a revised shape. I have always fought shy of the second course which
too often leads to re-submission of a manuscript which is still unsatisfac-
tory but comes back after the author has done more work at the publisher's
behest so that the publisher feels under an obligation to be kinder. He ends
up taking on a book in which he has less than the desirable confidence.

In this particular case more was in the wind. A Conservative MP, a
former teacher and later a Thatcherite junior minister, more intelligent
than many in her coteries but also a touch ridiculous, circulated a memorandum alleging that Penguin – and he named myself and one of my

senior editors – had rejected the book not on its merits but on ideological grounds and out of political prejudice. He sent his memorandum to all the directors of Penguin and Longmans and to the press but not to me. Only one of all these people took the trouble to ask me for my version of what had occurred and he was a former Conservative cabinet minister, Edward Boyle, who advised me to make light of the whole affair. Pearsons on the other hand made heavy weather and Penguin's chairman was jolted into drafting an apology to the MP without first asking me for the facts. I had no intention of wasting time over this business but since charges had been made against the integrity and professionalism of one of my colleagues as well as myself I sent it to my solicitors who replied in a matter of days – a record in legal celerity – that it was actionable. I asked my colleague what he wanted to do, promising my support. He replied that he had better things to do than sue a person whom he despised – with which attitude I heartily concurred. At the next meeting of the Penguin board all the members except one wanted the matter buried without further ado. I said that I did too, but I desired the secretary to record in the minutes my dismay at the disloyalty shown to me by Pearsons in the handling of an unsavoury episode. They failed to show me the consideration which I had shown to my subordinate. The truth was that they panicked, and they panicked because they were in unfamiliar territory. You are apt to go wrong if you have your feet off the ground.

This unsureness, to use no harsher word, surfaced again in an entirely different context. Because Penguin was big business in the world of books and because it was famous it specially attracted the attention of trade unions which had not previously seen much point in proselytising in this segment of white collardom. Apart from the warehouse Penguin staff knew little about unionism and were not much attracted; directors were just as ignorant and not attracted at all. There was no great hostility but there were questions which invited union intervention. Salaries, which had been distinctly low in Allen Lane's time, had been raised to the top of the publishing scales, but staffing levels were a latent bone of contention. There was overstaffing in some areas and Pearsons were naturally irritated by this slackness. With my special responsibility for the editorial departments, where overstaffing was undeniable if not precisely quantifiable, I drew up a plan whose rigour jolted not only the possible victims but also my chairman and other senior colleagues who thought I was asking for trouble. But I insisted that it was right, and after much argument union representatives said that they would swallow it whole against their own judgment if I would personally give them my word that my proposed cuts were both necessary and workable. I did so and went off to New York on business with this problem, as I thought, settled. But while I was away some of my colleagues decided that they might after all go one better and they added a rider to my plan which caused the whole thing to unravel amid a good deal of indignation and bad feeling. Shortly after this affair

Pearsons despatched one of their own people to show Penguin the ropes in dealing with staff. After one of his visits I gave him a lift in my car and as he got out he turned to me with the words: 'I suppose you know that your problem is not your unions but your colleagues.' This little drama, which did not improve my confidence in my superiors, was sharpened by an absurdly ill timed decision by Pearsons to give rises of 30 per cent to the top four people in Penguin – at a time when Penguin was cutting costs by getting rid of staff for the first time in its history. This was an early example of the insensitive folly which was to grow to scandalous proportions in Thatcherite Britain. My protests were vain, overridden with something like scorn. I was given to understand that I was ignorant of the real world. I thought they were. I was told that nobody would know of the increases – an argument which, even had it been reputable, was absurd since at least the accounts department must know of them and was not staffed by Trappists. (I never drew my share of this handout.)

Before this date my position in Penguin had changed. Within a year of my appointment as Editorial Director and for reasons which I never discovered Pearsons suddenly lost faith in Chris Dolley, who had seemed set for a prosperous upward career in the Pearson empire, and abruptly fired him. I got on well with Dolley for, although we were different kinds of person, our views about where Penguin should go were sufficiently congruent and each of us welcomed the other's decisiveness. Dolley did a good job in Allen Lane's last years and as his successor as chairman. He was respected but he also trod on toes and was suspected by the purer spirits of caring too little about the books and too much about the monthly profit figures. But even those who were uncomfortable with him were shocked by the manner of his removal. One colleague, shocked by Pearsons' crude behaviour, remarked to me that although Allen Lane 'could be a bastard' Penguin was at least his firm and he was always around; and I was astonished to notice a photograph of Dolley make its appearance on the desk of somebody who had not been a particularly warm admirer.

I was summoned to Pearsons' headquarters and offered Dolley's job as chairman. I without hesitation accepted it. It was a complex and demanding job but exhilarating, and thanks to my training at school and after I knew how to reach decisions and formulate them – advantages which save a lot of time and make life easier for other people as well as oneself. Gibson said he thought Pearsons should have two representatives on the Penguin board to which I agreed on the dual grounds that it was their right as owners and that it would be to Penguin's advantage that Pearsons should know early and directly what was going on in Penguin. Gibson added that he would prefer his representatives to have specific duties with Penguin, to which I replied that I would have to give this idea some thought. Two days later I returned to tell Gibson that I could not see anybody from the Pearson stable filling a specific publishing job and in order to meet his concerns I proposed that his two representatives join the Penguin board as part-time non-executive directors, one of them to be (if he wished) non-executive chairman provided I were left to perform with some other title the duties already offered to me. Gibson immediately accepted these proposals and I was given the title of Chief Executive. Jim Rose, a close friend of mine and Gibson's brother-in-law, was chosen to be part-time non-executive chairman and I went around telling people at Penguin what a good choice this was. And so it could have been. But not long afterwards a most extraordinary and discreditable event occurred. Without a word to me Pearsons translated Jim Rose into full-time executive chairman. I discovered the change by chance. I immediately protested to Gibson that, besides being made in a startlingly shabby way, this change was contrary to the agreement between us and furthermore was unworkable in practical terms since there was no room in a business like Penguin for a full-time Chief Executive and a full-time chairman. It was both a breach of faith and a breach of practical good sense and in the end it proved harmful not merely to me but to all concerned, including Jim Rose who was transported into a position for which he was not qualified. He too was a victim of a sort: I do not suppose that he was happy at Penguin or felt that he did a good job there. Gibson, using a phrase about himself which I have never used about anybody, promised to restore the situation and did not. I was so astonished by this episode that I failed to draw the obvious conclusions from it.

I made the mistake of trying to make things work. About a year later I prepared a long memorandum on the working of Penguin and the alloca- tion of authority within it. Its first section put the question: Who runs Penguin? and began the answer with the words: Nobody knows. To predictable confusion were added distrust and intrigue. Eventually my most senior colleague bluntly besought me to use my personal links with Gibson to effect drastic changes at the top without courting unpleasant publicity (which Penguin abhorred) and with the minimum of pain and humiliation to any individual. 'You can do it. Will you?' I refused point blank: 'I can but I won't.' This was an automatic reaction derived from a deep-seated principle that personal relations come before everything else. Yet general principles, however sound or admirable, are no more than guides. To apply them automatically in a particular case may be an alibi for hard thinking. They provide a ready answer but not always the right one. In this case my instinctive reaction led me astray and benefited nobody.

At the same time my own removal was in the making and it was accelerated by a ludicrous and not very seemly chain of events. I had agreed to serve until my sixty-fifth birthday. I was asked to accelerate my departure by a year and was offered in return a pension of £400 – accompanied by the suggestion that it would be a nice touch if I were to write to Gibson to thank him for this munificence. I agreed to the first part of this proposal which, since Pearsons were Penguin's sole owners, amounted to rather more than a proposal. But when it became known that

I would be leaving sooner than expected a strange commotion ensued. I got a call from the *Sunday Times* which wanted to know why. The paper scented a story but what the story turned out to be came as a total surprise to me.

Pearsons were still very much a family business. The line between family loyalties, solidarity and drive rightly acclaimed in Victorian novels and, on the other hand, an excessive and debilitating nepotism is a fuzzy one. The Second World War appeared to give nepotism a bit of a shove into the dustbin of economic and social history but in the worlds of finance, as distinct from industry, the cousinage proved unexpectedly resilient and Pearsons was reputed in the City to be a bastion of old ways and values. Yet it had never occurred to me that anybody in Fleet Street or anywhere else might assume that I had been recruited to Penguin by Pearsons because I (or my wife) had a supposed relationship with the ruling dynasty, or that I had been used as a pliant stopgap until Pearsons could take full control through a man of their own, or that I was about to be cast aside because I had served my purpose. Yet this was what was being said.

To the newspaper's original inquiry I had responded by refusing to discuss anything on the telephone or so long as my chairman was in hospital (where he happened briefly to be). A week or so later I went to the *Sunday Times* where a deputy editor whom I knew – Jack Lambert – had been designated to talk to me. Before we got going he told me that nothing would appear in the paper until it had been approved personally by the editor, but he added, in a confidential tone and laying a finger along the side of his nose, that the editor was determined to print something because he was incensed by attempts made by telephone to get him to say nothing. So I knew at the start that the *Sunday Times* would run a story, but what they first had in mind took me aback.

Jack Lambert then launched into his story about my supposed family connections. I killed this story stone dead. I told him that there was no such connection and that if the paper printed anything of the sort it would be making a fool of itself. Clearly surprised he asked me whether, even if there were no kinship, I did not think that my friendship with members of the family amounted to the same thing. I told him that if he had made similar suggestions a year earlier I would have laughed in his face but that the way Pearsons had treated me gave me pause for thought; that nevertheless I still believed the whole story was a myth. As a result nothing of all this appeared in the paper which contented itself with reporting that I was leaving a year ahead of time in consequence of differences between myself and Pearsons: the phrase used was differences over 'styles of management'. It was a mild and correct report but it had an unwholesome sequel. When I got to my office the following day I found that without a word to me my principal subordinates had been told that the story was false and that its publication had been secured by threats. This *fracas* over an anodyne story was symptomatic, a consequence of far-reaching mismanagement. It caused my abrupt departure from Penguin. I was given two reasons, both – to put it obliquely – ill grounded. It was suddenly alleged that I had lost the confidence of all the senior editors – which later they one and all angrily denied having said. I was given ten days to get out and my salary for six months.

Since Penguin was entirely owned by Pearsons and since Penguin's chairman spoke with the full authority and backing of Pearsons I did not question their right to remove me. Nor did I try to contest their decision to do so. Nor, to some people's chagrin, did I publicise their dubious dealings. But perhaps I was wrong. My standing may have been stronger than I thought it was and the issue was one in which I had an obligation, since what was at stake was the survival of Penguin. Pearsons destroyed Penguin – not in the sense of rubbing it out of existence but in the sense that they changed what they had bought from Allen Lane's executors into something very different. They did not intend to do this, for they were proud of acquiring Penguin. Nor were they the villains of popular anti-capitalist mythology. But they were ignorant, not always straight and mediocre. Villainy is rare but mediocrity, although less repulsive, can be just as disastrous. This is not an isolated story nor one confined to publishing. It is an aspect of the subversion of the commercial ethic based on expertise, thrift and fair dealing by the ugly greed, lax morality and wasteful exhibitionism of much modern capitalism.

They were not even, in my experience of them, much good with money. Penguin was a spectacularly successful publishing business which made Allen Lane a millionaire at a time when millionaires were not all that common. Pearsons, on a much larger material scale, had also been outstandingly successful in the postwar years, so much so that they had more money than they knew what to do with in their existing operations. They even mooted a return of capital to shareholders but since they too had more money than they could easily spend or give away the controlling shareholders did not want it. On buying Penguin Pearsons impressed on Penguin how much financial strength they could bring to it by lending money at the best, or better than, going rates and by providing new investment capital. In the event things turned out differently. I wanted to borrow as little as possible (outside the points in the publishing year when publishers need unusual amounts of cash to pay royalties) and I had no difficulty in getting what we wanted from our regular commercial bank. I was indeed invited to lunch at its West End headquarters where I gave an account of where we stood and where we wanted to go, answered some intelligent but not very searching questions and was then politely pressed to borrow more. When I said that we could borrow from our proprietors at favoured rates my hosts offered to match any rate Pearsons might offer, but they did not succeed in getting me to borrow money which I judged we did not need. (Banks were more successful in pressing money on publishers like Robert Maxwell but whether successful is the right word may be left an open question.) When the economic climate got choppy in the mid-seventies Pearsons, so far from providing the promised financial support, pressed Penguin to generate bigger profits and more cash for them. They demanded that Penguin retrench even to the extent of cancelling existing publishing contracts. I rebelled against a course which was not only dishonourable and potentially disastrous to Penguin's reputation but also unnecessary in financial terms. Although I did not entirely get my way I did so substantially enough to save our good standing and I also proved my point by turning in record profits that year. In my last year as Chief Executive Penguin's profits were again higher than at any time in its history. Soon afterwards it went into the red, also for the first time in its history but not the last. At various points Pearsons injected large amounts of capital into Penguin but without raising the rate of return on capital. During my years their financial support was not much more useful than their advice on how to handle stroppy unions.

A little while after I left Penguin I received a short note from Gibson saying how sorry he was that things had turned out the way they had. I did not doubt that his letter was well intentioned but it is one of the very few that I ever received to which I felt unable to return an answer.

Penguin's fate was not unique or even uncommon. In the seventies and eighties there was, in New York as well as London, a spate of forays into publishing by non-publishers with more money than they could spend in their own affairs. Their motives were financial. Publishing, they believed, could be made more profitable through better management and economies of scale. But these premises were largely false. Some publishers certainly were incompetent or, more probably, less competent than they might be, but by and large publishers knew what they were about and the comic stereotype of amiable nincompoopery was wide of the mark. It prevailed in publishing no more than it did in the worlds of finance; bankers, stockbrokers and other merchants of money provide equally risible performers. In my experience publishing businesses bought by non-publishers became on the whole less, not more, efficient. Nor was it true that the costs of publishing might be substantially reduced by amalgamations and the creation of super-publishers. Publishing is by its nature personal, not only because each book is different but mainly because publication of a book requires a series of operations, all of which need the touch of personal attention. These operations can be economised only by homogenising books, turning them (or as many of them as possible) into products with more similarities than dissimilarities. Revealingly, some of my colleagues at Penguin took to referring to books as units. In doing so they were applying to publishing language, habits of mind, methods and aspirations which do not properly belong to it.

Or rather, do not belong to a lot of it. To some publishing these attitudes may be applied and to that segment the new proprietors gave a boost which, however, tended to damage other segments and to distort book publishing as a whole. The new proprietors' chief impact came as much from their ignorance as from greed. The distinction is crucial, for a greedy man may be conscious of his greediness and may therefore restrain it, whereas the ignorant man is prevented by his ignorance from realising how ignorant he is. 'We knew,' somebody once remarked to me about one of these ill-versed invaders, 'that X did not know much about publishing but we did not know how little he knew.' 'Nor,' I replied, 'does he.' There is a story about a famous newspaper tycoon who, picking up a paper he did not own, asked: 'Why can't we produce a paper like this?' Nobody said anything, but they all knew that the answer was: 'Because of you.'

For good publishing to revive and flourish there must be good publishers and they must be the persons in charge. There have always been good and bad publishers. The curse of the seventies and eighties was the incursion of non-publishers and – an allied consequence – the corruption of a number of publishers by greed as the invaders persuaded publishers that they could become millionaires in next to no time by pursuing the fast megabuck. The essence of publishing is judgment. Good publishers are the ones who make more good judgments than bad; bad publishers are the ones who do the reverse. But non-publishers are not qualified to make publishing judgments at all; they downgrade those who can and entrust the business to those who cannot. In the course of doing this they may or may not make a lot of money.

The judgments required of a publisher are two: on the intrinsic quality of a MS which he is asked to publish and on its saleability. In making these judgments he may seek advice about the quality of the MS and also about its probable sales, but he reserves the publishing decision to himself. He does not begin by asking his salesmen whether they can sell the book: one of the ground rules in publishing is that you consult salesmen before deciding how many copies of a book to print but not about whether to publish it. Salesmen at the helm of publishing businesses owned by non-publishers direct their efforts to selling more and more of books that are easy to sell and construct sales departments accordingly. Marketeers like to spend lots of money on promoting books which will sell anyway and then claim the credit for the sales – and ask for yet bigger budgets. But it is the business of the publisher also to sell books that are less easy to sell. The salesman turns these books down. The publisher tells his salesman to get on with selling them.

The pre-eminence of the publisher/editor is crucial for a second reason. He is the link with the author. Books are written by authors and authors look to publishers to do a professional job for them, to keep in touch and answer queries (some of which may be irritating, even paranoid, but nevertheless that is the author's right and it is not removed if he abuses it). When editors are compartmentalised and downgraded, as happens in businesses run by non-publishers and their accountants and marketeers, the editor loses sight of the book halfway through its production process with the result that more often than not he cannot answer the author's legitimate questions about what is going on – or can answer them only after tiresome delays. Nor will the author have confidence in an editor who appears to be a minor cog in the machine. As incompetence proliferates redress, even attention, is hard to secure.

There remains a serious problem. Unwelcoming and damaging changes have been made to publishing but it is not enough to decry them. They have happened. In particular, a part of the publishing scene has been transformed by turning some books into 'properties' for which huge sums, irrecoverable from sales of the book, are paid in the hope of recovering that outlay and much more from the entertainment industry – to the considerable benefit of the lucky authors of these plums if and when expectations are fulfilled. These 'properties' are keys giving access to the plush fields of movies, T-shirts, picture mugs and other Aladdin's caves. These things are not be derided. The question is not the specious one whether they sap our culture but what they do to the publishing trade. There is nothing inherently wrong with this kind of commerce, however unattractive its ways and practitioners may appear; but the impact on publishing is serious if, as is almost certainly the case, these money-spinners have been permanently appropriated by non-publishers. The question that arises is whether publishers can do without them.

In the past the best-seller was a cheering bonanza but no solid publishing firm relied on having a best-seller every year or even every five years. Some never did. Their businesses were conducted on the basis that the best-seller might come along but the firm would prosper whether it did or not. Efficient publishers knew how to get along without them. (A useful distinction can be made between a best-seller and a block-buster. The best-seller is a book with sales out of the ordinary. A block-buster is not so much a book as a launch pad; its sales, however large, are less significant financially than the gains or expected gains from non-book revenues, notably films and serialisation in newspapers. A best-seller is by some standards and in some sense a good book. A block-buster need not be good by any definition.)

Big sales bring big money but the key to a decent profit is printing what you can sell and no more, getting the equation right. There is a lower limit below which no profit can be made even if the whole edition is sold at a properly costed price, but more important for the publisher than the odd best-seller is his ability to gauge each book's sale and achieve it with due competence. Every publisher knows this. Non-publishers, however, and their acolytes act as though quantity, not measure, is the key. They are wrong. Quantity entails expansion and what usually expands in these businesses is the tail – more accountants and marketeers wagging few editors and designers in desperate or greedy attempts to chase the books, or non-books, which are seen as the golden nuggets of the trade. But if new books published over a given period cover their costs and produce in addition profits yielding on average an acceptable return, then there is no need for the best-seller. It is welcome but not necessary for salvation. It is necessary only if the list as a whole is being published unprofitably so that the best-seller is needed to subsidise incompetence. The loss of this segment of the trade is fatal only for the publisher who believes that, in competition with the conglomerates which can afford to buy up the big names, he will not be able to acquire for his own list the authors who fall short of the best-seller category but are nevertheless necessary to keep him in business. That is the crucial question and there is no demonstrably certain answer to it. But given the great number of authors who write good books and the even greater number of people who – as a visit to a bookshop will show – want to buy and read them, the answer ought to be yes.

The upheaval has been most obvious and destructive in fiction. For publishers and also for the literary agents who handle (or refuse to handle) the works of aspiring novelists the novel has become the path to a crock of gold and the novel which lacks the glint of instant gold finds scant welcome. The highbrow novel, the trashy novel and special categories such as crime or sci-fi survive but the middle-of-the-road, middlebrow novel – entertaining, literate and mildly literary, a good read, here today if gone the day after tomorrow – needs a great deal of luck and influence to get into print. This is not a great cultural disaster, but it is a pity, and who knows how many good novels never emerge from the chrysalis because what matters to the publisher is not the writer's talent and its possible development but just one book at a time: the culture of the jackpot.

The picture is not all gloom. The damage done to publishing by nonpublishers has been considerable, not least by the dispersal of talent and the depression of standards, but dark clouds have silver linings and one consequence of the havoc in the trade has been to put a premium on publishing skills in editing and design. They may have to be even more rigorous than before but they are still there and they can still be rewarded.

For myself extrusion from Penguin was not quite the end of my life in the worlds of publishing and commerce. The Open University, of which I was from its birth an enthusiastic admirer, had set up a wholly owned company to sell beyond the university and all over the world the books, videos and other educational trappings which it produced to give to its own students. As an ancillary to these marketing activities it started a University Press with a small publishing programme of academic books. I was asked to be chairman of this company. After ten years the university changed its mind, partly because it was strapped for cash, and decided to sell the Press and handle its other commercial business as a department of the university and not through an incorporated company. The Press was sold for £1.3 million, a staggering price for something that had not even existed ten years earlier. My part in these matters had always been very much part-time and became more so after I had assembled a team able and eager to assume fuller responsibility. I became a minor Cartesian deity, watching the workings of a machine which I had helped to wind up in the first place. Upon retiring from this diminishing scene I was accorded an honorary Doctorate. It was an award that I greatly cherished. Whether earned by literary or commercial acumen I was not sure but if it was a bit of both I could gratifyingly interpret it as an appropriate signal of the end of what had been in more senses than one a hybrid career.

Note on Penguin Education

I append to this chapter this brief account of a special episode because I believe myself to be the only person in possession of all the facts. It concerns the downfall of Penguin Education. This latest addition to the Penguin brood did not fit comfortably in the nest. It was not popular with some of the old hands who saw it as a rival with esoteric skills which they imperfectly understood. This separateness was accentuated by its being physically located, for purely practical reasons, over a mile away from the Penguin headquarters at Harmondsworth, where there was no room for it. And whereas its editorial and production sections were under its own control its sales, marketing and distribution were handled at Harmondsworth by the central machine which was famously efficient at getting books into bookshops but had less experience in, and less time for, the quite different channels through which educational books have to go. Penguin Education was geographically split from the main body with awkward practical and psychological consequences. For all these reasons it was ill adapted to weather a storm and in the seventies two storms began to buffet it. There was the general inclemency of the post-1973 inflation and these breezes (for in publishing they were really no more than that) coincided with the launching of an expensive and controversial new publishing venture called the Penguin English Project (PEP).

Chris Dolley, who had been the first manager of Penguin Education in the sixties, and I both realised that its position was uneasy and puzzled over schemes to move it to Harmondsworth or to some other place where all the Harmondsworth operations and Penguin Education could be amalgamated. But neither he nor I had found a way to do this when the alarm bells began to ring. The PEP was well received by the teaching profession or at any rate by its more articulate and progressive elements, but its initial sales were poor and it was going to absorb a lot of money over the next few years with a problematic rate of return on a substantial investment. Controversial and expensive, it became the focus for a debate over the professional and managerial skills in Penguin Education as a whole with people taking sides on various and not always relevant grounds. Senior directors of Penguin were poorly informed as well as a bit scared; they hardly ever visited Penguin Education except for the Christmas party and matters were so confused that the chairman was able to write to *The Times Educational Supplement* a letter in which he said that Penguin

Education was losing money – which was untrue and caused a lot of offence. To Pearsons it looked like a black hole into which their money was going to be sucked.

Given these doubts and stringencies, the whole future of Penguin Education was properly brought before the superior board of which Gibson was chairman with other Pearson representatives and four from each of Penguin and Longmans. I was in a small minority who actively wished to find a way to keep Penguin Education going. The majority – perhaps all except me – wanted it ditched for one reason or another. Gibson ruled that the decision should be left to Penguin and said that he would personally back the decision, whatever it was. This well-meaning gesture was a trifle ingenuous since it was apparent to all that what we were talking about was the possible drain on Pearson, not merely Penguin, money. Gibson added one condition: that if Penguin resolved to carry on with Penguin Education it must co-opt to its managerial board a member of the Longman board. Gibson presumably did not know, although he should have known, that this was tantamount to putting the cat among the pigeons – not because Longman directors were personally obnoxious in Penguin but because they were more or less hostile to the PEP and to Penguin Education itself. Longmans regarded Penguin Education as a bunch of dangerously wilful amateurs who were probably heading for disaster or, alternatively, could become awkward competitors in educational publishing. Penguin Education on the other hand regarded Longmans as crusty, if successful, professionals temperamentally averse to new ventures such as Penguin existed to explore. Gibson's recipe was therefore unworkable and he should have known it.

I was fairly sure that my own colleagues, while wanting to kill off Penguin Education, would not override me if I took the opposite view, but after a night's unhappy reflection I decided to close it. I concluded that any attempt to save it would be no more than a reprieve. Early next morning I drove to Harmondsworth where I had bidden the managing director of Penguin Education, Martin Lightfoot, to meet me. I told him that I had resolved to close his show; that I believed I could save it for a while; but that with other problems looming I felt unable to guarantee more, and that was not justification enough for carrying on. My decision was a dreadful disappointment to him. He had fought his corner with skill and also loyalty, but he now generously told me that if he had been in my position he would probably have done the same. He asked me if he might try to sell Penguin Education as a going concern and so ensure its survival in some form and the jobs of as many of its staff as possible. I telephoned Gibson who immediately gave his consent. But in the ensuing negotiations my colleagues made greedy reservations which made a deal impossible (it was never going to be easy) and Penguin Education was sunk with all hands and even more gnashing of teeth.

9

Apologia

This book is a record from a personal stance but, since some of what it records is far distant, some quite close, it is not a personal record: it is not just about me, not does it even try to depict or explain or reveal me. I am necessarily central to it but – if not off stage – yet back stage. Its first main thread is provided by the fortunes over centuries of a small community or group of families which was forced by a cruel blow to flee home and fortunes, find new ones in foreign parts and adapt. This is a relatively obscure story but also one which sheds some light on the larger and more distressing movements which have become horribly commonplace in the second half of the twentieth century. The history of the island of Chios and of some of the families who lived there is unusual, intriguing, largely unknown and worth attention on its own account. The network of Chiot families to which I belong was devastatingly disrupted, but it re-formed and recovered. To the outside observer, so far as he is aware of it at all, this process may look like a smooth and ultimately happy transition, but for those directly involved there was great uncertainty and, before recovery, fear. From my own vantage point a century and more after the massacre of 1822 I have observed these varied emotions still at work in my parents' and my own generations.

Greeks of my kind who, after centuries of comfortable existence under Turkish and other foreign rulers in a small island off Asia Minor, moved perforce to fairly democratic and fairly liberal England at the height of British imperial world power had to find a way to fit and be accepted in new homes where they intended to stay. At one level they were far from ignorant about England and some of them had even been there, but the world they left and the world in which they settled were in many – and unsuspected – ways profoundly different. They needed to assimilate and wanted to; and yet, up to a point, not: *vorrei e non vorrei*. They were, it seems to me, about as successful as it is possible to be in a situation where success entails some abandonment of past habits and attitudes, some sense even of betrayal. To assimilate, however, is not to be engulfed. Assimilation means becoming like something else, not becoming the same as something else. Newcomers are entitled to preserve their own beliefs but they are also under an obligation to observe and accept the reasonable requirements of the community to which they have more or less willingly come and in which they plan to remain.

There is a crucial distinction between migrants and refugees. Refugees, who arrive in a foreign country in a pitiable condition and cannot return to their own without real fear of death or torture, are hardly ever welcome (particularly when numerous) but they have an overriding right to succour and asylum, however financially burdensome and socially tiresome the implementation of this principle may be to the host society. Migrants, by contrast, owe as well as being owed. They are not colonists and not entitled to create in their adopted country enclaves of their old. They have to adjust.

This process of adjustment is frequently obstructed by those among the migrants who most acutely suspect or resent assimilation as the thin end of a wedge and regard yielding a little as the primrose path to losing all: they equate, often perversely, adjustment with loss of identity. Such defenders of cultural or religious identities see salvation only through an aggressive separateness which reinforces alienation, negates assimilation and causes much strife and personal distress. In seeking to preserve a compact whole they risk maiming many of the individuals who make up that whole. Their motives may be good or bad. They may venerate and love traditions which they see slipping away; or they may be narrowly benighted or have a quasi-political interest in posing as saviours – too often self-righteous saviours. In either case they elevate group rights above individual rights and demand of members of their own community an insistence on the group's distinctive values which may be at variance with the individual's happiness and his right to choose for himself. At their worst such attitudes smack of moral blackmail.

I have spent some of my time in defence of minority rights both internationally (at the United Nations) and domestically (in the operation of the first British Race Relations Act). The need to define and protect the rights of members of minorities cannot be questioned and should never be skimped but I have come to doubt whether groups, as distinct from the individuals in the group, have rights and I have also come to believe that demands for rights for groups as such too often do individuals more harm than good. The concept of rights pertains to individuals, not to groups; it is ancillary to individual freedoms, opportunity and happiness. Leaders of groups who seek rights for groups come hazardously close to maintaining that minority groups are entitled to a distinct political or constitutional position in the state instead of demanding from the state the same rights which are owed to all its inhabitants (for example, the right to worship their own gods). There is a cleft between the distinctiveness of the group and the happiness of individuals and so a necessary, sometimes painful, choice has to be made. But the choice belongs to the individual and should be neither exercised nor imposed by other persons on his or her behalf. Leaders may claim that the preservation of group attributes overrides personal choice but for me this claim is spurious. It is part of the perpetual conflict between the collective and the personal, between the *polis* and the citizen, and to my way of thinking it is imperative that where this conflict cannot be comfortably adjusted the latter should prevail and be allowed to prevail. This is a question of principle and it cannot be fudged. Furthermore the champions of collective values and collective identities, however persuasive their arguments, cannot escape the charge that every collectivist, however laudable his motives, conceals a latent dictator. He is apt, with more determination than sensitivity, to see life in terms of conflicts to be resolved by obstinacy rather than adjustment and so far as he does so he downgrades personal rights and endangers personal happiness. Small is not beautiful when it is tight: consider the Wee Free Kirk, Afrikanerdom, Israel – small, sturdy, even inspired, but far from beautiful. There is here something of the difference between the ruling French and German political ideologies of the nineteenth century: the French committed to the Rights of Man, the German centred upon the mystique of the *Volk*; the French in the steady mainstream of descent from Rome and the traditions of Roman lawyers who constructed their systems upon the rights of individuals, the German with its new-found enthusiasm for classical Greece, the centrality of the *polis* and the apotheosis of the German state. (The English, exhibiting the strengths and weaknesses of the hybrid, fought shy of the Rights of Man when they became associated with French revolutionary violence and equally shy of the blood-and-soil imagery out of which the Germans fashioned a German nation and a German state. Have the English had it both ways or neither?)

The story of Chios and the Chiot migrants is an historical vignette with broader associations. Migrations and the fate of migrants have become a major theme of contemporary history. Some turn out comparatively well, like the Chiots themselves or the Huguenots who fled from France to England and Prussia in the seventeenth century, but the larger the tide the more frequently is it disastrous. Some of the causes of migration remain the same – religious intolerance, national hatred, wars. They are exacerbated by sheer numbers. There are far more people in the world, and numbers alone create pressures which, independently or in concert with prejudices and calamities, get treks going. The collapse of empires from 1918 to 1985 has taken the lid off many temporarily repressed conflicts, and the yeast of self-determination has gone on fermenting in and fragmenting the states which emerged from the empires. New states promising their peoples a better life have put more resources and energies into arming the state than feeding its citizens and, like older states, a great deal into corruption. Poverty has added to the need to flee.

At the heart of most of these migrations is the existence of groups with consciously separate identities nursing real or imagined inter-group conflicts which, however irrational in themselves and baffling to outsiders, persist underground even when the groups live peacefully intermingled for long periods: Serbs with Croats, Armenians with Azerbaijanis, Uzbeks with Pathans. The sources of their conflicts are various but most commonly they derive from a language or a religion distinguishable from the language or religion of neighbours. The conflicts are easily exhumed, excited and exploited by appeals to loyalty, pride or fear and each time they recur – whether reanimated by accident or malice – they stiffen ancestral hatreds and end or devastate more lives. Ethnic diversity is attractive when viewed from outside and for those within ethnic minorities who comfortably straddle two worlds – witness colourful cosmopolitanism, cross-cultural music and painting – but for many it is a trap, even a death trap. At the root of the killing in Yugoslavia after the collapse of the communist regime was the sense of separate identities and their direful inflammation by politicians, clerics and the foreign champions of one faction or another whose rhetoric mirrored the conflicts instead of trying to compose them.

These issues lead to a question which is at the core of this memoir's second main theme – international relations. The very term discloses the problem. International relations means not relations between nations but relations between states. And, if the state and the nation are not the same thing, what is the state? Once upon a time the state was defined by power; it was a territory where the sovereign's power was legitimated by conquest and continuing effective authority. In more recent times the legitimacy of the state has been found in popular consent elicited by democratic choice or self-determination. But this doctrine leads to indefinable fragmentation as ever smaller national groups claim the right to be recognised as states. It is no longer clear what a state is, nor is it clear what are the proper functions of an international organisation which is in fact an association of states clearly marked on the map and pledged not to interfere in each other's affairs.

Further: attempts to strengthen international law and order – to reduce the number of wars between and within states – are bedevilled by a change which goes deeper than political definitions. The general mental climate has become less propitious. People in optimistic mood behave differently from people with doubts and forebodings and the twentieth century is markedly less certain, more hesitant, than the nineteenth. So the management of divisions in the world – political, economic, religious, cultural – is rendered more difficult and these prime sources of preventable human misery are less easily controlled.

Much of the turmoil and tribulation around the world may be ascribed to human incompetence and human beastliness, but not all of it. Human history records man's increasingly assured dominance over the world but this success has brought mankind in the twentieth century to a profoundly disquieting point. Although the world's physical contours, its climate and other properties, are much the same as they have been throughout human history, and although the scope of human activity in the world has increased dramatically, the balance between man and the world about him has shifted, or seems to be shifting, against man. Man has come to know vastly more about the world, to be able to do vastly more to it, and to be continuously in touch with all parts of it and all peoples in it, but it is open to question whether all this knowledge and capability have commensurately added to man's control over what is going to happen. The past record created confidence and optimism but the present reckoning induces doubt and pessimism as human powers seem to be running ahead of human controls. As human power over the world increases, the exercise of that power is bedevilled by the very magnitude, speed and complexity of mankind's own discoveries. More knowledge may connote less control. This conundrum is something new to this generation. It arises less from changes over five centuries than from the speed of the changes in the last.

The growth of knowledge and the capacity to handle it have been the main instruments of man's dominance over animate and inanimate non-man. This growth has been exponential. In Europe the Renaissance, the Enlightenment and the Industrial Revolutions have all contributed through discovery and education to striking increases in knowledge and therewith power. They had a happy duality. Advances in material production and wealth were accompanied by comparable advances in welfare – in, for example, medicine and public health and the availability of food (which made life in cities possible and so did more than anything since the Ice Ages to change the pattern of human distribution over the land). The duality was not invariably happy: science and technology powered discoveries by sea and land with contrasting consequences, for knowledge of other peoples entailed also exploitation of some by others. But on balance it seemed reasonable to be hopeful. In the present century the pace has continued to quicken but the outlook has become more troubled. Populations have continued to grow – mainly through reductions in mortality – but the consumption of foods and minerals has grown faster. City life has become a worldwide phenomenon but also economically unstable and humanly unsafe in rich countries as well as poor, in the United States as alarmingly as in Africa. The century's outstanding miracles, in electronics for example or space travel, offer no obvious cures for the century's characteristic ills nor any welfare benefits to match the threatened degradation of the human condition. Words like advance and progress no longer have clear meanings. Yet there is no going back: man has little, if any, control over the direction of change. Opponents of nuclear energy cannot disinvent it, however dangerous they may show it still to be. Above all there is no discernible acceleration of human thought processes, so that things now seem to be changing faster than mankind can devise ways of mastering and directing the changes. We seem to be moving headlong towards something which we may not like when we see what it turns out to be. The overall effect is a sense of opportunities which can all too easily be perverted or simply run out of control: alarm and pessimism.

The world into which I was born on the eve of the First World War was

optimistic with an optimism bred by the conquests of science and technology which were still in those days specific to parts of Europe and North
America. These conquests derived from the intellectual and scientific
revolutions of the sixteenth and seventeenth centuries in western Europe
which created a European dominance and therein a European mentality
(later inherited and engrossed in the United States) which have passed
into history. History, when I started learning it in the 1920s and 1930s,
was understandably but perhaps arrogantly European history and not
much more. Europe's history is rich, exciting and rewarding. Few other
areas give as much. But there comes a time when no single area gives
enough, when all areas are subsumed or entangled in global happenings.
In European history, when I was at school, the Congress of Vienna which
set about putting Europe to rights after the phenomena of the French
Revolution and Napoleon was a major landmark – both positive and
negative since the Congress dismantled Napoleon's achievements but
could not kill off the ideas behind the Revolution. In world history,
however, the Congress of Vienna amounts to little. So too even greater
European landmarks such as the Renaissance and Reformation which in
my adolescent scheme of things divided history into its two major compart-
ments of the medieval and the modern but mean little in Japan or Iran or
India and not much in Australia.

World history has other guideposts. Francis Bacon said that the three
inventions that transformed the world in his time were printing, artillery
and the needle (i.e. the compass): triumphs in technique. Only scientific,
technological and imaginative revolutions have global, more than local,
significance: the scientific and technological because all peoples want to
annex them; the imaginative because, with the easy transmission of ideas
in the modern world, all peoples have to wrestle with the choice of what to
assimilate into their own cultures and what to repel – in reaction, for
example, to Europe's offerings, Newton and Einstein yes but Rousseau and
Mill *quaere*.

The singularity of the globe brought about by the revolution in communications from air travel to the fax machine has introduced perplexity
which is in itself an intellectual challenge. Economics, the science of the
oikoumene or inhabited space, is forced to deal with larger and larger areas,
and yet the economics of large areas are imperfectly understood and the
areas themselves do not accord with our mental images of how the world
is divided – into states or political leagues. Adjustment is peculiarly taxing
for Europeans whose recent history has taught them a certain disregard
for other parts of the world and has given them rather too good an opinion
of themselves: the opinion which a century ago prompted the warning
proffered by Mrs Ponsonby de Tompkins to Sir Gorgeous Midas to 'endeavour to draw a veil of reticence over the effulgence of consummate
achievement'. Yet Europe never did run the world. A few Europeans ran
large parts of it but most Europeans neither did so nor wanted to.

The second half of the twentieth century was the period when Europe was forced to confront the consequences of a loss of weight in world affairs, hitherto only lackadaisically apprehended. In doing so the two leading continental states, Germany and France, had the paradoxical advantage of defeat and deflation in war which purged a number of prejudices and pretensions and inclined them to accept their smaller neighbours' radical ideas for converting a patchwork of declining sovereignties into a tighter union. Britain, however, having escaped these pressures partly by ending the war on the winning side and partly through its ambivalent position on Europe's margin, remained addicted to a European states system even if it entailed redefining Europe to include the United States and exclude Russia. The ensuing forty years saw therefore two separate developments – on the one hand the Cold War for which the United States was co-opted into Europe in order to fend off a Soviet threat, and on the other hand the formation of the European Community of western European and Mediterranean states, beginning with economic measures but looking forward to some kind of European, not Euro-American, political union too. The principal concern of the Cold War was the fate of continental Europe but its initial inspiration was Anglo-American and its strength American. The fashioning of the European Community was almost exclusively the work of continental Europeans. By the eighties, after Gorbachev had overturned the Soviet system but failed to maintain the Soviet union, the Cold War was over and Nato was an honourable anachronism, while the European Community, although still embryonic, was besieged by new applicants for membership and appeared anxious to embrace in some form all central and eastern Europe, including the European remnants of the Soviet Union.

The Cold War had a deceptive effect. It made European affairs after the Second World War look like a version of European affairs in the thirties, with a Russian substituted for a German threat. Further, it made world affairs look like a worldwide contest between two equally matched Superpowers. While there were reasons for this depiction of the way of the world, it was, as I have said in an earlier chapter, a delusion because it grossly overestimated the capabilities of the Soviet Union which, besides its all but lethal battering in the Second World War, was ruled with exceptional incompetence and corruption and could not sustain the economic imperatives of the Superpower conflict. If and so far as the possession of nuclear weapons made the Soviet Union a Superpower, it was nevertheless never the equal of the United States and its collapse and disintegration put an end not only to the Cold War but also to the assessment of power in terms of nuclear weaponry. The Superpowers, if any, were the United States and Japan with some prospect of a third, the European Community, provided it could match its economic strengths with appropriate political apparatus, coherence and authority. This distribution of world power represented the universalisation of world affairs more accurately than had the Cold War. During the Cold War power was represented as lodged in and radiating from two centres, Washington and Moscow, and power meant military power. After the Cold War power was more clearly seen to be located where science and technology were breeding economic power, however that power might then be used.

The Cold War had two legacies of prime importance. It precipitated the collapse of the Soviet Union and of the communist parties within it. These parties – the central party or CPSU and its provincial counterparts – had long ceased to care about communism or any other set of ideas and had become corrupt cliques interested only in themselves, their power and their perks. They had, however, held the state together even while they were corroding it, so that their disappearance threatened anarchy, aggravated by the simultaneous disintegration of the Soviet Federal Union and the publicisation of its economic devastation. The ancillary upheavals in the Soviet satellite states greatly extended the areas of uncertainty and distress to the alarm of the rest of Europe, already engaged in the painful, contentious and incomplete business of radically recasting its own political and economic framework. Confusion was compounded when Yugoslavia, the one communist state in Europe not dominated by the Soviet Union, also disintegrated with peculiarly vicious violence and the flight of hundreds and thousands of refugees into other countries. Within a few years nearly twenty new states emerged in Europe, all of them with severe or very severe economic problems.

The Cold War, although it ended with a spectacular demonstration of the vices and ineptitude on the communist side, did not leave 'the West' untainted: the term explains the infection. It was invented to define the associated enemies of the Soviet Union and of communism but it did more than define. It laid claim to virtue. As a definition it was a handy way of defining Europe minus central and eastern Europe but plus north America. As a claim to virtue it was useful against the Soviet Union but distasteful and even offensive. The virtue claimed was political: the virtues of democracy over authoritarianism (or, for many Americans such as Ronald Reagan and his friends at home and abroad, communist authoritarianism only). Apart from overlooking embarrassing defects in western democratic societies this arrogation of superiority reminded the rest of the world of attitudes in the West in the nineteenth century. In particular it fuelled hostility in Islam where the West, its technological pre-eminence undisputed, exhibits also evil qualities in sexual licence, capitalist crime and corruption, social carelessness and tawdry commercialism – the modern Deadly Sins. Islam claimed against the West the high moral ground which the West had held against Soviet communism, and this contest – more truly ideological than that between communists and anti-communists – was the more important because Islam's adherents were very numerous and some of its component states were very rich from what the rest of the world could not do without – oil. The Cold War, I have argued, developed in its earliest stages through mutual incomprehension and mistaken

calculations. Between the West and Islam lies a more profound gulf –
historically profound because it is old, a revived version of the conflict
between Christendom and Islam which was waged through centuries in
Spain, in the Holy Lands of western Asia and in eastern Europe; and
ideologically profound because in Christendom the force of religion had
declined very much more than in Islam.

Europe has been distinguished by more than its achievements. Its
nature too evolved in a distinctive way. While on the one hand its material
pre-eminence in modern times propelled European skills and inventions
and power throughout the world, Europe's history gave it a civilisation
which has marked it off from much of the rest of the world. Long ago Europe
was secularised. Europe might have become a more or less unified society
dominated by Christianity and aptly denominated Christendom in much
the same sense as another and larger chunk of the world is called Islam.
So: two large areas each permeated and dominated and in large measure
united by a religious faith – two of a kind. But that is not what happened.
Islam acknowledges, in theory and often in practice, a single authority in
which church and state are not so much conjoined as identical and
inseparable. In Islam the notion of a division between church and state is
either incomprehensible or vile. This belief may or may not survive the
coming centuries; probably it will not. Although Muslims have adhered
atavistically to the singularity of church and state the vision of Islam as a
single society has been undermined by the very spread of Islam from its
native core as far as South East Asia in one direction and west Africa in
the other. Islam has spread too far to remain coherent. Muslims have
therefore the problem, by no means new but never palatable, of jettisoning
the notion of Islam as a single political entity while preserving and even
in recompense sharpening its fundamental Islamic values and tenets
within the several and distinct Islamic states and against the outside world
– no single Islamic state but each state a unified Islamic society exempli-
fying these Islamic verities, linked in a special relationship with all other
Islamic states and distinguishing itself from non-Islamic states sharply
and often self-righteously. This process entails a heightened hostility to
non-Muslims, partly out of conviction and partly as an aspect of the
competition for purity and influence among the various Muslim states
themselves. Europe, which (isolated pockets apart) rejected its fundamen-
talists long ago, is easily misled into regarding the manifestations of this
overall Islamic consciousness as a kind of extremism which has to be lived
with and is at least half mad. This is a dangerous misconception.

There is not going to be a violent clash between Islam and the West
because there are no political, economic or military entities corresponding
to these general terms; nor will there be. There is nevertheless a cultural
antagonism which underlies particular, narrower disputes, sharpens them
emotionally and has the capacity to push them over the line which divides
a conflict under control from a conflict out of control. This underlying

cultural antithesis is the more dangerous when the antagonists fail to understand one another, misrepresent one another ignorantly or deliberately, and allow their mutual irritations to spice political and economic rivalries with hatred and contempt. The conflict between Islam and the West is not the only one of its kind but it is the outstanding example and it overheats international relations in a way in which other conflicts – the bid for economic supremacy, for example, between the United States and Japan – do not.

The conflicts within Islam to which I have drawn attention do not make it unique or even special. Europe has experienced similar tugs and tears but at a wholly different time. Europe embarked centuries ago on a destiny ruled by secularisation and fragmentation: the two trends which Islam most committedly seeks to repel but which it may itself be beginning to undergo. The Roman empire split into two in the fifth century, and the Christian church likewise in the eleventh; in western Europe, and largely at the instigation of the church, authority was divided between church and state with the consequence that the church, by asserting its sovereignty in spiritual matters, allowed emperor and monarchs to claim sovereignty in secular affairs. There is no more telling epitaph on medieval aspirations for a united Christendom than the simple fact that the cohabitation of Pope and Emperor in one capital city was always inconceivable. The separation of church and state strengthened both in their several spheres but it destroyed the idea of Christendom and inaugurated Europe's profound and persisting distrust of ideologies. (The anti-communist ideology which animated the Cold War meant much less in Europe than it did in the United States.)

Further, on both sides of the division strife ensued. The conflict between church and state in western Europe was sublimated and stifled, but at the expense of increasing conflicts within the church and between states. Anti-popes made their first appearance in the twelfth century, the papacy split into two in the fourteenth (and for a brief time into three) and the Reformation put an end to its spiritual authority in much of western and central Europe. The fragmentation of the church was followed by the attenuation of its god, degraded from unqualified omnipotence to a subject of debate, marginalised by the scientific revolution of the seventeenth century and the Enlightenment – a fate which may yet overtake the god of Islam but so far has not. On the secular side fragmentation was even more marked. The Holy Roman Emperor, never more than a German supremo, lost his pretensions and his authority to princes within Germany while separate sovereign states multiplied and still do. This secular fragmentation nourished a fruitful variety and provided a pattern which was copied all over the world during and in the wake of the age of European expansion but in Europe it proved in course of time all but fatal when, sharpened by nationalist emotions and technical efficiency, it produced a culture regulated in the last resort by war and culminating in the two great wars of the twentieth century. To the question whether this European catastrophe, aggravated in half Europe by Soviet misrule, has amounted to irreversible decline I have given in my book *Resilient Europe* an optimistic answer but it is one of those questions which cannot be finally answered until the next century. On its evolution depends the future role of Europe in world affairs – whether as a major actor or as an assortment of minor ones, as a colossus like North America or a bunch of (mostly) risible delinquents as in South America.

In the West that term was invented to stress that the Soviet Union and half Europe did not belong to it. So the West never meant Europe. It was a convenient and sometimes self-righteous way of defining the *ad hoc* Euro-American alliance against an enemy which, however, vanished, leaving behind an uncomfortable feeling that nevertheless Europe still needed a Euro-American alliance against something and could not modify or redefine its association with the United States without doing violence to some spiritual or ideological verities – a strikingly unsound basis for political thinking.

At the end of the present century the main sources of conflict and danger in the world are the destructive forces of ideologies, whether religious as in Islam or secular as for communists and anti-communists; and secondly, the destructive forces of nationalisms and other separate identities, mostly expressed and concentrated in the form of states or groups trying to become states. These sources are mutually reinforcing for (as Albert Hourani pointed out in reference to the Arabs) religion is an aspect or form of nationalism; a Croat nationalist is by definition a Roman Catholic and Greek leaders have recently asserted that a Greek is no Greek if he is not an Orthodox Christian. The intolerance and belligerence of these forces are aggravated by two other sources of conflict: first and most frightening, the exceedingly rapid growth of populations and therewith of want, an urgent competition for food and other basic stuffs and an inevitable fierceness in struggling for them in order to keep alive; and second, the formidable difficulties – psychological, organisational – in the way of managing the diversities which drive men in the mass to fight and prevent men in authority from reconciling these prejudices and inequalities without fighting. My own position in this complex and perplexing scene has been that of the observer and analyst. I have not had public position or authority and I have more than once observed the imprudence of those who allow themselves to be seduced from one walk of life to another where the discipline and cast of mind are quite different. The business of the observer is to observe, report and expound – and to stick to that role. While enjoying the privileges of critic he must forego those of action and direction. It is natural to be tempted into the fields of action, especially if you feel you know better, but intellectuals who have taken over the reins have proved with few exceptions ineffective and disastrous, while the reflections of retired men of action are with fewer exceptions embarrassingly superficial and misleading.

It is risky and generally myopic to make big claims for one's own times and I am temperamentally opposed to such claims, but I find it hard to resist the conclusion that I have lived at a time of unprecedented transformation. There are such things as turning points whether in the history of small communities or great nations or yet wider civilisations or even the whole of human kind. The present age has seen the effective unification of the world, not politically or culturally but in terms of the accessibility of its parts and their economic interdependence, coupled with their continuing diversities and incomprehensions. It has also expanded knowledge and power, often beyond the understanding of most people and perhaps beyond the sagacity of all. It has been enthralling to live in such times. To leave without knowing the sequel is vexing.

Index